Strategic Survey 2017
The Annual Assessment of Geopolitics

published by

for

The International Institute for Strategic Studies

was sorely tested by intramural tensions with Poland and Hungary. Instability in the Western Balkans, fomented by a toxic mix of nationalist politics, Russian meddling and organised crime, put Europe's southeastern neighbourhood at heightened risk. Without any realistic or imminent prospect of EU membership, the incentive for regional leaders to adopt more responsible policies was weakened. In the Middle East, the one regional institution that appeared at least reasonably stable, the Gulf Cooperation Council (GCC), began to tear itself apart as Saudi Arabia, the United Arab Emirates and Bahrain presented Qatar with a list of demands while closing borders and cutting off relations. The US, the UK and France all sought to mediate and support regional efforts led by Kuwait to repair relations, but the strident nature of the public diplomacy conducted by the principal stakeholders, on both sides, left the impression that damage to the integrity of the GCC could well be permanent. In Asia, America's key partners and allies mainly worked hard to keep the US committed to the region. Pyongyang's persistent missile testing and provocations kept North Korea at the very top of President Donald Trump's security agenda. Even here, alliance solidarity was tested as South Korea's new president, Moon Jae-in, chose to freeze and, later, only 'temporarily' resume the US deployment of the Terminal High Altitude Area Defense missile-defence system, meant to protect the Republic of Korea, and US troops serving there, from North Korea's shorter-range missiles.

The fracture of these various partnerships and alliances, mainly from the inside, is opening up more opportunities for large countries, who perceive the status quo to be stacked against them, to exploit and widen these fissures. Political leaders focused on domestic challenges, both economic and political, will have great difficulty maintaining a strategic sense of purpose in repairing these international relationships. Protecting long-standing alliance structures from external pressures is diplomatically labour-intensive; in Europe, the Middle East and Asia, the status quo challengers may have a stronger focus and a longer attention span than the status quo defenders.

Policy towards Russia in Europe has been shaped since 2014 by the Ukraine crisis and the sanctions policy that arose in response to Russia's involvement there. Nearly four years on, Russia continues to poke and prod at the status quo, frustrated by the refusal of the West to accept its status or bend to its regional interests. Military developments and deployments, including ones that probably breach the 1987 Intermediate-Range Nuclear Forces Treaty, are overt and threaten Europe's balance of power. These military challenges will force NATO continually to develop more robust policies of deterrence and defence. Yet while these classic challenges start to multiply, Russia is also engaging in a policy of what might be styled 'disruptive engagement', using the full sweep of state power and capacities to disturb at multiple points Europe's security. Intelligence professionals and others point to a witches' brew of cyber activity, information warfare, support for political movements and tacit promotion of various types of illegal activity, all combining in vulnerable parts of Europe to destabilise and discomfort.

While Russia has apparently been refining its techniques in these areas, there is a sense that Western capabilities to counter these persistent but *sub rosa* activities have waned. To the degree that Western states retain capacities to counter Russian disruptive engagement, these still need political direction. Europe and NATO's ability to shape a coherent and balanced policy towards Russia turns heavily on what President Trump ultimately decides is US policy. It is probable that clear guidance and a consistent approach will not come soon from Washington, and so there is a risk that without US leadership, European vulnerabilities in the east and to the south could be uncomfortably exposed to Russian meddling. Without clear US leadership on Russia, the Europeans may struggle to agree on how seriously to regard Russian provocations and what action should be taken in response. US sanctions on Russia, led by a Russo-sceptical Congress, are too robust for the liking of some Europeans but they signal a strong concern over Russia's recent direction. Yet the US president's sympathetic approach to his Russian counterpart appears to give some licence to Moscow's disruptive engagement, testing the tolerance and resilience of European societies, particularly in the Western Balkans.

In the Middle East, a degree of US disengagement from the Syrian conflict has led to Russia and Iran consolidating their dominance of the battlefield and left their client, President Bashar al-Assad, in a stronger position internally than at any time since 2012, even if in control of limited territory. The soft partition of Syria is becoming a fact, with the regime-controlled west and centre; the Kurdish Rojava in the northeast and northwest; the Islamic State, also known as ISIS or ISIL, in the east; and small groups of rebel holdouts in the north and south. Apart from ISIS, each entity is heavily dependent on external support and protection. Russia has consolidated its military presence in Syria, begun to explore economic opportunities in oil and minerals there, and taken control of the international diplomatic activity surrounding potential resolution of the Syrian conflict. More disturbing for the regional balance of power, however, is the way in which Iran has used the Syrian conflict to extend its reach into the Levant. Through its support of various Shia transnational militias in the south of Syria, and given its other proxy relationships, Iran has effectively established political influence and territorial contiguity from Iran to Lebanon.

The extension of Iranian influence in this way is disturbing to Israel and several Arab Gulf states. Yet a coordinated strategy with the US to deal with these encroachments does not appear to be in the offing. While Iran has verifiably abided by the nuclear agreement negotiated and agreed under the Obama administration, its regional ambitions executed through the Islamic Revolutionary Guard Corps have not been satisfactorily checked – and this at a time when the GCC is divided. The decision by Saudi Arabia, UAE, Bahrain and Egypt to sanction Qatar for its alleged financing of terrorism and interference in internal affairs – key elements of their 13 demands, later repackaged as six principles – created an important split in the region.

The UAE, in particular, has argued most vociferously for the development of a new set of relations in the Gulf, potentially to replace the old ones. Qexit – the prospect of Qatar leaving the GCC – has not yet become an accepted neologism, but it was a prospect openly discussed by many influential figures. An organisation established in large measure to stand up to Iran appeared willing to lose one of its members that had been suspected, inter alia, of having too close a relationship with Tehran. Arguments that such action would push Qatar into Iran's embrace were dismissed breezily, on the basis that Qatar was already there. In time, the all-too-public diplomacy might give way to discreet talks and a resolution. Regional organisations are usually strongly favoured by their most powerful members, as an amplification of their own power, so Saudi Arabia may come around to the view that fracturing the GCC is not strategically smart. Qatar has long been linked with extremist movements, while its GCC neighbours have long been irritated by the editorial line taken by the Arabic version of Al-Jazeera. It is plainly the case that the complainant states will seek moderation in Doha's policies as a precondition for resumption of normal relations. This will have to happen at some speed if relations are not to be tarnished beyond repair and the GCC as an organisation to wither away. Even if a satisfactory solution is found, there is a sense that new political alignments are taking shape that may change the strategic dynamics of Gulf politics.

The focus of the Trump administration in Asia was on North Korea's nuclear and ballistic-missile programmes. North Korea was the one foreign-policy issue that seemed consistently to seize the president's interest, but six months into his administration, North Korea's pace of ballistic-missile testing and provocations was breathtaking. North Korea very likely has the capacity to hit South Korea, Japan and US forces in the region with a missile-delivered nuclear weapon. Its longer-range capabilities are in much greater doubt. The two-stage *Hwasong*-14 has a maximum range in excess of 7,500 kilometres, and may be able to reach the US West Coast if armed with a warhead weighing 650 kilograms or less. However, the prototype tested in July 2017 was not optimally designed to achieve maximum range but rather to strengthen the probability of a successful maiden flight by relying on flight-proven stages. A new design, one that also has the range to threaten the entire

US mainland, could emerge in late 2017 or early 2018. North Korea might, in theory, couple two *Hwasong*-14 engines to power a larger first stage, and build a second stage using a single engine.

In addition to launches associated with the development of an intercontinental ballistic missile, Pyongyang will continue its efforts to create a submarine-launched ballistic missile. The *Pukguksong*-1 has been test-fired from a launch tube fixed to a submerged barge, but not from a deployable submarine. Future tests will feature launches from its one submarine. In the longer term, North Korea will need to build at least two or three more submarines before it will have an operational sea-based missile force. In parallel, flight trials of the land-based version of the sub-launched missile, the *Pukguksong*-2, will continue.

Efforts to press China into using its leverage over North Korea to curb Pyongyang's persistent efforts to improve its ballistic-missile capacities has not produced results. North Korea will not agree to arms-control measures to limit testing, in the absence of a major US diplomatic initiative focused on Pyongyang (which does not appear likely). No one believes that a direct military attack on North Korea will end in anything other than catastrophe. There will be more attempts to get China to do more to pressure North Korea, but breaking the rhythm of North Korean activities will require concerted diplomatic effort with allies and partners, and a departure from the so-far iterative efforts to implore change. Perhaps other measures might be undertaken to slow the pace of North Korea's progress. The fuel – a form of hydrazine – used by the *Musudan*, *Hwasong*-12 and *Hwasong*-14 is produced in only three countries: the US, Russia and China. Cutting the supply, or introducing contaminants to the fuel, would seriously impede North Korea's missile programme. Similarly, as Pyongyang also relies on imported electronics, the introduction of computer viruses or other defects could complicate North Korea's efforts. However, using cyber tools to disrupt missile launches in real time is more challenging, especially against North Korea's older missiles. *Scud* and *Nodong* missiles do not contain digital hardware, and are therefore immune to cyber and other electronic countermeasures.

Such tactical measures, or others that may imaginatively be developed, could form part of a broader strategy. For that to succeed, the US will need to gain greater purchase on China's attention. As President Xi Jinping approached the late-2017 Chinese Communist Party congress, his efforts to consolidate his position and announce China's powerful arrival on the global stage intensified. In spring 2017, the Belt and Road Summit brought together 29 heads of government and 1,000 other participants to Beijing to promote Xi's signature geo-economic project, which involves more than 60 countries. At the end of July, the 90th anniversary of the People's Liberation Army was celebrated in Inner Mongolia at an event at which the president commanded his troops to display full loyalty to the party. China is quickly developing high-tech weaponry and platforms that will in time make it a peer competitor to the US, and is extending its reach beyond its immediate region, most symbolically by its opening on 1 August 2017 of a logistics base in Djibouti. Once his new term and politburo are formalised, President Xi can be expected to insist more resolutely that the Chinese point of view on regional and international matters be more widely respected – and even catered to. The states of the Association of Southeast Asian Nations (ASEAN) are already alert to the strategic swagger demonstrated by a confident Chinese leadership and the approach, akin to the Monroe Doctrine, that it is taking to South China Sea issues. ASEAN celebrated its 50th anniversary in 2017 but its efforts to present a coordinated approach to regional security were hobbled by some of its members adopting a hedging strategy towards China. Any Code of Conduct ultimately agreed between China and ASEAN would probably not be robust enough to ensure uncontested and unfettered access to the international waters of the South China Sea and its features. Washington's engagement with the region will have to be resolute and consistent if the 'principled approach' to regional security it favours is to be maintained.

An important element in this dynamic will be the attitude of India. The Modi administration is taking a much firmer approach to regional security issues and, specifically, to the challenges it sees not just in China's military posture but also in its geo-economic policies. The fast pace of Chinese military modernisation is of at least as much concern to India as it may be to the US. The BRI project, especially the China–Pakistan Economic Corridor element of it, has irritated the Indian leadership. The prominence of territorial disputes with China has risen within India's national-security debate. Tensions in the tri-border area known as Doka La, Donglang and Doklam in India, China and Bhutan respectively are especially high and strain India–China relations. Indian concerns have not yet, however, been translated into a security policy in the region or in the wider Indo-Pacific that fully engages the many countries who would be sympathetic to more practised security and defence collaboration. Carefully developed, the US would find in India a partner that did not define itself principally as a non-aligned power and did not have the aversion to defence collaboration with a Western state that may previously have dominated Indian thinking. How India chooses to play a role in the defence and security architecture of Asia in 2018 and beyond will be crucial in determining whether there can be a regional concert or a balance of power that does not rely uniquely on the nature of the US–China relationship.

Asia, like Europe and the Middle East, has been increasingly affected by ISIS-inspired terrorism that only exacerbates a sense of strategic frailty. Indonesia, Malaysia and the Philippines strengthened their counter-terrorism cooperation in the year to mid-2017. There was an emerging sense that security cooperation had to be improved within the region on the counter-terrorism challenge but also between the region and key players in the Middle East. Crafting transregional cooperation when regional organisations appear fragile will be a daunting task.

These trends indicate that the issues that will dominate the geopolitical agenda in 2018 will be nuclear proliferation (North Korea), terrorism (ISIS and others), information warfare (largely Russia) and the use of proxies by state actors (principally Iran). There is a limit to what ad hoc coalitions and state-to-state collaboration can do on these issues. A rebuilding – and, in some cases, a repurposing – of regional institutions and security partnerships is needed. It used to be said that a sign of a great power was the ability to lead large groups of countries in the service of a larger public good. China's leadership does not yet inspire that magnetic attraction – states are bending to its will, but not moved by its values – while America seems to have put down the baton of leadership in favour of a series of transactional and conditional arrangements on particular issues. Strategic unease could morph into strategic chaos unless greater discipline is introduced into policymaking processes. This is not an injunction aimed uniquely at any one country. There are many states where individual leaders make frequent adjustments in policy without reference to government colleagues, legislative branches or the policymaking institutions that normally would produce considered options and measured outcomes.

The volatility of policymaking, in turn, induces a sense of permanent unease in populations, who are moved regularly to protest informally rather than speak through established political structures to appeal for better governance. Dealing with the politics of the street is no longer a challenge associated principally with governments of the Global South in Asia, Latin America, Africa and the Middle East; it is also a feature of Western political life. A loss of confidence in the competence of government is a widely felt political emotion. Leaders with many domestic challenges are not often able to focus effectively on international strategy. Yet in today's networked world of transnational threats, immunity from the outside world is impossible to achieve. The tempo at which threats emerge and crises evolve, demanding a response, is stretching government capabilities and invites principally reactive approaches. Striking a pose, making a complaint, challenging an opponent, sanctioning an enemy, signing one agreement and renouncing another are the entrances and exits, alarums and excursions on the strategic stage. They are the sounds of activity that all too often muffle the reality of a stalled strategy. Aside from several authoritarian regimes that are able to summon the full range of state power in the service of their strategic goals, most states are finding that the range of international-security issues they confront is testing their resilience and the capacities of the machinery of government.

The goal of shaping the international strategic environment seems out of reach even for the larger powers, unless resources are made available to meet the complex and hybrid threats that have emerged. America's strategic shrinkage, a consequence of the plethora of unfilled posts in the US departments of state and defence, means that only a few issues are addressed at any given time. State and non-state actors that resent the status quo can nimbly disturb and infect the strategic landscape. Their appetite to take risks to change facts on the ground to their benefit has increased. It should surprise no one if this happens on numerous fronts at the same time. For strategic overload to be avoided, some revival of the strategic partnerships and alliances that have in the past been stabilising is required.

Chapter 2

Drivers of Strategic Change

In the following pages, IISS experts seek to highlight developments and themes that have the potential to drive strategic change in individual regions, and in the world as a whole. They do not offer forecasts of specific future events: this annual book remains a review of international affairs covering a 12-month period, in this case from mid-2016 to mid-2017. However, regional experts use their analysis of developments in this and recent years to identify strategic risk factors. This section is not a comprehensive list of risks facing the world, nor does it attempt to assess or quantify threats. World events will remain unpredictable. But we hope our analysis is useful for the identification of key drivers of strategic change.

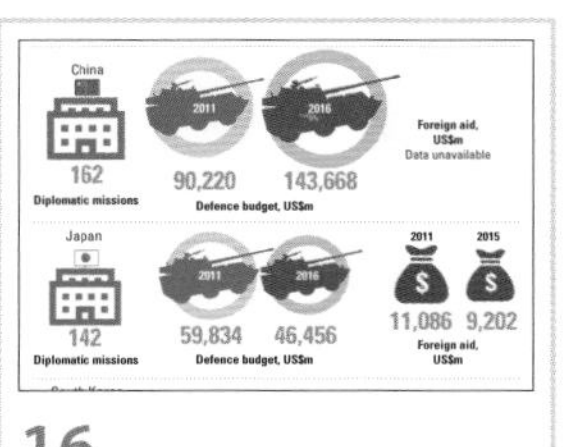

16

Asia-Pacific

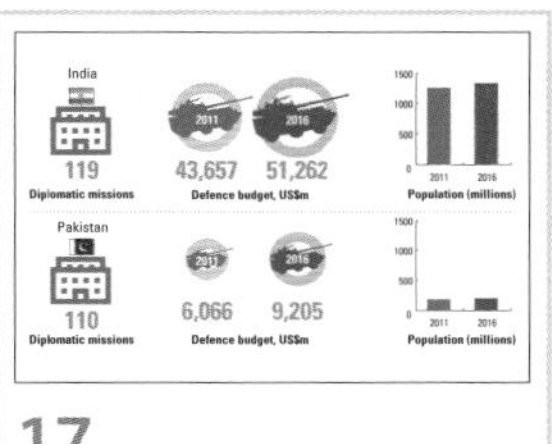

17

South Asia and Afghanistan

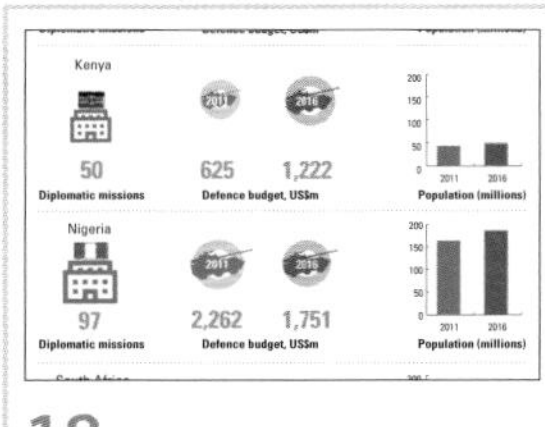

18

Sub-Saharan Africa

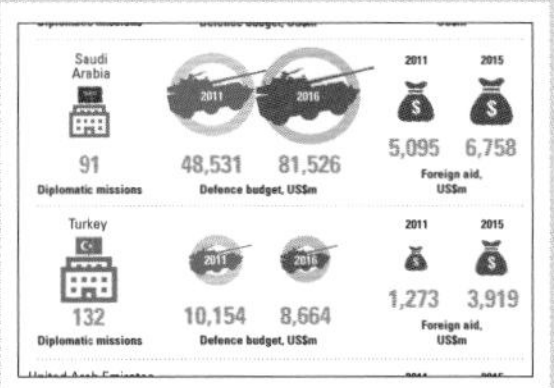

19

Middle East and North Africa

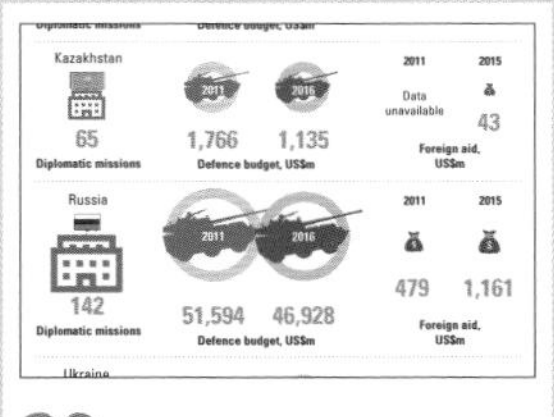

20

Russia and Eurasia

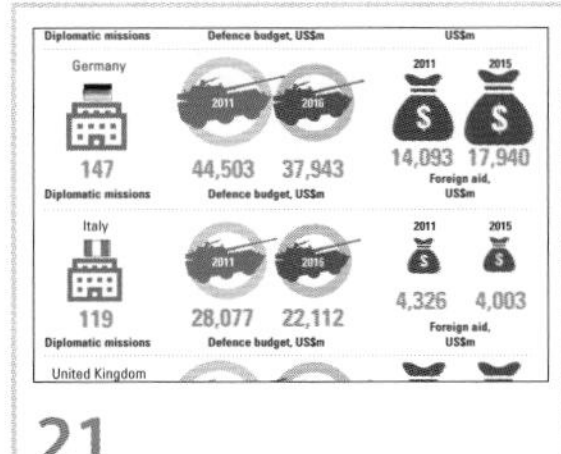

21

Europe

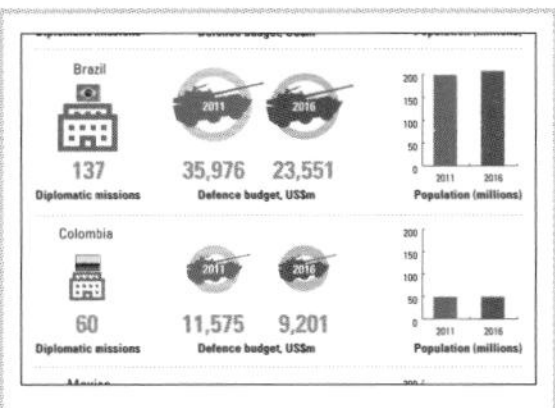

22

Latin America

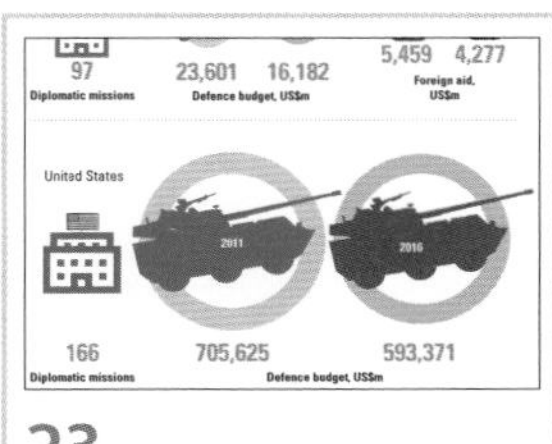

23

North America

Sources: IISS *Military Balance*; IDMC; Lowy Institute; OEDC; UNHCR; World Bank

Asia-Pacific: drivers of strategic change

- Accelerating North Korean nuclear-weapons and missile programmes continue to encourage cooperation between Washington, Seoul and Tokyo; Beijing's growing economic and diplomatic pressure on Pyongyang in response to the programmes has yet to yield results.
- Due to the uncertainty created by Washington's questioning of US security guarantees and abandonment of the Trans-Pacific Partnership, US allies are hedging to preserve the regional security architecture and rules-based order in the Asia-Pacific.
- Some Southeast Asian states appear to show increasing deference towards China, yet there has been no significant reduction in the nationalism, competition over resources and geopolitical rivalry behind territorial disputes in the South China Sea.
- Japan continues to strengthen its security cooperation with other Asian democracies, as its government steps up efforts to revise Article 9 of the constitution, which strictly limits use of the military.
- Concerned about the increasingly complex and challenging security environment, Australia is increasing its defence budget and pursuing greater intra-regional collaboration.

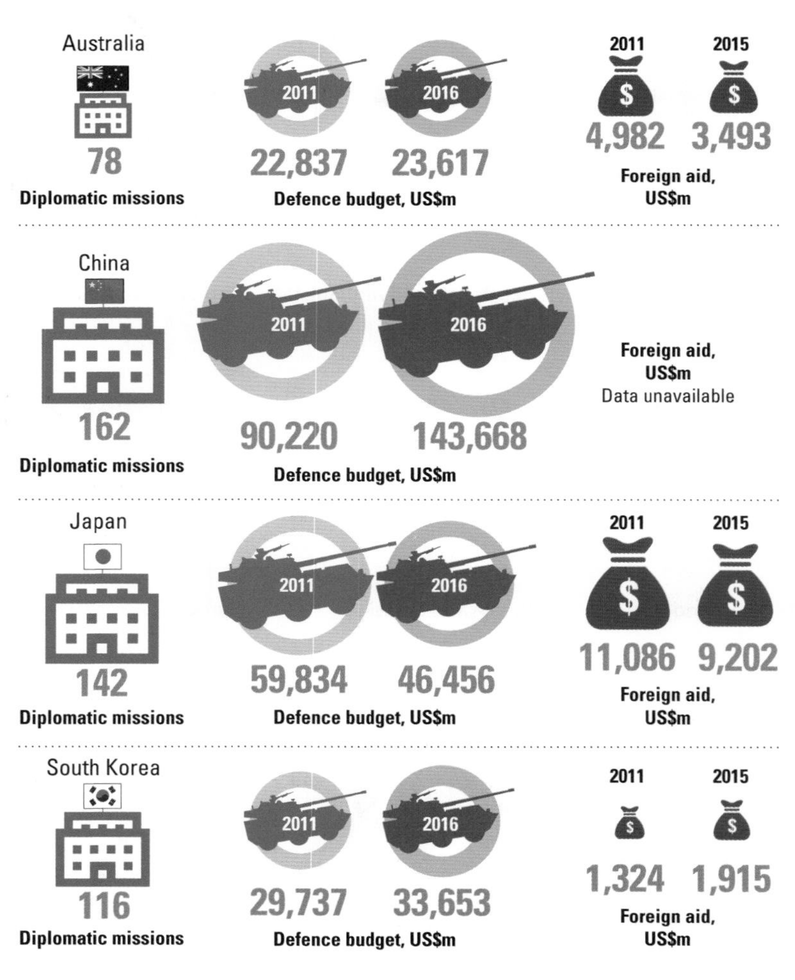

South Asia and Afghanistan: drivers of strategic change

- India is deepening security, economic and development cooperation with other states in the Indian Ocean, making considerable progress towards its goal of becoming a leading power in the region.
- Islamabad continues to strengthen its economic ties with Beijing through the China–Pakistan Economic Corridor, amid persistent concerns about the debt burden the initiative is placing on the Pakistani economy.
- India's relationship with Pakistan is deteriorating further due to cross-border terrorism, economic competition and rising tension in Kashmir.
- India is undertaking fiscal and monetary reforms that have the potential to significantly boost its economy, which remains the fastest-growing of any major developing country.
- Major powers are engaging in increasingly fierce competition for influence in Afghanistan, largely failing to pursue the kind of multilateral cooperation needed to resolve the conflict there.
- India continues to be concerned about China's growing influence in South Asia, amid a stand-off between the countries in a territorial dispute near the Siliguri Corridor.

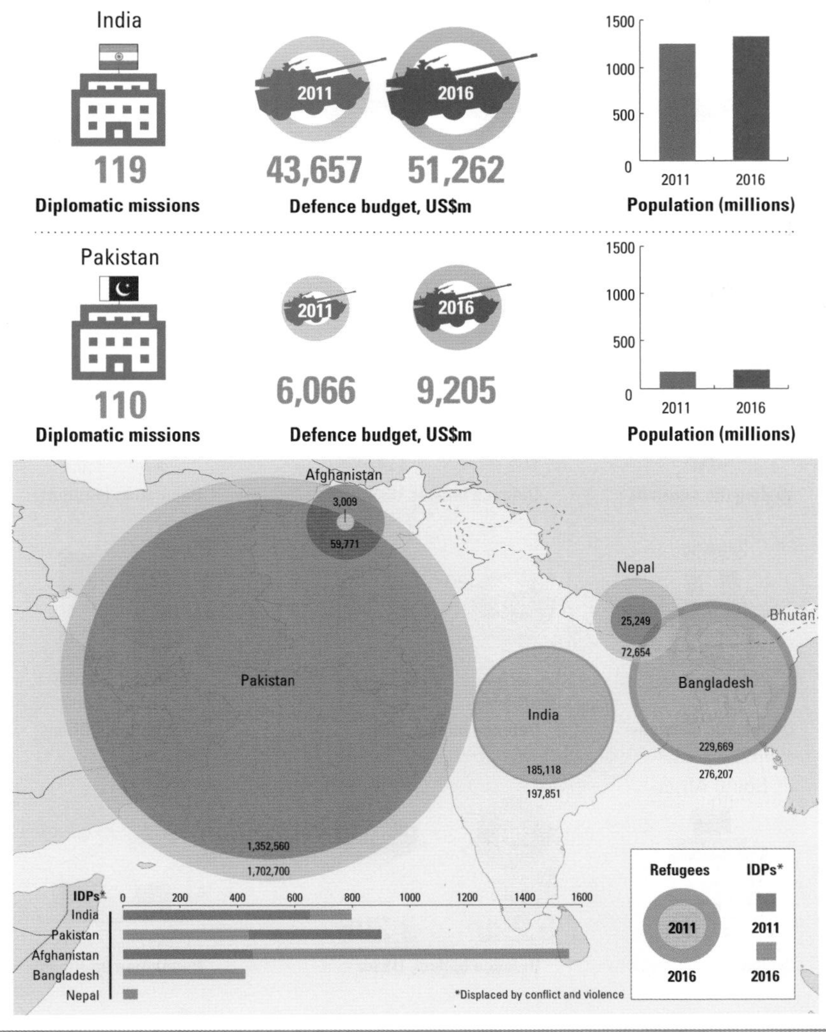

Sub-Saharan Africa: drivers of strategic change

- Funding constraints on several of sub-Saharan Africa's main powers are leading them to focus on multilateral responses to security threats and democratic failures.
- Some West African states are demonstrating reduced tolerance for autocrats, integrating their efforts to provide security and strengthen democratic practices.
- Domestic turmoil is preoccupying several military powers in sub-Saharan Africa, straining their resources and thereby reducing their capacity to participate in regional initiatives.
- Beijing's desire to secure long-term supplies of oil and minerals from sub-Saharan Africa is fostering increased Chinese engagement with the region.
- A history of impunity among leaders guilty of large-scale human-rights abuses is encouraging the development of regional judicial institutions, particularly the Extraordinary African Chambers.
- The new US administration's cuts to foreign-aid spending are threatening to have a particularly severe impact on sub-Saharan Africa, not least in the security sector.

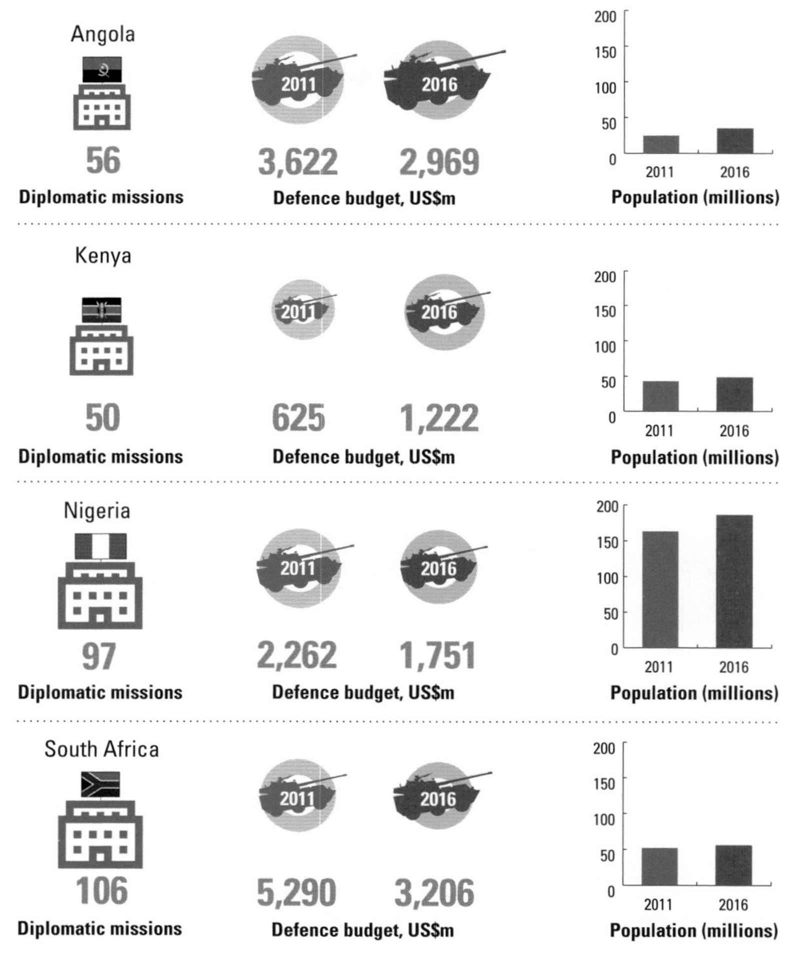

Middle East and North Africa: drivers of strategic change

- Wars across the region are killing tens of thousands of people, displacing millions of others and, in Syria's case, dividing the country into zones of influence dominated by competing major powers.
- Deepening rivalry and mistrust between Iran and Saudi Arabia continues to foster proxy conflict and economic competition across the Middle East.
- The stand-off between Qatar and Saudi Arabia, as well as their respective allies, is threatening to fracture or refashion the Gulf Cooperation Council.
- The rapid erosion of the Islamic State, also known as ISIS or ISIL, is encouraging territorial and political opportunism by state and non-state actors wherever the group is driven back, as well as spurring it to carry out a greater number of terrorist attacks outside the Middle East.
- Turkey's descent into authoritarianism is undermining its relationships with Western states, likely ending the country's chances of accession to the European Union.
- Israel's interests are converging with those of some Gulf Arab states, increasing the incentives for cooperation between them on issues such as counter-terrorism.

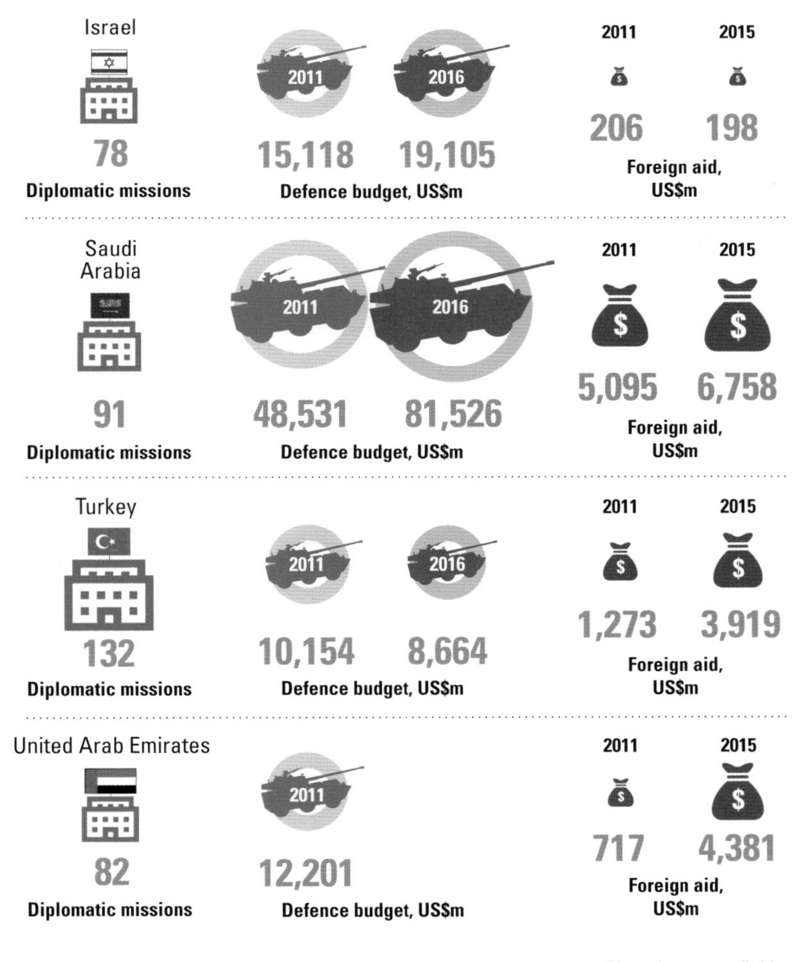

Russia and Eurasia: drivers of strategic change

- Russia's involvement in the Syrian conflict has restored its status as a great power in the Middle East while further damaging its relationship with Western states.
- Moscow and Western capitals are maintaining fundamentally opposed views of Europe's future security architecture, undermining measures on arms control and the development of the post-Soviet region.
- Russia's and NATO's perception of each other as a defence priority continues to encourage militarisation on both sides.
- Ukraine's government remains constrained in its approach to the conflict in the east of the country, due to domestic unpopularity and a desire to avoid being outflanked by Ukrainian-nationalist forces.
- Russian information operations against the United States are ensuring that US sanctions on Russia will remain in place for the foreseeable future.
- The fallout of low commodity prices and the contraction of Russia's economy is hampering growth in Eurasia, inhibiting some regional states' attempts to maintain a paternalist approach to governance.

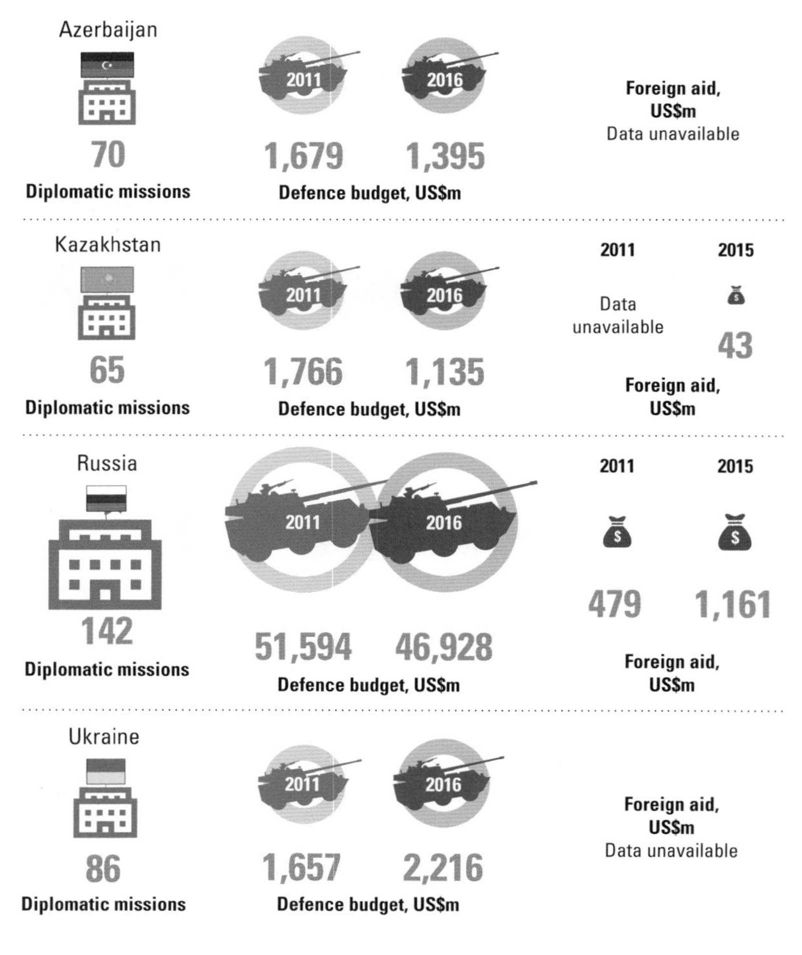

Europe: drivers of strategic change

- European electorates are increasingly discontented with the performance of ruling elites and even the workings of democracy, generating electoral volatility.
- The need to maintain a common negotiating position on the United Kingdom's exit from the European Union, and relations with Russia and Turkey, is stretching the EU's capacity to pursue regional integration.
- The Polish and Hungarian governments are attempting to secure control of domestic politics at the expense of democratic checks and balances, bringing them into conflict with EU institutions.
- Rising major-power competition is combining with poverty, high unemployment and the growing threat of terrorism to destabilise the Western Balkans.
- High-casualty terrorist attacks continue to spur many EU countries to bolster intelligence-sharing and related security measures.
- Instability on Europe's periphery continues to exacerbate a migration crisis in Europe, disproportionately affecting southern European countries.
- Due to the uncertainty created by Washington's questioning of US security guarantees and the global trading system, European countries are exploring ways to reduce their reliance on the United States.
- The legacy of the economic and financial crisis continues to create divisions among EU member states that run between West and East, North and South.

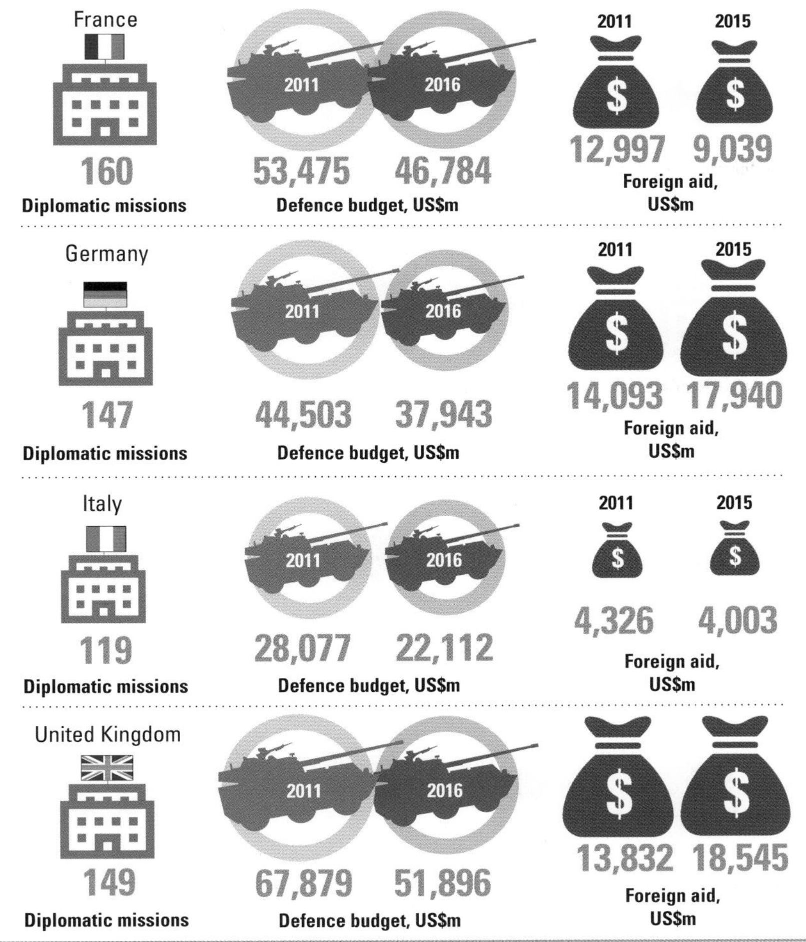

Latin America: drivers of strategic change

- The election of Donald Trump as US president is unsettling most Latin American countries, as he calls into question Washington's long-standing positions on regional integration, security cooperation and development aid.
- The United States' withdrawal from the Trans-Pacific Partnership and renegotiation or withdrawal from the North American Free Trade Agreement is threatening to inhibit trade in many Latin American countries, potentially facilitating expansion of Chinese influence in the region as they look for new commercial partners in Asia, Europe and elsewhere.
- Many Latin American countries are considering a uniquely concerted and confrontational diplomatic response to the political and economic crisis in Venezuela, which has the potential to destabilise the region.
- A general shift towards market-friendly politics in Latin America, as well as Trump's election, is creating impetus for greater integration between states in the region.
- Lacklustre economic growth and a series of corruption scandals are generating instability and public discontent, as many Latin American political and judicial systems attempt to implement anti-corruption reforms.
- Implementation of the peace accord between Colombia's government and FARC is being threatened by the agreement's rejection in a national referendum, growing political polarisation and significant financial and logistical challenges.

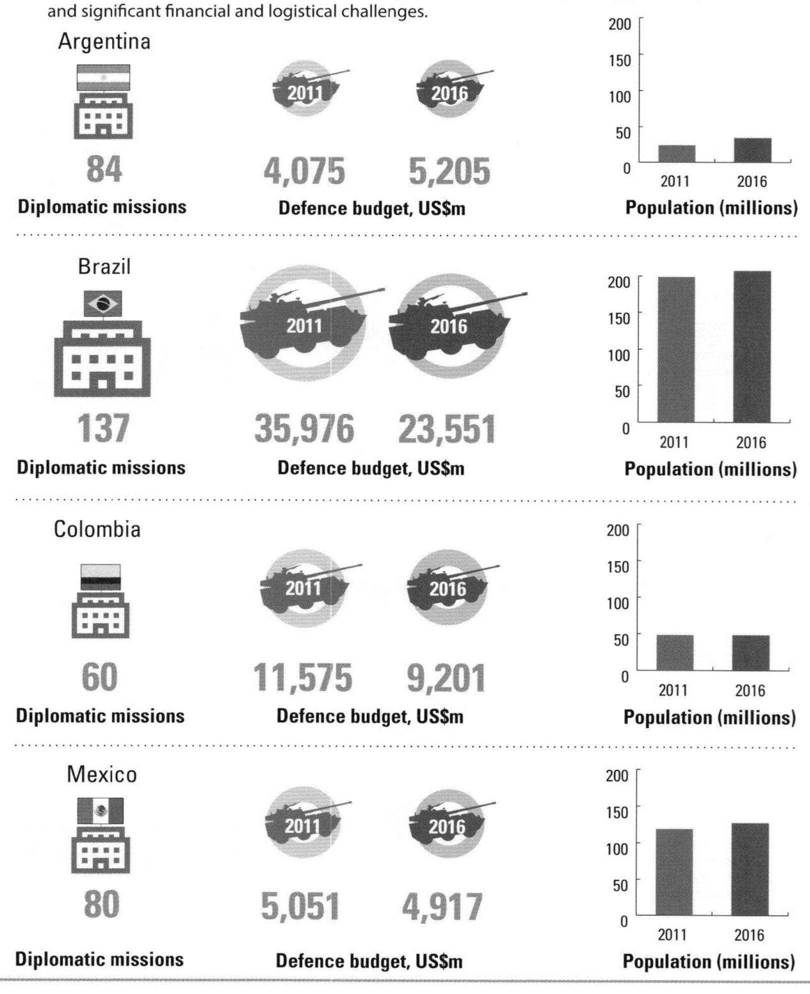

North America: drivers of strategic change

- The presidency of Donald Trump is forcing governments around the world to plan for scenarios in which the United States turns away from its commitment to key alliances and the global rules-based order.
- The US withdrawal from the Trans-Pacific Partnership and pursuit of protectionist measures is posing a growing threat to the global trading system.
- The new US administration's failure to fill major vacancies in government departments is inhibiting the United States' capacity to formulate and implement strategy, and to engage in diplomacy.
- Trump's inconsistent approach to diplomacy is escalating tension on the Korean Peninsula, increasing the risk of conflict there.
- Alleged Russian interference in the US democratic process is accelerating a years-long deterioration in relations between Washington and Moscow.
- Concern about the effects of the Trump presidency is spurring Canada to increase defence spending, and to reaffirm its commitment to rules-based international order, free trade, gender equality and measures to combat climate change.

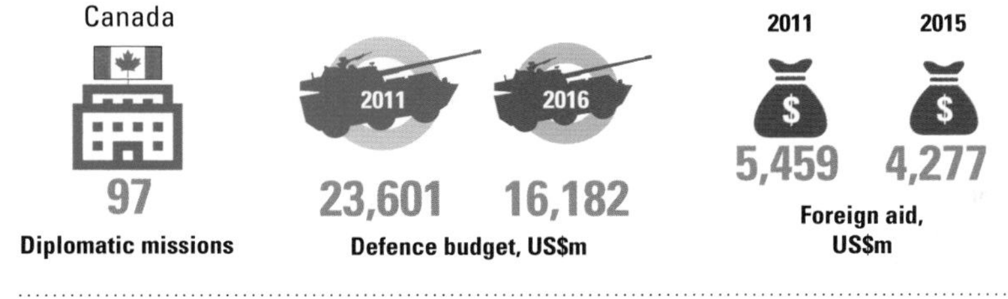

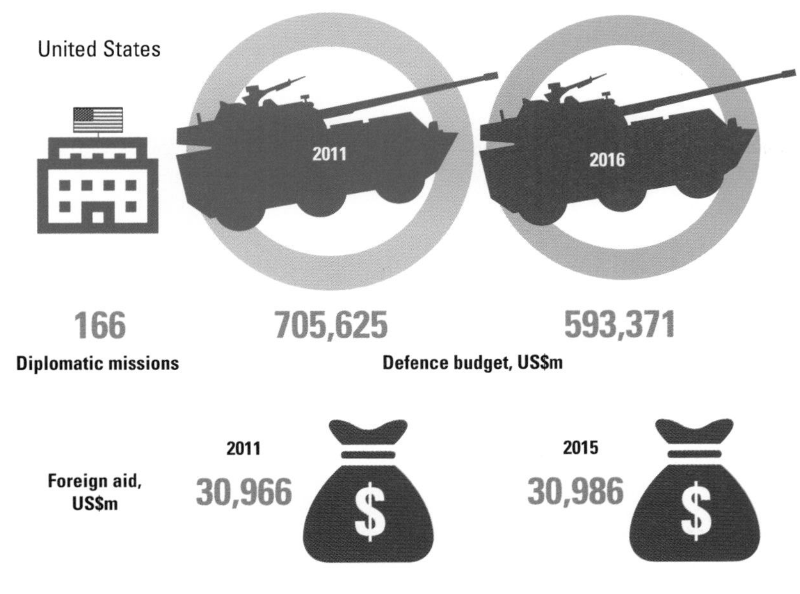

Chapter 3

Strategic Policy Issues

Future of the World Trade Organisation

The foundation of the World Trade Organisation (WTO) in 1995 was less a birth than a transformation. The event created a permanent, international organisation from a lesser-known but long-standing multilateral agreement on global trade. In the aftermath of the Second World War, major industrialised economies met routinely and developed a sustainable, rules-based and non-discriminatory trading system designed to prevent a repeat of the nationalist, protectionist mistakes of the Great Depression.

Twenty-three countries established the General Agreement on Tariffs and Trade (GATT) in 1947. They initially wrote rules for non-discriminatory treatment of member-country trade, then used GATT as a forum for engaging in periodic, multi-year 'rounds' to reciprocally cut tariffs. They completed eight such rounds between 1947 and 1994; GATT membership expanded continuously over time.

The foundation of the WTO came at the end of the final GATT round, which kicked off in Uruguay. The new organisation institutionalised a functioning, inter-state dispute-settlement procedure for easing trade friction. The WTO immediately became consensus-based, and by the end of the twentieth century had built on GATT to create an open, rules-based trading system that could address the needs of the industrialised world. By 2016, its membership had grown to include 164 countries. However, politico-economic shocks, along with institutional design flaws, now place the future of the WTO in peril.

Struggle to accommodate developing countries

Although GATT and the WTO established a trading system that worked effectively for the industrialised world, the organisations ignored many of the needs of developing countries. Dozens of these states joined GATT, albeit mostly in name only. Through a system of 'special and differential treatment', developing countries were not expected to engage in reciprocal tariff negotiations and thus take on standard GATT commitments to liberalise their markets for international trade. As members, they received some benefits that made this worthwhile, such as access to high-income-country markets. Benefits arose simply through membership that entitled their exports to the low tariffs that rich countries negotiated, applied to imports from one another and extended to all other members through GATT's rules of non-discrimination. By the 1970s, developing countries received greater export-market access, as rich nations voluntarily, unilaterally offered even lower tariffs on some export products through what developed as the Generalised System of Preferences.

Yet within this voluntary – as opposed to reciprocity-based – approach, the special access freely granted to developing countries left out the export sectors of greatest interest to them, such as agriculture and labour-intensive apparel manufacturing. Industrialised countries largely failed to liberalise these sectors. As developing countries were not asked to come to the bargaining table and offer something in return, GATT's reciprocity approach – which might otherwise have been used to liberalise trade in their true export interests – was never harnessed in a way that would meet their needs.

At the Uruguay Round, rich countries for the first time promised to bring sectors such as agriculture, textiles and apparel into the agreement's disciplines. As part of this grand bargain, rich countries would benefit reciprocally by expanding the trading system's rules beyond goods to start including services, as well as important commercial issues such as the protection of intellectual-property rights.

However, by the early 2000s, it had become clear to most of the WTO's developing-country members that the gains they expected from the Uruguay Round would never materialise. Some of their disappointment stemmed from unrealistic expectations and rich countries' failure to follow through by liberalising agricultural trade. But equally important was the unexpected rise of China.

Having begun negotiations on entry into the multilateral system in 1987, China was finally allowed into the WTO in 2001. Opening rich countries' markets to foreign textile and apparel manufacturers failed to evenly distribute benefits. Instead, as a labour-abundant export powerhouse, China captured much of the new export business other developing states had anticipated during the Uruguay Round.

By the early 2000s, the mismatch between reality and the expectations of the Uruguay Round was already apparent. Rich countries were happy that their services and intellectual-property rights had been introduced into the system, and wanted to negotiate on issues such as foreign investment and competition policy. But developing-country WTO members refused, feeling cheated out of their anticipated gains in agriculture, textile and apparel trade.

Due to the organisation's consensus-based approach, developing countries had the power to block new arrangements. Facing an impasse, WTO members attempted in 2001 to reach a compromise for a new round of negotiations, the Doha Development Agenda. But, even from the start, the agenda's objectives promised to disproportionately favour developing countries in redistributing unrealised Uruguay Round benefits. This imbalance precluded the reciprocal-gains approach of the eight prior negotiating rounds. More than 15 years later, the objectives of the Doha Round have still not been met – and they may never be. Perhaps more importantly, the stalemate reflected a failure to address other areas of stalled reform that threatened the WTO, especially given the rise of China.

China's entry into the organisation shocked the system. On the positive side, it has been a transformative humanitarian achievement: the country's export-led growth model lifted hundreds of millions of people out of poverty in less than two decades. The phenomenon occurred directly within China through the migration of seemingly an entire generation of Chinese citizens from rural agrarian regions to urban areas focused on manufacturing. It also occurred indirectly and outside China, as the country's insatiable demand for natural-resources imports fuelled growth in commodity-producing countries in Africa and Latin America.

Furthermore, China did not receive the free pass gained by developing countries that entered GATT. As a condition of its entry into the WTO, China was forced to cut import tariffs to much lower levels than had been demanded of developing countries that were already part of the system. China also had to undertake other large-scale market-oriented reforms, most of which it successfully completed.

But China's entrance also posed challenges to, and exposed several weaknesses in, the WTO system. The rapid growth in Chinese exports coincided with a broad decline in manufacturing employment in the United States and elsewhere in the West. Although economists have ascribed some of the decline to increased imports from the so-called 'China shock', they have attributed most of these job losses to technological advances that allowed for greater automation of production, and to changing product demand. Nonetheless, the coincidence of Chinese-export growth and Western-manufacturing decline has political implications: it is likely to have at least partly contributed to the narrative behind the recent populist backlash in the West.

The enduring impact of China's entry into the global trading system originates in the country's incomplete transformation into a market economy. China made considerable efforts at reform in the 1990s and early 2000s in particular, introducing private firms to compete with state-owned enterprises. Yet Beijing's more recent activities suggest a resurgence of state intervention in the Chinese economy. This trend has generated concern within a global trading system designed around cooperation between market economies. The system has never before been forced to manage trade between market economies and such a large non-market, state-driven economy, whose policy decisions can have profound implications for its trading partners.

Washington arguably recognised this looming problem during the presidency of George W. Bush. With the collapse of the Doha Round talks at a ten-day ministerial meeting in Geneva in July 2008, it became clear that the US lacked the leverage within the WTO framework to address its concerns about China and a handful of other major developing economies (such as India). As the US and most other industrialised countries had largely opened their economies to trade, they had little to offer to these latecomers to the system as an incentive to undertake liberal reforms. As a consequence, Washington implemented a plan to secure its long-term trading interests within the system through other means, not least the negotiation of mega-regional agreements.

Responses to the China challenge

The Obama administration began in 2009 by conducting trade talks with a small group of Pacific Rim states, before expanding the process to include 12 countries under the Trans-Pacific Partnership (TPP). The economic anchors of the agreement were to be the US and Japan – which joined in 2013, when the talks were already well under way. Signed in 2016, the final deal also included Canada and Mexico – thereby updating the trilateral North American Free Trade Agreement (NAFTA) – as well as Australia and major emerging economies such as Vietnam, Malaysia and Peru. Combined, TPP countries accounted for more than one-third of global GDP and engaged in roughly one-quarter of world merchandise trade.

China was notable in its absence from the TPP. Indeed, the areas covered by the US-led agreement made clear that it was intended to establish the rules of trade in the region, with a view to setting the terms of eventual negotiations between Washington and Beijing. The TPP introduced labour disciplines and environmental standards while expanding protections for intellectual property – all of which could be enforced through trade sanctions on non-compliant member countries. Importantly, the TPP also included competition and anti-corruption provisions, as well as new rules for electronic commerce and digital trade – an area of growing concern for US technology companies such as Google, Facebook and Amazon, which feared exclusion from, or limitations in, a Chinese market that favoured national champions. Finally, the TPP imposed disciplines on state-owned enterprises, an area of long-standing US concern about China.

The agreement included an accession clause that, in line with long-term US strategy, would give Washington leverage in its stalled trade talks with Beijing. Members of the TPP such as Vietnam and Malaysia – and perhaps Indonesia and other countries in the future – would receive the kind of trade preferences in American markets that the US could use to tempt China back to the negotiating table, and thereby to address its systemic concerns about the Chinese economy.

Washington built on this approach in 2013, launching negotiations with the European Union on the Transatlantic Trade and Investment Partnership (TTIP), a separate mega-regional trade deal intended to cover everything in the TPP, along with other areas. The agreement was designed to tackle regulatory cooperation, a lack of which implicitly impeded transatlantic commercial integration. Multinationals such as those in the automotive sector aimed to benefit from a single regulatory model that would meet the high safety standards of both the American and EU markets. Despite the fact that both sides had relatively high standards, inadequate engagement had often resulted in costly regulatory divergence, involving redundant testing and product modifications that were expensive but did little to improve safety. Other examples include the development of new pharmaceuticals and medical devices, areas in which there was sometimes a legal need for scientifically redundant clinical trials.

Even in the best circumstances, negotiating a deal such as TTIP would be a daunting challenge requiring years of sustained political commitment. The only point of comparison for this type of international regulatory cooperation was that which arose as part of the decades-long politico-economic integration project that culminated in the EU itself. Although it was not designed to achieve anything near as deep as EU integration, TTIP was likely to require new long-term, living and breathing institutional relations to manage ongoing change. It would involve far more than the one-off paperwork of an old-fashioned trade agreement.

The successful implementation of TTIP could have provided the US and the EU with strategic leverage they needed elsewhere in the trading system, including in their efforts to address the challenge posed by China. By acting as first movers, the US–EU partnership could have established a new template for trade and regulatory rules in the inevitable next set of trade negotiations with the rest of the world. But all of this seemed to have been cast aside with two votes in 2016. The first of these came on 23 June, when the United Kingdom chose to leave the EU; the second on 8 November, when the US elected Donald Trump as president.

Potential threats to the global trading system

The UK's decision to negotiate a departure from the EU created complications for, and posed technical questions to, the WTO – although the task facing the organisation appeared to be relatively manageable. More challenging was the UK's and the EU's attempts to settle on the form of their future trade relations. It was unclear whether the sides would trade with each other 'only' as WTO members; negotiate a full free-trade agreement that would remove tariffs on exports; retain or form a customs union, in which they would not only have a free-trade agreement, but would share a common external tariff on imports from third countries; or even agree to the UK remaining in the single market. By mid-2017, London seemed increasingly unlikely to remain in the customs union, due to its desire to retain control over external trade policy and negotiate free-trade agreements with countries such as the US and Australia – and potentially India and even China.

One of the main uncertainties that arose from the UK–EU talks involved the many regulatory functions and governance rules that

Britain had adopted in line with other members of the Union. It was unclear whether London would regain control of these measures or instead negotiate a regulatory-sharing arrangement with the EU. Given that negotiations on regulatory arrangements are of growing importance to other countries – as reflected in the TTIP talks – the UK needed to resolve these issues before other rich countries would know how to engage with it in trade negotiations. Nonetheless, the UK's decision to leave the EU potentially allowed for a move in a different globalist direction rather than simply a turn inwards.

Yet such a turn inwards was a distinct possibility on the other side of the Atlantic, following the election of Trump. He had campaigned not only as a political outsider, but as an opponent of trade agreements he regarded as unfair to the US. In signalling his disdain for these arrangements, Trump was especially critical of mega-regional and multilateral deals such as that behind the WTO.

During his first week in office, President Trump fulfilled a campaign promise by withdrawing the US from the TPP. Because the agreement had not been ratified by Congress, this did not change US law. However, the move sent a strong signal to TPP countries that the US was disengaging from their regions – a particularly worrying prospect in an Asian politico-security environment troubled by North Korea's increased missile testing, an impeachment scandal and presidential transition in South Korea, and Beijing's growing assertiveness in territorial disputes in the South China Sea.

By mid-2017, contrary to his claims during the election campaign, Trump had neither withdrawn the US from NAFTA nor imposed tariffs of 45% on Chinese imports. But the new US administration had undertaken several other, subtler forms of import protection that could equally undermine the WTO and the rules-based trading system. During his first 100 days, Trump initiated government investigations into whether imports of steel and aluminium were a threat to US national security under a rarely used trade statute. These investigations had the potential to lead to the introduction of an expansive set of trade barriers.

Washington's new approach put US trade partners and the WTO in a potentially unenviable position. If Trump imposed import restrictions with dubious legal justification, these partners would have the option of challenging them through the WTO's dispute-settlement procedures. But such an explicit challenge to America's sovereignty and right to defend itself – regardless of how ill-conceived the claim – could exacerbate Trump's disdain for multilateralism. It could also provide him with the requisite support among Republicans to withdraw the US from the WTO – as he had withdrawn it from the COP-21 agreement on climate change in June 2017. Yet by failing to resist the Trump administration on the issue, US trade partners would risk encouraging other countries to invoke the national-security exception on protectionist measures of their own. Either way, the process could slowly destroy the essence of a rules-based trading system.

The Trump administration was also heavily critical of the WTO's dispute-settlement procedures, viewing a handful of legal rulings on technical issues – such Washington's use of anti-dumping policy – as an unjustifiable encroachment on American sovereignty. But although the administration exaggerated the economic importance of these issues, in other areas it was more forward-looking. The White House correctly identified the contemporary WTO's powerlessness in addressing major US concerns about China, particularly its overcapacity in industrial goods such as steel and aluminium, and its failure to complete the transition to a market economy.

Before 2016, there seemed to be a real possibility that the global trading system's largest problems would be fixed through a process involving long-term re-engagement with the WTO. It was conceivable that – in contrast to the stalemated Doha Round – successful TPP and TTIP negotiations would have developed new rules that excluded, and thus frustrated, China. This frustration could have been used to draw Beijing back into negotiations on the additional market-oriented reforms sought by the West. Any resulting points of agreement could have been combined into a multilateral deal and shepherded through the WTO.

Procedurally, if the main concerns of the West and China were not of interest to other WTO members, their negotiated solutions could have been implemented through what are known as 'plurilateral' deals. Historically, the plurilateral approach had been used when only a small group of GATT countries wanted to implement new rules. So long as the rules did not discriminate against non-participating members – and those countries were also afforded the benefits through most-favoured-nation treatment – these rules could be introduced by a critical mass of concerned countries, even if they were a minority of the membership. The members of GATT most often adopted this approach during the 1970s, when a small group of mostly industrialised economies wanted to introduce rules on new non-tariff barriers.

Following the failure of the Doha Round, there was some momentum within the WTO to rejuvenate the plurilateral approach. In summer 2016, a group of 24 economies began implementing coordinated tariff cuts under the second Information Technology Agreement. Although they were only a fraction of the WTO membership, the countries involved in the deal accounted for an estimated 90% of the US$1.3-trillion global trade in affected products.

At the time, there were also plurilateral discussions on a potential Environmental Goods Agreement and a Trade in Services Agreement (TiSA). The former was an attempt to reduce trade barriers on goods that might help improve environmental conditions, such as solar panels, wind towers, equipment for water-treatment facilities and electronics to better regulate heating and cooling systems. In parallel, TiSA involved market-access negotiations and rules for licensing, covering areas such as financial services, e-commerce and professionals moving abroad.

President Trump's policy priorities seemed at odds with both initiatives. His decision to pull the US out of the 195-country COP-21 agreement reflected scorn for environmental concerns. And his quixotic attempt to return 1950s-style heavy-industry and blue-collar jobs to the US – despite the persistent downward trend in US-manufacturing employment since the second half of the twentieth century – would seem to rule out TiSA. Moreover, reliant on an internationally mobile workforce, much of the services trade was threatened by Trump's executive orders seeking to restrict immigration into the US, including that of highly skilled professionals, under the H-1B visa programme.

As he signalled with his national-security exceptions on steel and aluminium imports, Trump looked set to ignite several conflicts within the WTO system – none of which had an obvious solution. Beyond the intractable problems introduced by Trump's election and the UK's decision to leave the EU, the WTO confronted a series of longstanding, systemic challenges, not least those involving the Chinese economy. Yet, at the same time, the organisation's rules, disciplines and dispute-settlement procedures seemed more necessary than ever. The survival of the WTO would require some combination of resilience, cool-headed deliberation and luck.

Electoral Disruption and the Liberal Order

In *Postwar*, Tony Judt's history of Europe since 1945, the author observed – from a vantage point in the first half-decade of the twenty-first century – some sociological patterns of attachment to, and alienation from, the idea of the European Union:

> To one side stood a sophisticated elite of *Europeans*: men and women, typically young, widely travelled and well-educated, who might have studied in two or even three different universities across the continent. Their qualifications and professions allowed them to find work anywhere across the European Union ... This new class of Europeans travelled with confident ease across their continent – communicating, like medieval *clercs* wandering between Bologna, Salamanca and Oxford, in a cosmopolitan *lingua franca*: then Latin, now English.
>
> On the other side of the divide were to be found those – still the overwhelming majority – who could not be part of this brave new continent or else did not (yet?) choose to join: millions of Europeans whose lack of skills, education, training, opportunity or means kept them firmly rooted where they were. These men and women, the *villeins* in Europe's new medieval landscape, could not so readily benefit from the EU's single market in goods, services and labour. Instead they remained bound to their country or their local community ... and [were] often more hostile to 'Europe' than their cosmopolitan fellow citizens.

Since Judt wrote those words in 2005, the transatlantic West has suffered an epochal financial crisis, failed military interventions in the Middle East, successive bouts of terrorist violence and the depredations of a reactionary if not revanchist Russia, as well as more European-specific crises involving the EU's single currency and massive inflows of refugees and other migrants. But Judt's decade-old story of winners and losers from the process of European integration seems to include a starkly prescient warning about the problem of winners and losers from globalisation writ large. And that broader story appears to be part – if only part – of the crisis of liberal disorder that shook the West in 2016, with the United Kingdom's referendum decision to leave the EU (nicknamed 'Brexit') and, five months later, Donald Trump's election as president of the United States.

This crisis in its acute 2016 manifestation was distinctly *political.* After more than a decade of turmoil in economies, diplomacy, international security and various national societies, the crisis was manifest in the political choices of voters, and the subsequent policy choices of the governments that they elected (or, in the case of the UK, instructed by referendum). These choices were presaged by the political embrace of anti-liberal authoritarianism in two formerly communist EU states: Hungary, where Prime Minister Viktor Orbán's Fidesz-led government came to power in 2010; and Poland, where the Law and Justice government took power in 2015. Of greater global import, however, were the political choices in the US and the UK, which repudiated key institutions and tenets of the post-Second World War liberal order that both countries had done so much to construct.

What liberal order?

There is ambiguity and tension in the word 'liberal'. This starts with the fact that the word has different meanings in Europe and in the US. In Europe, it can mean, at least in a reductionist version, 'capitalist'. Within this meaning, the post-war liberal order includes an open, rules-based international trade regime. But in addition to the Bretton Woods institutions of international economic order, the post-war project rested on extensive state planning for ambitious national welfare states. This was true not only in Western Europe but also in the US, where the word 'liberal' connotes something closer to 'social democratic'. In the conceptions of Bretton Woods, in the formation of NATO, in the reconstruction of Europe – in large measure under the Marshall Plan – and in the institutional beginnings of European integration, crucial leadership came from British Labourites and American New Dealers (many of whom were social democrats at heart, even if they could not embrace full socialism given the constellation of American politics and society).

The continental Europeans who participated in the project included not only socialists but also the conservative Christian Democrats who were in power for most of the years in which Europe's social-democratic welfare states were built.

Catholic conservatives and social democrats in Europe were united with liberal Democrats and even Eisenhower Republicans in the US by a conviction that there was no going back to the arrangements of interwar Europe and Depression-era America, which were laissez-faire in domestic political economy and protectionist in international trade. Of course, a post-war regime of welfare, state planning and open trade embodied the tension in the hybrid, transatlantic concept of liberalism. To begin with, trade liberalisation did not happen all at once: stages and degrees of protectionism were deemed necessary to protect welfare states. Over time, however, the two meanings of liberal order were to a great extent bundled together. This process required conservatives to accept the state's responsibility for general welfare and socialists to embrace capitalist markets, including open international markets, as engines of wealth creation. Arguably, the apotheosis of the latter is the EU single market promoted by then EU Commission president Jacques Delors, a French socialist, in the late 1980s and early 1990s. The UK's leaders wholeheartedly supported the single market after Labour returned to government in 1997; for years thereafter, the marked success of the EU appeared to reflect the wealth-creating magic of globalisation.

Yet after the financial collapse of 2008, many in the West viewed that magic as systemic fraud. Recovery in the US was painfully slow, and it was even slower in an EU constricted by fiscal orthodoxy and the monetary straightjacket of the euro. The European project was further undermined by a failure to cope with massive inflows of refugees and other migrants from the Middle East and North Africa, as well as terrorist attacks that were blamed, tendentiously but nonetheless effectively, on the Schengen Area's open internal borders. The UK belonged to neither the monetary union nor Schengen; it had a high degree of sovereign control over its economy and borders – even while accepting large numbers of workers from EU states in Central and Eastern Europe – but its Conservative-led government, in power since 2010, shared the inclinations towards austerity of German policymakers.

These difficulties aggravated the raw politics in the UK, continental Europe and the US in 2008–16. (Barack Obama's election as US president inspired hope among those who had voted for him but racial panic in smaller quarters of the electorate.) The general mood was bitter and sullen. This was especially the case in lower-middle-class areas of the American Midwest and South, and in the poorer areas of England and Wales. Still, the vote for Brexit and the victory of Trump took much of the world by surprise.

Brexit, Trump and populism

The apparent commonalities between Trump's election and the outcome of the UK referendum stirred widespread debate as to whether they were discrete events or part of a single phenomenon. It was, after all, Trump's prediction that his election would be 'Brexit times five'; and it was Trump who, after the referendum, invited UK Independence Party leader Nigel Farage, Brexit's most notorious advocate, to join him on the campaign trail in Jackson, Mississippi. There, Farage told Trump supporters that they could do in the US what the campaign to leave the EU had done in the UK. Five days after the election, Farage became the first British politician to meet president-elect Trump, posing with unrestrained glee for a photograph in front of Trump Tower's gilded lift doors.

Brexit-and-Trump has since become a cultural signifier, especially for the losers of the two votes. A neat, if unscientific, analysis by the *Economist* shows a geographical correlation between signatures on a UK petition against a state visit by Trump and support for Remain in the EU referendum. To put it another way, those who dislike Brexit also dislike Trump.

The comparison is resisted most fiercely by the supporters of Brexit, for understandable reasons. Trump's campaign was, at times, overtly racist, starting with his embrace of the 'Birther' claim that the Hawaiian

Barack Obama was actually born in Kenya. His positions on Islam and immigration also put him far outside of the mainstream of UK politics. If the British electorate had selected the US president, polling suggested that Hillary Clinton would have won by around 30 percentage points. There may have been a personal overlap between Trumpism and the more hardline Brexit elements, but many Brexit supporters would not recognise these elements as representative. Farage had failed to gain a seat in Parliament seven times, and led a party whose vote share peaked at 13% in parliamentary elections. The referendum campaign group Farage represented, Grassroots Out, was not recognised as the official advocate of the Leave vote, on the basis that, according to the UK electoral commission, it was less capable than its competitor, Vote Leave, of representing the views of the Brexit movement as a whole. Moreover, although leaving the EU might expand the powers of the UK executive and stir a great deal of angst over separatist pressures in Scotland and Northern Ireland, these and other problems would be very different from the incipient constitutional crisis in the US over alleged links between the Trump campaign and Russian intelligence agencies, and Trump's obfuscatory and domineering response.

There were, however, two similarities that made the Brexit-and-Trump comparison more than an effete sneer. The first was a similarity of message: a focus on immigration, both for its own sake and as a symbol of sovereign control, and a classic populist critique of an unrepresentative elite out of touch with the will of ordinary people.

The second was a similarity of demographics. The constituencies voting for Brexit and Trump are difficult to compare, of course, for the obvious reason that they reside in different countries with their own history, culture and politico-economic conditions. A national referendum in which each vote counts is different from the disproportional Electoral College, for instance; and race relations, although perhaps represented by proxy in the Brexit vote, are far more salient in US elections. Bearing these qualifications in mind, a responsible comparison might involve two questions: which features of the votes were different from the normal patterns of national electoral politics in each country? And, overall, what did the 'typical' Brexit voter and Trump voter look like?

An atypical feature of both votes was the correlation between educational levels and choice of vote. Trump won among non-university graduates by an eight-point margin, and among white non-university graduates by a 39-point margin – both markedly larger gaps than in previous elections (in 2012, for example, Obama won non-university graduates by four percentage points). According to analysis by the BBC, in the UK referendum, voters' educational levels had a higher correlation with their propensity to vote Remain than any other demographic indicator. Although British university graduates in recent years have tended to vote for left-leaning parties in general elections, this was a much sharper divide.

Another noticeable feature was geographical realignment. Trump won the presidency through an Electoral College majority despite gaining a smaller share of the popular vote than his opponent, Clinton. He did so by flipping so-called 'rust belt' states that had been expected to vote for Clinton such as Michigan, Wisconsin and Pennsylvania (which had last voted for a Republican presidential candidate in 1988, 1984 and 1988 respectively). The EU referendum saw traditional Labour Party strongholds in the north of England, as well as in Wales, vote Leave by wide margins. For example, the Leave campaign won 60% of the vote in the northeastern city of Sunderland, which only a year earlier had comfortably elected a Labour member of parliament.

Although these were the most obvious shared features of the two votes, inferring causation from voter demographics is fraught with analytical danger. Nonetheless, it is still possible to observe from exit-poll data that a randomly selected Trump or Brexit voter was more likely to be male than female, older than younger, less educated than more educated and white than from an ethnic minority. And if social status is zero-sum, then the average older, white man without a university degree believes he is the clear loser of recent economic and cultural change in advanced Western economies – or what might be called liberal progress, together with the effects of globalisation.

A study of the rise of populist parties in Europe up to 2014 by social scientists Pippa Norris and Ronald Inglehart noted that although populism received greater support among the less well-off, it could not be straightforwardly called the result of inequality. Populist sentiment was stronger among the lower middle class than among unskilled manual workers, the authors observed – but it was closely linked to cultural factors. Older, white, less-educated men were 'most likely to feel that they have become strangers from the predominant values in their own country, left behind by progressive tides of cultural change which they do not share'. Writing in August 2016, Norris and Inglehart went on to suggest that Brexit and the rise of Trump could be attributed to this kind of cultural backlash, enabled – but not necessarily caused per se – by economic discontent.

This cultural interpretation of Brexit-and-Trump, as described by the economist Anatole Kaletsky, holds that 'when free-market economic liberalism failed in the 2008 crisis, political challenges to social liberalism could no longer be deflected by invoking impersonal economic laws'. To put it another way, a shift in social values might have been tolerable to Judt's *villeins*, albeit resented, during a period of broad economic growth. But in conditions of recession and inequality, it was enough to shift voting behaviour.

In this sense, the two votes resembled, and appeared at least partly driven by the same causes of, a long-term phenomenon. By 2016, as the academic Cas Mudde has observed, populists were earning more than 10% of the vote in 16 European countries; in Hungary and Poland, they were in charge of governments intent on remaking the state; in Austria and – to a lesser degree – France, they had threatened to claim the presidency; in the Netherlands, they could have become the largest parliamentary party. The definition of the term 'populism' remains a matter of internecine dispute among political scientists, depending on whether it is considered to be an ideology, a rhetorical style or an organisational practice, but at its core it rests, as Mudde defines it, on presenting a dichotomy between 'the pure people' and 'the corrupt elite'. The combination of this basic ideological device with types of far-right and nativist political movements should, despite Emmanuel Macron's victory in France and Mark Rutte's in the Netherlands, be considered a long-term threat to the Western political order – for it is exclusionary, anti-pluralist and, partly as a result, hostile to the European project. It has opened more fissures in the EU, turning both Hungary and Poland into near-pariah member states, and in the long term could drive them out of it.

Whatever the role of a populist surge in events in the UK and the US, of course, no political event is mono-causal. The ideological tradition of British euroscepticism might have contained some strands of cultural resentment, but it also drew on a desire for national sovereignty as a legal and constitutional matter, present on the political left as well as the right, and predating the ascendancy of economic and social liberalism. And if Trump was an extraordinary Republican candidate for the presidency, he was still *the* Republican candidate; support for him was rationalised on the basis that he would install at least one conservative Supreme Court justice and sign into law the products of a Republican Congress.

The other overlap between Brexit and the election of Trump – one that is much less a matter of simple academic speculation – is in their effects. In the first place, the two votes together dramatically reconfigured the existing and planned architecture of international trade. If the UK leaves the single market, as both Prime Minister Theresa May and leader of the opposition Jeremy Corbyn have said will happen, it will mark the most dramatic reversal in trade liberalisation since the establishment of the post-Second World War economic order. This is not to say that the UK will be unable to reach a free-trade agreement with the EU or with the third-party countries that the advocates of Brexit claimed would be keen to negotiate such a deal. But, by definition, the free movement of goods, services, capital and labour enshrined in the European single market permits the 'freest' trade on offer with what is currently the UK's largest trading partner. The two votes also killed off the already uncertain prospect that the EU and the US would finalise the Transatlantic Trade and Investment Partnership – Brexit helping to do so via its shock to the European political system, and Trump by virtue of his avowed protectionism. That position also led Trump to sign an executive order withdrawing the US from the Trans-Pacific Partnership; to modify the G20's position on free trade to recognise the role of 'legitimate trade defence instruments'; and to demand a renegotiation of the North Atlantic Free Trade Agreement as the price for retaining it.

Less tangibly, but no less significantly, the two votes damaged transatlantic solidarity. The West – loosely defined as the democracies of Europe, North America and a handful of allies elsewhere – is, in material terms, strong: it accounts for one-third of global GDP and more than half of global military spending. But its ability to confront current challenges depends on the political solidarity that underpins collective action. Europe is large enough to be able to take care of even a few million refugees, but only with a plan for spreading the financial and political burden of doing so among its member states. Russian President Vladimir Putin's threats to Europe may be primarily defensive bluster, but the more divided the Western alliance becomes, the more Russia has to work with. A vote for Brexit marked a symbolic and substantive retreat from cooperation, a decision that the UK's freedom of action was more important than the shared gains offered by a limited pooling of sovereignty. Moreover, Brexit will remove UK resources and influence from EU responses to Europe's crises. These resources are likely to be diminished: there are few credible scenarios under which Brexit will not disrupt UK economic growth. In theory, all of this could be compensated for by the UK's stated desire to seek a 'deep and special partnership' with the EU; in practice, the complexity of Brexit negotiations will hinder the ability of the British government to make substantive progress on any new areas of cooperation, and failure to reach an agreement on the terms of the UK's exit – with manifold dire consequences – would strike a blow to European solidarity unlike any since the Second World War.

Russia's win?

In March 2016, before the two consequential votes, *Washington Post* columnist Anne Applebaum recalled previous threats to the Western alliance: in the 1950s, 'when the institutions were still new and shaky'; in the 1970s of Vietnam and Red Brigades terrorism. But she concluded,

> in my adult life, I cannot remember a moment as dramatic as this: Right now, we are two or three bad elections away from the end of NATO, the end of the European Union and maybe the end of the liberal world order as we know it.

At the time, it was only a question of a possibility of Trump becoming the Republican presidential nominee, but it was a real possibility and, as Applebaum noted, 'elections are funny things': Republican nominee Trump could, conceivably, become President Trump. In France, National Front leader Marine Le Pen, who shared Trump's affinity for Putin's Russia and hostility to both NATO and the EU, was a leading candidate for the presidency. It seemed likely that the French left and right would cooperate in second-round presidential elections to defeat her, but who could be sure? Finally, as there was a serious prospect of the UK voting in its June referendum to leave the EU, it was 'not hard at all to imagine a Britain unmoored from Europe drifting away from the transatlantic alliance as well'.

Two of Applebaum's 'bad elections' have transpired. She had further worried about a chain reaction of EU withdrawals, a British electorate facing post-Brexit economic turmoil turning to the only viable alternative – Labour under the leftist Corbyn – and the US empowering Trump's innate hostility to the institutions and practices of liberal order.

What has surprised, perhaps, is that of the three sides of the triangle, it is the continental EU that has proven most resilient. By mid-2017, the euro-area economy was performing better than that of the UK and on a par with that of the US. Perhaps chastened by the US reminder that elections have consequences, voters in the Netherlands and Austria turned decisively against right-wing populists. The Austrian case was a kind of controlled pre-Trump and post-Trump experiment: due to minor technical irregularities, the Austrian Supreme Court had ordered a rerun of the presidential elections, with the result that an extremely narrow win by the centre-left candidate was turned into a more decisive defeat of his extreme-right rival. German politicians, including Chancellor Angela Merkel and Minister of Defence Ursula von der Leyen, found their voices with strong proclamations of liberal values and direct criticism of the US president. Finally, Le Pen was soundly defeated by the charismatic Macron, a technocratic centrist who touted his commitment to the EU and free-market liberalism. Across much of the EU, opinion polling showed a marked uptick in public support for the Union. NATO too appeared reasonably safe, for the moment. Trump's persistent refusal to reaffirm the commitment to collective defence under the North Atlantic Treaty had the side effect of demonstrating that most of the US national-security establishment, including his top foreign-policy aides, believed in the commitment. (Trump eventually reaffirmed the commitment, but did so under pressure and with palpable reluctance.) And yet, Trump's nomination and election had revealed that a large swathe of the Republican electorate was at least indifferent to their candidate's heresies on NATO. Thus, American allies were forced to think about fallbacks and hedging strategies.

The electoral triumph of Trumpism and the similar dynamics in Hungary and Poland, as well as Turkey's regression towards a presidential dictatorship, suggested the demise of any remaining confidence in the inevitability of liberal-democratic progress. Macron faced a formidable task in reforming France's economy, while the Dutch prime minister felt the need to embrace some populist themes in order to defeat his hard-right rival. The presumption that Le Pen's defeat marked the turning of the tide for Western populism may not be sound.

It is unnerving, moreover, that the political travails of Western liberal order have coincided with geopolitical disorder worldwide. And it is reasonable to inquire whether the two things are related. Certainly, the epochal breakdown of the 1930s – still, barely, part of the collective living memory – featured historically established connections between socio-economic disruptions, the rise of fascist extremism and consequent geopolitical revanchism in an international system that had not been adequately reconstituted after the First World War.

Resort to historical analogy is inevitable, but sometimes misleading. A crude analogy has framed the disorder as a product of moral weakness. In this telling, President Barack Obama failed in 2013 to enforce his red line over the Syrian regime's use of chemical weapons; this failure convinced adversaries and potential adversaries that the US no longer had the will to play the role of global hegemon; this spreading conviction that the hegemon had lost its nerve encouraged Chinese aggression in the South China Sea and Russian aggression in Ukraine; and, ultimately, Moscow came into Syria to fill the vacuum left by the US. As a consequence of deflated American credibility, world disorder has accelerated.

Obama was asked about this directly during his final year in office, when *Atlantic* journalist Jeffrey Goldberg challenged him on whether 'deterrent credibility' had been undermined by the red-line episode, leading President Putin to 'push him a little further' in Ukraine. 'Look', Obama responded,

> this theory is so easily disposed of that I'm always puzzled by how people make the argument. I don't think anybody thought that George W. Bush was overly rational or cautious in his use of military force. And as I recall, because apparently nobody in this town does, Putin went into Georgia on Bush's watch, right smack dab in the middle of us having over 100,000 troops deployed in Iraq.

On these terms, the then-president was right; both historical evidence and common sense suggest that the more important source of credibility is an adversary's assessment of capability and interest, not a generalised willingness to use military force. In Georgia in 2008, and in Ukraine in 2014, the balance of interest favoured Russia. And Obama's example suggests, among other things, that there is an opportunity cost to using force for the purpose of making future threats more credible.

None of this, however, refutes the geopolitical significance of historical shifts undermining the stability of alliances. To a significant extent, these shifts are the delayed result of the end of the Cold War.

In the Middle East, much of the discord between America and its Arab partners, as well as Israel, stems from the simple fact that their interests are no longer clearly aligned. Thus, the Obama administration determined that US interests required the negotiation of a nuclear deal with Iran rather than cooperation with Saudi Arabia, other Gulf Arab states and Israel in a fierce cold war against the Iranians. The Trump administration has made a different determination – promising to join Sunni autocracies in a maximalist front against Tehran – but it is hardly clear that this will lead to a more peaceful or secure Middle East, or a sustainable course for the US. America's Asian allies were understandably discomfited by Trump's early rhetoric of abandonment, but they were already anxious due to China's growth – potentially, into the first real peer competitor that the US has faced since the nineteenth century.

In material terms, the Russian challenge to America and its allies is far less potent. Although its intervention in Ukraine and annexation of Crimea have transgressed important principles of European order, it is strategically significant that these conflicts are on Russia's borders, far to the east of the inner-German central front of the Cold War. By providing security guarantees to the Baltic states, NATO may have overextended: there are plausible scenarios in which Russian forces seize territory in a fait accompli that would seriously challenge any campaign to take it back. But, due to the plans and deployments the Alliance made after the Ukraine crisis began, it is highly likely that they could only do so by risking dangerous, potentially nuclear, escalation.

Russia has been most successful, however, in exploiting recent political disorder. Russian leaders seem to operate on the basis of assumptions promulgated in a seminal 2013 article by Russian Chief of the General Staff Valery Gerasimov: the continuum between kinetic and politico-information warfare is seamless; the political end of that continuum is deadly serious and even existential; the West through political means of destabilisation turned stable Middle Eastern states – Libya and Syria – into places of anarchy almost overnight; the West intends, and has some strategies, to do the same in Eurasian states partnered with Russia and even Russia itself; and this matter is existential and therefore – this part is implied, not stated, in the article – Russia should employ the same strategies against Western democracies.

In doing so, Moscow has benefited from the decentralisation of the production and distribution of news, embracing a dystopian online media environment within which no narrative is uncontested. Contrary to early techno-utopian forecasts, this connectivity has not promoted the best of human nature or critical understanding. With the demotion of traditionally important editorial gatekeepers, Russian propagandists have, for example, exploited Western Europeans' anxiety about mass migration to cultivate virulent false narratives, such as the January 2016 story of the kidnapping and rape of a Russo-German girl by Arab migrants.

Both Le Pen and Farage have enthusiastically abetted such new-media propaganda campaigns. In Le Pen's case, the French state and mainstream parties mounted an impressive defence against attempts to hack Macron-campaign emails and disseminate them strategically before the second round of the presidential election. Brexit, with its effects on EU and NATO solidarity, seems a strategic fruit for any opponent of that solidarity, but it is a fruit that fell mainly unassisted into Moscow's lap.

The Russian role in the 2016 US presidential elections is more troubling, even dire. American intelligence agencies determined, with a stated 'high level of confidence', that their Russian counterparts covertly intervened in the process to harm Clinton and help Trump. This included various familiar forms of disinformation and, apparently, even efforts to hack into individual states' computerised voting systems. The main vehicle, however, was the successful hack of emails to and from Democratic National Committee staff and Clinton campaign chief John Podesta. The hacked emails were transmitted to WikiLeaks, which published them in strategically timed tranches.

The real possibility that Russia influenced the outcome of the presidential elections – and might have colluded with the Trump campaign to do so – constitutes a significant blow to US democracy and, by extension, a significant Russian victory. The blow is not diminished by recognising that the pre-existing disorder, polarisation and acrimony of American politics is what made it possible – as seen when, during the campaign, Senate Majority Leader Mitch McConnell rejected President Obama's appeal for a bipartisan warning to Moscow about the hacking, with the claim that Obama was merely trying to discredit the Republican nominee. To say that Russian strength in a contest with Western democracies is mainly a function of these democracies' internal problems is not so different from the assessments, in the early years of the Cold War, from analysts such as George Kennan, who insisted that the Soviet threat primarily resided not in the strength or position of the Red Army but rather the fact that post-war Western Europe was cold, hungry and scared.

The Western alliance is no longer hungry or cold, or weak by any relevant material standard of measure. Russia today is, in relative terms, far weaker. But the Anglo-Saxon powers' loss of faith in their domestic arrangements, and in the post-Second World War global structures they did so much to create, could foreshadow many more years of crisis.

Urbanisation, Violence and City-Led Policymaking

As the global population is increasing – especially in Africa, Asia and Latin America – and ever more people are moving to cities, urbanisation is shaping the security environment. Although urbanisation is often associated with higher levels of socio-economic development and prosperity, the phenomenon also creates societal problems, particularly when combined with rapid population growth. Fast-paced, unmanaged and poorly serviced urbanisation generates an array of infrastructural, economic, social and security challenges. These problems are most apparent in slums and other informal settlements, where unofficial, often illicit governance and economic structures challenge the host state and licit economy. Many such areas become disputed territories: pockets of high-intensity armed activity in which governance challenges and the activities of non-state armed groups converge.

More people, more cities

For most of human history, the global population grew slowly. However, in recent centuries, the pace of growth dramatically increased: between 1900 and 2000, the world population rose from 1.5 billion to 6.1bn. The trend is likely to continue, according to the United Nations. By the end of the twenty-first century, the population is expected to reach 11.2bn. Much of the growth will occur in a handful of regions. Africa, which has the youngest population of any continent, is expected to account for more than half of population growth by the middle of the twenty-first century. Between 2015 and 2050, half of the world's population growth is expected to be concentrated in nine countries – all of them, bar the United States, in Africa or Asia.

Rapid population growth has coincided with large-scale migration to urban centres. In 1950, more than two-thirds of the global population lived in rural areas; today, approximately 55% of people live in urban centres. This proportion is projected to rise to 60% by 2030, at which point an estimated one-third of people will reside in either a large city or a megacity (comprising more than 1 million or more than

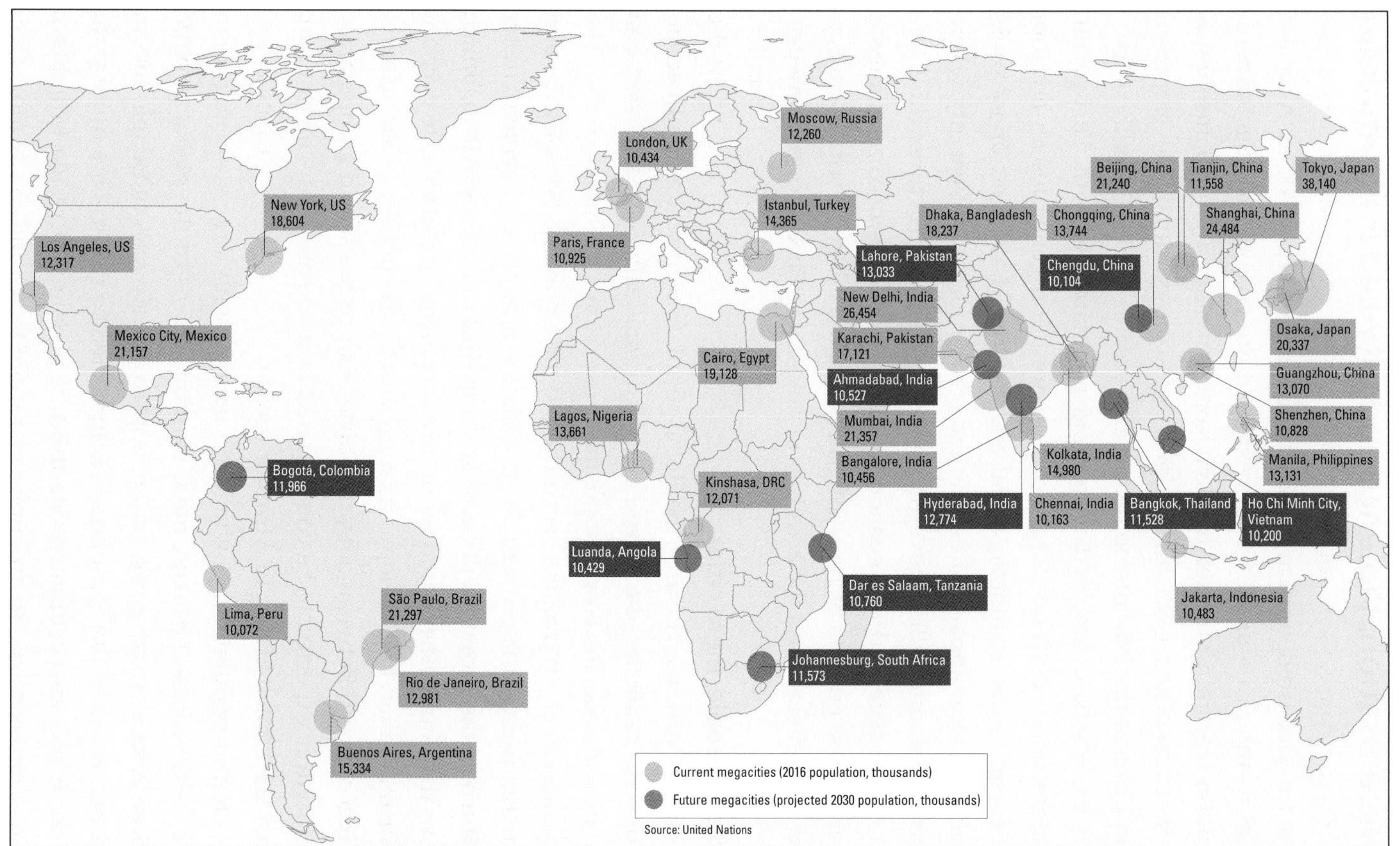
Moscow, Russia 12,260
London, UK 10,434
Beijing, China 21,240
Tianjin, China 11,558
Tokyo, Japan 38,140
New York, US 18,604
Istanbul, Turkey 14,365
Dhaka, Bangladesh 18,237
Chongqing, China 13,744
Shanghai, China 24,484
Los Angeles, US 12,317
Paris, France 10,925
Lahore, Pakistan 13,033
Chengdu, China 10,104
New Delhi, India 26,454
Osaka, Japan 20,337
Mexico City, Mexico 21,157
Karachi, Pakistan 17,121
Cairo, Egypt 19,128
Guangzhou, China 13,070
Ahmadabad, India 10,527
Lagos, Nigeria 13,661
Mumbai, India 21,357
Shenzhen, China 10,828
Kolkata, India 14,980
Bogotá, Colombia 11,966
Bangalore, India 10,456
Manila, Philippines 13,131
Kinshasa, DRC 12,071
Hyderabad, India 12,774
Chennai, India 10,163
Bangkok, Thailand 11,528
Ho Chi Minh City, Vietnam 10,200
Luanda, Angola 10,429
Dar es Salaam, Tanzania 10,760
São Paulo, Brazil 21,297
Jakarta, Indonesia 10,483
Lima, Peru 10,072
Johannesburg, South Africa 11,573
Rio de Janeiro, Brazil 12,981
Buenos Aires, Argentina 15,334
Current megacities (2016 population, thousands)
Future megacities (projected 2030 population, thousands)
Source: United Nations

10m inhabitants respectively). India, China and Nigeria will account for more than 30% of additional urban residents by the middle of the century. Combined with the new urban dwellers expected to live in the Democratic Republic of the Congo, Ethiopia, Tanzania, Bangladesh, Indonesia, Pakistan and the US, by 2050 around 55% of the global urban population will live in ten countries, according to the UN's *World Urbanization Prospects 2014*.

The distribution of megacities will also continue to be uneven. Among the world's 31 megacities in 2016, 26 were located in developing regions. It is projected that, by 2030, ten more conurbations will have become megacities. Six of them are in Asia, three are in Africa and one is in Latin America.

The speed at which these changes are occurring places intense pressure on infrastructure, security structures and economic activity. Johannesburg, one of the urban centres expected to become a megacity by 2030, is a case in point. As shown in the *Atlas of Urban Expansion*, between 1990 and 2013 the city's population grew by 154%, while the territory it covered expanded by only 60%. This trend reoccurs across the Global South, sometimes bringing with it rising social tension and burgeoning illicit economies.

Local authorities are often unable to meet the needs of the large number of people who converge on cities seeking employment, better prospects and security. This lack of capacity fosters the establishment of slums and other informal settlements. In poor, fragile or conflict-affected countries, more than 60% of the urban population lives in slums in which the state has a limited presence, allowing for the rise of informal governance and illicit or informal economies, as well as the proliferation of non-state armed groups such as criminal gangs and violent extremist organisations.

The development of sprawling, poorly serviced peripheries often accompanies urbanisation in these settings, a phenomenon UN-Habitat describes as 'peripherisation'. This process occurs when a metropolis is only able to absorb large numbers of new people by expanding into surrounding areas in an unplanned – and often illegal – way, depriving new residents of secure land tenure and basic urban services such as sanitation. The UN estimates that since 2000, despite international efforts to address the global expansion of slums under the Millennium Development Goals, 6m people have joined informal settlements every year – or 16,500 every day. There are currently 881m people living in slums. Peripherisation forms part of a vicious cycle in which poor people are forced to move after being unable to access affordable housing or public transportation, which in turn increases the cost to the government of extending public services to their areas.

Urbanisation often has many economic benefits, with cities accounting for much of a state's tax base. For example, Karachi is home to around 10% of Pakistan's population but generates more than half of the country's tax revenue. It is also a megacity that faces multiple security problems, requiring the continuous deployment of the Pakistan Rangers to contain violence and criminality, particularly in informal settlements with poor sanitation and water supply. Many other cities in developing countries encounter similar challenges. These problems have raised new concerns about security among policymakers, analysts and state employees. For instance, urban planners have been forced to account for risk factors associated with violent crime and terrorism when designing urban areas. This trend is reflected in the *New Urban Agenda*, a document that UN member states adopted at the Habitat III conference, held in October 2016, to guide urbanisation in the following two decades. By adopting the document, the states committed to urban-development initiatives that 'integrate inclusive measures for urban safety, crime and violence prevention'. They also called for 'special attention' to urban development in post-conflict settings, where political tension and the activities of non-state armed groups often manifest as terrorism or crime.

Their increased concern about violence in urban areas stems from a combination of organised crime and armed violence in a growing number of Latin American, African and South Asian cities. In fact, even the world's richest country, the US, faces high levels of criminal violence in large urban centres such as Chicago. In a 2014 study,

UN-Habitat warned about 'autonomous and "no-go" zones such as slums and other informal settlements that effectively lie outside local and central government control'. These are the areas in which old and new security threats exacerbate mismanagement of urban social and spatial dynamics.

Urban warfare and disputed territories

Military analysts and practitioners have long focused on the challenges of urban warfare as an all-out struggle in built-up areas. The perception of urban environments as battlefields has led to a silo mentality in urban-security policy and insufficient cross-sectoral cooperation. This has limited the options available to urban planners, development experts and institutions such as UN-Habitat. As a consequence, frameworks for violence prevention, gang rehabilitation and community policing frequently crumble in the face of highly organised violence in unstable peripheries. However, effective urban-security policy requires a perspective that reaches beyond urban warfare to encompass the ways in which the changing character of conflict affects cities.

Put forward by US General Charles Krulak (Retd) in 1999, the concept of the three-block war describes the complex demands placed on security forces in unstable peripheries: combating non-state actors in one block, conducting peacekeeping operations in the next block and delivering humanitarian aid in yet another block. The concept rests on an acknowledgement that conflict increasingly involves a mixture of state and non-state actors, in multiple domains, who challenge established security mechanisms. These problems are familiar to local authorities in Medellín, which were forced to adopt a series of improvised policing, military and architectural solutions to stabilise *comunas* (slums) controlled by left-wing guerrillas and powerful criminal groups during the 1990s and 2000s. They are also familiar to US special forces deployed to Mogadishu in 1993, as part of a humanitarian-support operation that quickly descended into a bloody urban battle.

As seen in cities such as Kabul and Karachi, rural warlords have proven capable of adapting to urban environments. More broadly, insurgencies and other types of conflict involving non-state actors in rural areas have spilt into cities through flows of weapons and militant activity, exacerbating political tension and fuelling illicit economies there. Analysts Nils Gilman, Jesse Goldhammer and Steven Weber describe such flows as moving through cities in 'a de facto archipelago that runs from the inner metropolitan cities of the United States to the *favelas* of Rio de Janeiro to the *banlieues* of Paris to the almost continuous urban slum belt that girds the Gulf of Guinea from Abidjan to Lagos'.

Often described in popular culture as ganglands, 'no-go' areas or criminal enclaves, disputed territories exist at the convergence of multiple social and strategic challenges relating to demographic trends, governance and the activities of non-state armed groups. In these territories, rapid population growth can exacerbate risk factors associated with state fragility, armed conflict and the prevalence of illicit economies. Yet megacities are not inherently problematic: for instance, residents of Chinese megacities are remarkably safe from armed violence, while Buenos Aires recorded around four times fewer homicides than Rio in 2015 despite having a larger population than the Brazilian city. Rather, such challenges arise when specific territories, usually urban peripheries and slums, transform into disputed areas. Although these areas frequently create the same kinds of policy dilemmas, the forms of governance adopted by non-state groups there vary widely.

During the second half of the twentieth century, Medellín became a focal point of the armed conflict between the Colombian government and FARC. The city received flows of people displaced by guerrilla warfare in rural areas, as well as a mixture of armed insurgents, right-wing paramilitaries and criminal gangs. As a consequence, the population of Medellín grew fourfold between 1950 and 1985. Conflict and deployments of non-state armed groups were overwhelmingly concentrated in unstable areas such as Comuna 13 – a slum that was home to around 5% of the city's population but experienced a disproportionate share of the fighting between guerrillas, paramilitaries, gangs and state forces. In 2002 around 40% of the people who fled their homes in Medellín due to violence were residents of Comuna 13. The same year, a military operation launched by then-president Alvaro Uribe expelled FARC from the slum, only for the group to be replaced by right-wing paramilitaries and, later, criminal gangs. Despite the overall security improvement in Medellín in the past decade, Comuna 13 recorded the second-highest number of intentional homicides among the city's 16 areas between 2012 and 2015, according to official statistics. A press investigation revealed that 34 gangs operated in Comuna 13 in 2014, the second-highest number among these areas.

The authorities in Rio face challenges similar to those in Medellín. Although there is no armed conflict in Rio, armed groups control many of the city's slums. These organisations invade rivals' territory and expand their areas of control, establishing shadow economies that spill into the broader urban environment through extortion, theft and drug trafficking. The government attempted to regain control of the slums by launching in 2008 a pacification programme designed to protect their 1.5m inhabitants. The authorities established bases there staffed by heavily armed military-police officers and began peacebuilding efforts, urban-development initiatives and the provision of basic services such as rubbish collection and mail delivery – all of which had been unavailable. With intentional homicides across the city falling by 42.5% between 2008 and 2014, security experts and the international media vaunted the pacification programme, especially given Rio's visibility as host of the 2016 Summer Olympics.

But Rio and Medellín also demonstrated the challenges of sustaining security interventions in large, complex areas. Both cities experience fluctuations in the homicide rate and occasional clashes between criminal groups engaged in territorial disputes. Most of Medellín's criminals operate within small gangs known as *combos*. Rio faces a more dangerous threat due to the presence of much larger, transnational groups such as Comando Vermelho (Red Command). Brazil's 2015–16 recession also laid bare the difficulties in maintaining expensive, labour-intensive security operations in densely inhabited areas for several years. Eventually, Rio ran out of funds for the development and infrastructure investment necessary to support the pacification programme.

City-led responses to transnational threats

Although urbanisation is not a cause of conflict, Latin America's experience with high levels of criminal violence is linked to the fact that it is the most urbanised of all developing regions: approximately 80% of people in the region live in cities. Around 40–50% of Africans and Asians live in urban areas, but the proportion is growing fast. This is worrying not only because of the sheer speed with which metropolitan areas are having to absorb impoverished populations, but also because these regions are affected by ongoing conflicts. Sub-Saharan Africa and the Sahel host eight of the world's 15 UN peacekeeping operations, while many South Asian cities – which include some of the largest slums anywhere – are hubs for drug trafficking and the activities of armed groups.

Amid exponential growth in the number of people living in cities in low-income or fragile states, gaps in infrastructure, public services and security capacity will become more glaring in peripheral or slum areas. These shortfalls present opportunities to non-state armed groups, especially those involved in profitable illicit activities such as drug trafficking, extortion, money laundering, kidnapping, human smuggling and prostitution. In many cities rife with such activity, the authority of the state can be challenged or ignored with impunity.

Durable governance structures are crucial to addressing these problems. Adopted by UN states in 2015, the 2030 Sustainable Development Goals recognise the growing security and development challenge in cities: goal 11 concerns efforts to ensure that cities are inclusive, safe, resilient and sustainable. There is a growing consensus among local policymakers and urban planners about the importance of carefully combining security and development techniques. For instance, this involves establishing robust police forces that are able to fend off armed criminals, while also safely delivering public services. In post-conflict environments, new street layouts and transportation connections can help reintegrate communities who would otherwise feel excluded from a city's mainstream political and social life. Many of the challenges cities face can be addressed with initiatives ranging from improved rubbish collection to the introduction of advanced data-gathering technologies that help shape the strategies of local policymakers. As policymaking in cities is often more practical and less philosophical than state-level national-security discussions, it has an important role to play in tackling transnational threats. As argued by political theorist Benjamin Barber in *If Mayors Ruled the World*, cities are the most networked and interconnected of political associations and, ideally, are defined by collaboration and pragmatism. Notwithstanding corruption within many municipal authorities, cities can provide a structure on which to build evidence-based policy that avoids the politicised debates or sectarian divisions so often apparent within national governments.

The ambitious pledges made by UN member states under the Sustainable Development Goals and the *New Urban Agenda* could harness the potential of local governments to improve security in urban areas. However, this may be insufficient to break the silo mentality and old habits of agencies and professionals in disparate fields such as military stabilisation, policing, urban planning and rubbish collection. Nonetheless, as urban areas in developing countries continue to grow, citizens' demand for security will contribute to the momentum of city-led initiatives.

Resurgence of Information Warfare

The use and abuse of the internet for political effect was a major feature of several significant events in the year to mid-2017. State and non-state actors conducted information campaigns that exploited societal vulnerabilities in conjunction with complex cyber operations, generating renewed interest in the growing potential of information warfare.

In Europe and North America, Russia's subversive political activity exploited the hyperconnectivity of social media in a way that demonstrated the new power, reach and speed of its traditional information-warfare techniques when enabled by the internet. In most regions of the world, the Islamic State, also known as ISIS or ISIL, exploited the internet to radicalise target populations and gain recruits as its control of physical territory diminished. The rise of information warfare that posed a clear and distinct societal threat culminated in direct Russian interference in the US and French presidential elections, as well as a series of ISIS-inspired terrorist attacks in major cities across the globe. Together, these events eclipsed previous concerns about China as the world's leading threat actor in the cyber domain: high-profile press coverage of Chinese hacking exploits and theft of intellectual property faded in the face of direct attacks on nations, political processes and societies by Russia and ISIS. Similarly, the once-prominent debate about Western states' offensive cyber capabilities, and concern about privacy violations resulting from internet monitoring, abated as awareness of a new and immediate challenge grew.

The fundamental principles employed in the attacks are well established. Russia's contemporary use of information warfare rests on long-established techniques dating back not only to the Soviet era but also Tsarist times. Parallels have been drawn between ISIS public-relations/propaganda techniques and those adopted by Germany's Nazi Party in the 1930s and 1940s. Yet, in each case, the internet's capacity to exert direct, personalised influence on individual targets has transformed the effectiveness and reach of information operations. Both Russia and ISIS employ substantial linguistic and other human resources to translate content into the languages of specific audiences, and to adapt this content to regional and sub-regional requirements. Augmented by the 'filter bubble' effect of social media that tailors content to users' interests, this has enabled hostile messaging to penetrate target societies to an unprecedented degree.

Despite their mutual antagonism, Russia and ISIS have adopted similar tactics, techniques and procedures in disseminating messages via the internet. For the jihadist group, messages on social-media platforms that urge individuals to engage in acts of terrorism demonstrate the ways in which narratives can drive and enable violent behaviour. Russian trolls (false accounts operated by humans on social media or discussion boards) and bots (false accounts operated by automated processes) use the same platforms to reinforce false amplifiers upon audiences, diverting or suppressing debate for political effect or simply to discredit adversary state institutions. Both of them not only play on Western media behaviour to achieve maximum publicity for their activities, but also use approaches that are recognisable as commercial-marketing techniques designed to exploit Western internet users' responses, often imitating the manner in which celebrities build their social-media followings. Even the highly personalised mentoring programmes ISIS uses to radicalise vulnerable individuals have parallels with Russian subversion campaigns conducted by individually approaching and recruiting key influencers in a range of countries via social media.

In the United States and to some degree Europe, recognition of this phenomenon came in the form of widespread alarm over the prevalence of 'fake news' – a term that arose in mid-2016 to denote what earlier might have been called disinformation. Whereas in previous decades a painstaking, sometimes years-long process was required to plant false information in the mainstream media, the internet ensures that this can now be done almost instantaneously.

Intensifying Russian subversion

Russia's foreign-intelligence services utilised a range of information-warfare tactics and cyber capabilities to attempt to influence the 2016

US elections, in which Republican candidate Donald Trump unexpectedly triumphed over his Democrat opponent, Hillary Clinton. The reluctance of the outgoing Obama administration to publicly acknowledge these hostile Russian actions or to take countermeasures against them meant that they were effectively conducted unopposed. Details of the hacking of political-party servers, selective leaking of damaging information and direct attacks on state electoral systems slowly emerged in early 2017, after the election result.

Nonetheless, by the time of France's presidential elections in April–May, the French electoral authorities, media, government and political parties had sufficient details on the Russian approach to put in place countermeasures – above all, efforts to raise awareness of the likelihood of direct interference and leaks of sensitive information. As a result, while the controversy over the result of the US elections persisted, Russia was swiftly seen to have failed in its objectives in France. Not only was the Russian campaign unable to tip the outcome of the election in Moscow's favour, but it even enhanced the status of the winning candidate, Emmanuel Macron. Russian interference in this election was also counterproductive in that it alienated Macron, ensuring that he would have a wary relationship with Moscow long before the votes had been counted.

The French presidential elections demonstrated that information-warfare measures undertaken by Russia can be countered. But Moscow likely has substantial reserves of other such techniques to deploy in the future. Moreover, defeating the most ambitious Russian efforts, those to influence the selection of heads of state, does not deter secondary information operations, such as those to exert a more insidious influence on government policy or wider society. High-profile elections in larger countries were not the only targets of Russian influence operations: there was a noticeable increase in hostile Russian cyber and information activities against a range of countries across Europe in the first half of 2017. Western media outlets have highlighted the role of Russian disinformation in influencing political events in the Western Balkans, particularly in preventing countries such as Macedonia from joining NATO.

Following its annexation of Crimea in 2014 and the accompanying deterioration of relations with the West, Russia seized the opportunity for indirect power projection presented by information operations. In the absence of any significant reprisals, Moscow steadily escalated the range and scale of its cyber and information campaigns to the point of attempting state capture in the form of election manipulation. This reflects a rapid evolution of ideas in Russia on what can be achieved through information effects – one spurred by the experience of conducting operations in Ukraine and Syria. Although Russian military thinkers have long recognised that information campaigns can be used to achieve strategic goals, prior to 2014 they assessed that such efforts provided only the preconditions for a swift, effective military victory. Now, these thinkers are instead describing information warfare as replacing conventional military operations completely.

According to Russian Chief of the General Staff Valery Gerasimov, indirect and asymmetric methods such as information warfare can 'enable the opposing side to be deprived of its actual sovereignty without the state's territory being seized'. Andrey Kartapolov, commander of Russia's Western Military District and former chief of the Main Operations Directorate, has argued that 'information effects – including using the internet to affect mass consciousness – can in some cases replace armed intervention altogether'.

A key feature of Russian operations during this period was their mixture of pure 'cyber' activities with information operations in other domains, often using cyber effects as an enabler for broader efforts. This could be seen in Russia's alleged hack of the US Democratic National Committee email server and subsequent release of compromising material from it via WikiLeaks. The operation reflected the Russian approach in which computer-network operations are not treated as distinct from other information operations: Russian theorists tend to see as artificial the distinction between activities in cyberspace and those in processing, attacking, disrupting or stealing information. Instead of cyberspace, Russia (and other countries with a similar conceptual framework, such as China) refers to 'information space', which includes computer networks, the media and human information processing – in effect, the cognitive domain.

According to this approach, information is both the object of activities and the medium through which they are carried out. Furthermore, this information can be stored anywhere and transmitted by any means, so regardless of whether it exists in print media, on television or in a military officer's head, it is subject to the same targeting concepts as an adversary's computer or smartphone. Similarly, this information can be transmitted by any means, so introducing corrupted data into a computer across a network or from a flash drive is conceptually no different than placing fake news in a media outlet or causing it to be openly repeated by a public figure. Thus, Russia's holistic approach presented a fundamental challenge to nations that considered themselves to be well prepared for purely technical cyber aggression, but had no defences against a broader information offensive of which cyber attacks were only one component.

A wide range of state and para-state agencies are available to Russia to bring about the desired information-warfare effects. Both the military Main Intelligence Directorate of the General Staff and the notionally civilian Federal Security Service have been identified as sources of advanced cyber-enabled attacks on Western states. Russian state authorities remain adept at co-opting, cooperating with and exploiting criminal networks in cyber and information campaigns. After many false starts, the Russian armed forces announced the creation of 'Information Operations Troops' in February 2017. These troops were widely misunderstood as having a computer-network-operations function analogous to Western cyber commands; instead, they appear to cover a wider spectrum of activities, in keeping with Russia's broad definition of information warfare.

ISIS online

The increasing prevalence of deliberate disinformation on social media is also posing serious challenges to counter-terrorism work: ISIS has shown an aptitude for adapting marketing principles to attract followers and, like Russia, is unconstrained by any requirement to ensure that its information output is plausible. However, unlike Russia, ISIS has a brand to sell and a 'positive' message; even before it began to suffer substantial territorial losses, the group exaggerated the success of its enterprise while aggressively asserting that its enemies were fragmenting in response to its state-building activities. The manufactured perception that ISIS territories in Syria and Iraq constituted a flourishing 'caliphate' was persuasive enough to garner support from across the globe. As a result, some Muslims were encouraged to migrate to ISIS territories, while others were induced to commit violence in their home countries.

In these latter cases, ISIS propaganda was unlikely to have been solely responsible for radicalising individuals but rather to have catalysed extremists' development from tacit support to active participation. The group appears to have intensified its online incitement of violent attacks in response to territorial losses incurred amid the accelerating campaign of the anti-ISIS coalition. The prominence of ISIS online has remained relatively unaffected by the group's loss of territory and physical assets. This is partly due to its prior saturation of the online jihadist marketplace of ideas with content from 'official' outlets approved by the group's leadership, providing an abundance of raw material with which supporters produce their own propaganda. This distributed operation also facilitates resistance to attempts by states worldwide to censor or block distribution of ISIS content. The group's global campaign continues to heavily rely on these techniques to sustain its fundraising and recruitment capabilities.

The redundancy provided by the wide range of available media platforms has improved the survivability of ISIS information-warfare campaigns. As well as micro-targeting across social media – conscientiously tailoring centralised messages, narratives and propaganda to distinctly different audiences – the organisation makes use of the unregulated and hidden networks comprising the so-called 'dark web' to disseminate orders and intelligence, and to share tactical knowledge. Furthermore, ISIS is content to make extensive use of older internet channels, which many users overlook in favour of newer and more complex media platforms such as Facebook, Twitter, Snapchat and Telegram.

Openness, countermeasures and political disaffection

As the controversy over Russian interference focused public attention on the influential role of social-media networks in political processes, Facebook and Twitter were singled out as major channels through which to reach voters in both the US and French presidential elections. Equally, in the campaign leading up to the United Kingdom's June 2016 referendum on membership of the European Union, some groups appeared to exert disproportionate influence by using detailed profiling of Facebook users to conduct targeted outreach. These developments generated widespread concern about commercial entities' unprecedented power to influence political outcomes worldwide.

Facebook and Twitter had markedly different responses to requests for greater openness – requests intended to develop an understanding of the ways they are used to form and change opinion, and to prevent their abuse by malicious actors. Twitter's relatively open ethos and architecture lends itself to analysis; paradoxically, it also exposes the platform to abuse by bots. In contrast, Facebook has resisted calls for greater openness, citing commercial confidentiality. Facebook has acknowledged that social-media platforms can serve as tools for the collection and dissemination of fake news, false amplifiers and disinformation – all of which are exploited in information operations designed to distort public discourse, recruit supporters or financiers for hostile activities and, ultimately, achieve political or military outcomes. However, by mid-2017, the company continued to block attempts to clarify whether and how Russia exploited its platform to influence the US presidential elections.

Although global efforts to counter Islamist radicalisation are well established, Western states have also begun to search urgently for solutions and countermeasures to Russian information activities. The two campaigns face similar and overlapping challenges. In the Euro-

Atlantic area, steps to counter the spread of disinformation or radical messaging in the media and among the public are constrained by concerns about freedom of expression.

Countermeasures to information warfare by states – whose primary objectives include influencing government decision-making – are also hampered by the absence of any reliable metrics of the ways in which hostile campaigns have been successful. The dissemination of disinformation is the most easily detected form of Russian information activity, as its product can be accessed in open fora. As a result, a wide range of government and independent bodies have set up organisations to monitor the spread of disinformation, distribute information on narratives propagated by Russia and fact-check and debunk stories. But these efforts lack the means to critically assess the effectiveness of disinformation campaigns. Similarly, despite years of extensive, well-funded work on countering extremism, there is little convincing evidence of the success of these programmes in reducing Islamist radicalisation and violence.

In the long term, experts on media behaviour and fake-news campaigns advocate initiatives that build societal resistance to disinformation through media-user education. But, as yet, there seems to have been no concerted effort to provide education of this kind. Although undertakings by governments and non-governmental organisations seek to identify disinformation, there is still no dedicated agency or systematic effort to coordinate their findings or organise countermeasures. The problem is exacerbated by the fact that attempts to study the role of social-media networks in disseminating hostile messaging is only possible to the extent that these networks cooperate with investigations.

Nonetheless, the prevalence of fake news is a symptom as well as a cause of the growing frustrations of ordinary people with the political institutions and individuals that notionally represent them. The election of Trump, as well as the UK's referendum on the EU and June 2017 parliamentary elections, to varying extents reflected deteriorating trust in democratic institutions and in conventional authority figures.

To some degree, they constituted a protest vote against the established global political order.

Disaffection of this kind provides fertile ground for hostile information actors. Movements in Western society support Russian goals in Europe without any direct Russian input; Islamist radicalism feeds off a sense of alienation in Western nations. In this context, adversary information campaigns exploit rather than initiate social trends, and can ride the wave of pre-existing phenomena to achieve their objectives.

The Kremlin's methods of information warfare and disinformation are not solely calibrated to promote a Kremlin agenda but also to confuse decision-makers, undermine confidence in political leadership and institutions, and distract both their audiences and adversaries. The disinformation seeded by trolls, bots and fake media outlets comes in the form of both blatant, evident untruth and more subtle distortion of facts or statements, contributing to an environment of ubiquitous untruths competing through toxic tweets and posts.

Russia is particularly keen to create the perception that the US, rather than itself, is an irresponsible and aggressive actor. With the rapid erosion of faith in US leadership under the Trump administration, this argument has substantially greater potential to gain traction in European public opinion. Meanwhile, ISIS also targets people who are already disaffected with their home country or host nation. Both are aided by a trend of growing distrust in traditional news organisations, as well as increasing reliance on social media as a primary source of news and political information. Both also support their disinformation efforts with intimidation and harassment of journalists and commentators who seek to highlight, explain and discredit the campaigns.

Borderless warfare

Both legitimate and malicious uses of social media for political activism are certain to continue to grow in importance. Although ISIS may make fewer attempts at radicalisation and incitement to violence as its power diminishes, the techniques the group both established and refined will be available to its successors.

Personalised targeting of individuals will continue to gain prominence as a central aspect of successful subversive activity. Russia and ISIS have demonstrated their ability to gain influence by targeting not just communities but individuals, whether for espionage purposes, to persuade them to act in a particular way, to discredit them or for any one of a range of other objectives. Thanks to the reach of social media and the ubiquity of internet-connected devices, there is a far lower threshold for targeting individuals than in previous eras. Hostile targeting was once largely limited to highly influential people due to the intensive effort required to profile them and investigate their movements and vulnerabilities. But this information can now be harvested from smartphones and social-media profiles on an industrial scale, providing unprecedented access to their habits, interests and contacts.

Russia has particularly extensive experience in discrediting key individuals to reduce the effectiveness of organisations. Domestically, this kind of activity has focused on political opponents of the government or anti-corruption investigators. Abroad, Russia has repeatedly used disinformation – for instance, allegations of child rape or possession of child pornography – to neutralise important figures, including critics of Russia and, in at least one case, US Army officers. Campaigns of this sort usually intensify in times of crisis, given that these circumstances maximise their effectiveness in incapacitating the target and sowing doubt or dismay among his or her family and community. Russia also has a programme of testing and accumulating capabilities for targeting personnel en masse on a personalised basis, triaging individuals by location, activity or role. This programme has the potential to target individuals with false messaging on a large scale, imitating trusted sources to maximise the likelihood of success. The capability could be used to spread persuasive disinformation or false instructions at a critical moment in a crisis involving confrontation with Russia.

Technical aspects of information operations also continue to develop rapidly. Hostile actors are now increasingly using social media to conduct technical cyber attacks, exploiting targets' lower wariness in reading social-media posts from apparent friends than in reading emails. Fake news is likely to develop into 'fake video': the adoption of affordable, widely available computer-generated-imagery technology to fabricate compromising scenes of public figures engaged in disreputable activities or making false statements.

Russia has many options for achieving local information dominance to achieve strategic or operational effects, including technical, informational, physical and other means. Flooding social media with trolls and gaining physical control of civilian internet infrastructure are two techniques that the country has already employed. In this context, the April 2015 complex cyber attack on French television network TV5Monde was a trial run for neutralising civilian mainstream media outlets. Moreover, multiple Russian theorists suggest that in the initial phase of a conflict, electronic-warfare forces will be used to suppress an adversary's broadcast media and internet access.

Moscow has also been exploring ways to achieve information dominance through physical initiatives. During the seizure of Crimea, telecommunications engineers embedded with Russian special forces aided in the isolation of the peninsula from information from the outside world, thereby reducing the likelihood of organised resistance. Shortly afterwards, Russia intensified its programme of reconnoitring civilian internet-communications infrastructure abroad, including in the subsea domain, space and, more recently, US territory. Moscow is unlikely to replicate its striking success in achieving total information dominance in Crimea elsewhere, due to the uniquely favourable human terrain and telecommunications topography on the peninsula. But Russia's intense interest in probing Western civilian-communications infrastructure in recent years suggests that it is preparing to deny adversaries access to the information space in times of crisis, including by preventing political leaders from communicating with the public.

These possible applications of information warfare have led to renewed attention to the legal status of cyber and information activities – a debate long promoted by Russia and China, in which Western nations have traditionally been reluctant to engage. Cyber operations have already complicated the process of determining who is a combatant under the Law of Armed Conflict, as seen in discussion about whether a civilian cyber-security operative is a legitimate military target if his or her work contributes to a military effect. But the kind of information operations being carried out by both Russia and ISIS achieve local military effects by targeting individuals and communities on another continent. For instance, these actors can collect sensitive information on the families of enemy servicemen on the front-line. According to Gerasimov, modern warfare involves 'simultaneous effects to the entire depth of enemy territory, in all physical media and in the information domain'. In this conception of information warfare, there are no rear areas or non-combatants.

In May 2017, Microsoft caused controversy by backing a 'digital Geneva Convention' to regulate hostile activity in cyberspace, an initiative long called for by Russia and China. Accompanying proposals included the formation of an independent attribution authority to resolve controversy about the source of attacks. Yet neither approach would constrain state or non-state actors who were willing to violate international law. In the continuing absence of effective countermeasures or deterrents to such activity, malicious and borderless exploitation of information effects is likely to continue.

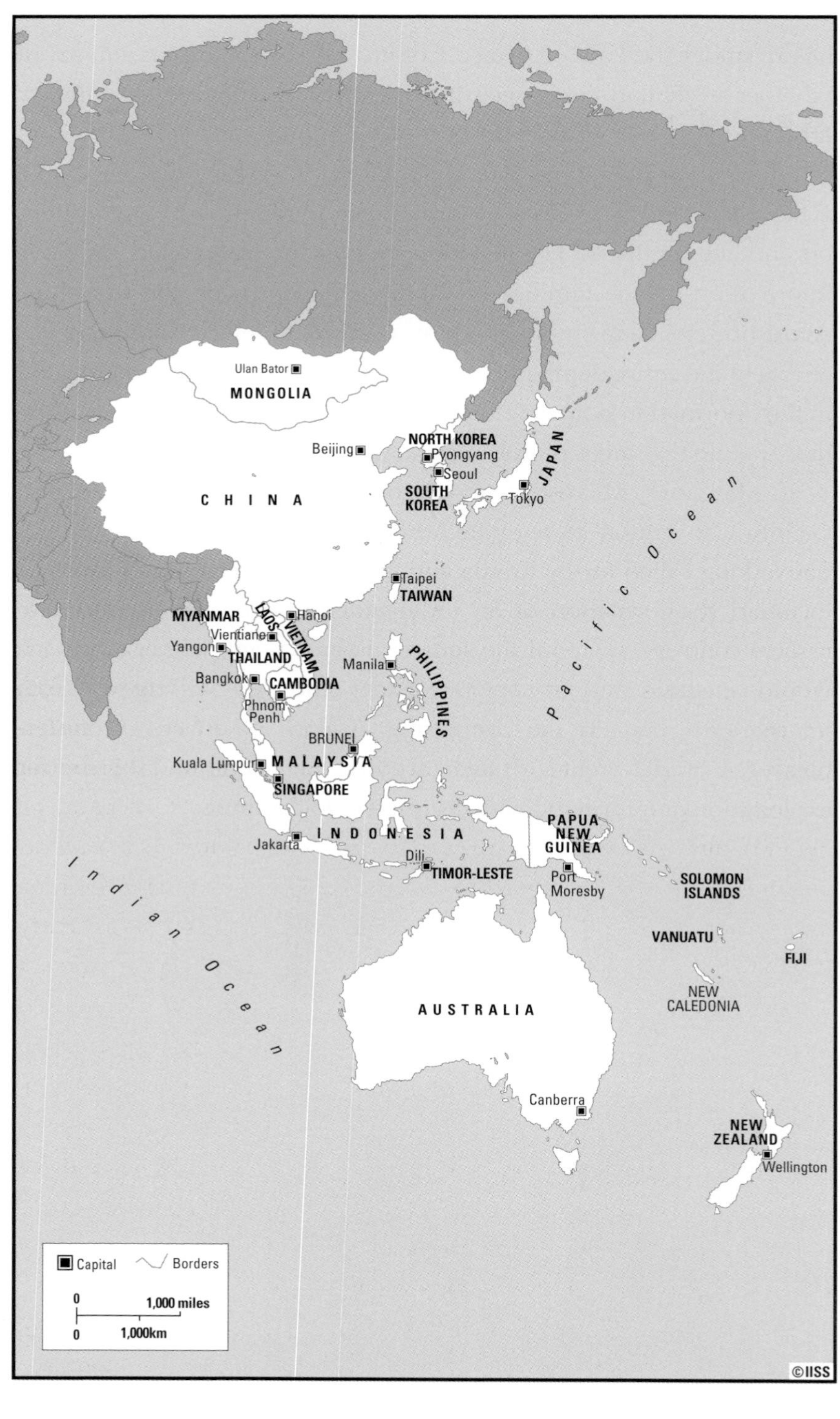
Ulan Bator
MONGOLIA
CHINA
Beijing
NORTH KOREA
Pyongyang
Seoul
SOUTH KOREA
JAPAN
Tokyo
Pacific Ocean
Taipei
TAIWAN
MYANMAR
LAOS
VIETNAM
Hanoi
Vientiane
Yangon
THAILAND
Bangkok
CAMBODIA
Phnom Penh
Manila
PHILIPPINES
BRUNEI
Kuala Lumpur
MALAYSIA
SINGAPORE
INDONESIA
Jakarta
Dili
TIMOR-LESTE
PAPUA NEW GUINEA
Port Moresby
SOLOMON ISLANDS
VANUATU
FIJI
NEW CALEDONIA
Indian Ocean
AUSTRALIA
Canberra
NEW ZEALAND
Wellington
Capital
Borders
0 1,000 miles
0 1,000km
©IISS

Chapter 4

Asia-Pacific

The ramifications of China's extrovert and confident foreign policy, together with concerns over the threat posed by North Korea's nuclear-weapons and missile programmes, continued to dominate the Asia-Pacific security landscape in the year to mid-2017. However, from late 2016 onwards, the approach of an extraordinary new US administration led by Donald Trump created uncertainty and complex problems for the region's states, particularly Washington's allies and security partners. Behind China's policies on the region lay President Xi Jinping's position as its 'core leader', strengthened through the intensification of a far-reaching anti-corruption campaign within the ruling Chinese Communist Party (CCP) that seemed at least partly designed to install a new generation of leaders. As China's economic growth slowed, the leadership emphasised the need for structural reforms aimed at stimulating innovation, creating jobs and reducing poverty. The party dealt firmly with dissent from non-governmental organisations, academics, Uighur separatists in Xinjiang and pro-independence activists in Hong Kong. Meanwhile, Xi and the party leadership continued to rapidly increase defence spending while also launching a major restructuring of the People's Liberation Army (PLA) to significantly enhance China's military capability.

In some ways, China handled its foreign-policy challenges adroitly. Importantly, the Belt and Road Forum for International Cooperation, convened in Beijing in May 2017, helped the country project its vision of a regional and global order that would satisfy not only its needs but also those of its international interlocutors. With the Brexit referendum result and Trump's election indicating the strength of unilateralist and protectionist sentiment in parts of the West, China used the Belt and Road Forum – as well as the earlier G20 summit in Hangzhou, the Asia-Pacific Economic Cooperation (APEC) summit in Lima and the 2017 Davos summit – to project its strong support for international trade and investment. The trade wars Trump spoke of while campaigning posed a serious threat to Chinese interests, but one result of Xi's summit with him at Mar-a-Lago resort in April was an agreement on a 100-day plan for talks to resolve disagreements over trade.

Nonetheless, there remained important differences between China and the United States on regional security issues. Beijing claimed that the US deployment of Terminal High Altitude Area Defense (THAAD) anti-missile systems in South Korea ran counter to Chinese security interests. In an apparent attempt to placate China and domestic critics, the new administration in Seoul led by President Moon Jae-in announced in June 2017 that it would suspend further THAAD deployments. Moreover, despite China's imposition of new sanctions on North Korean coal exports to the country in November 2016, the Trump administration condemned Beijing's failure to react with sufficient force to Pyongyang's continuing nuclear and missile tests. China might have had some success in influencing North Korean leaders, as Pyongyang conducted no nuclear tests between 9 September 2016 (the date of its fifth such test) and July 2017. Nonetheless, North Korea accelerated its missile programme during the period, conducting its first test of an intercontinental-range missile in early July and thereby increasing the likelihood of a US military response. Given the massive devastation and loss of life that would result from a conflict on the Korean Peninsula, President Moon wished to avoid war. There was a possibility that the sides would engage in a diplomatic initiative to reduce tensions and freeze Pyongyang's nuclear and missile programmes.

Beijing's continuing assertiveness in the maritime sphere complicated its relations with other Asia-Pacific states, as well as with the US. This was particularly true in the South China Sea, where Beijing's territorial claims and activities directly impinged on Southeast Asian states' interests. Although there were no high-profile incidents in the South China Sea in the year to mid-2017, Beijing nonetheless continued to build military infrastructure on occupied features in the Spratly Islands. China also dismissed the July 2016 ruling against most of its claims in the sea by the Arbitral Tribunal at The Hague, in a case brought by the Philippines. Perhaps surprisingly, Southeast Asian governments were muted in their reactions to the ruling. Crucially, the new Philippine administration under President Rodrigo Duterte effectively used the ruling as a bargaining chip to establish a new, more positive relationship with Beijing, which involved large-scale Chinese economic support for the Philippines. Duterte also questioned the merits of his country's alliance with the US. However, he was reminded of the importance of the relationship in mid-2017, when the Philippines' security forces relied on US military support to combat Islamist insurgents who had seized parts of the city of Marawi, on Mindanao.

Other members of the Association of Southeast Asian Nations (ASEAN) also de-emphasised their concerns about developments in the South China Sea. Beneath this veneer of ASEAN unity, some Southeast Asian leaders retained deep anxiety about the issue, but were often wary of challenging Beijing for fear of economic repercussions. Singapore was an exception, lending principled support to the Arbitral Tribunal ruling that severely strained its relations with China.

Developments in the South China Sea continued to concern the Abe administration, which recognised the importance of freedom of navigation there to Japanese economic and energy security. Following the introduction of new legislation, the Japan Self-Defense Forces (JSDF) were able to operate more closely with the US Navy in Asian waters – including the South China Sea – while also engaging in naval exercises with regional states and providing them with capacity-boosting assistance. Tokyo felt direct pressure from Beijing in the East China Sea, where

China deployed naval, coastguard and fishing vessels with increasing frequency and aggressiveness near the Senkaku/Diaoyu Islands, resulting in a growing number of confrontations with the Japan Coast Guard. In breach of an earlier agreement, China also emplaced gas-exploration rigs in the East China Sea. Meanwhile, in response to the growing threat from Pyongyang's missile programme, the JSDF also cooperated more closely with both US and South Korean forces, engaging in a trilateral missile-defence exercise. Despite this cooperation, historical issues continued to impede the development of relations between Tokyo and Seoul. As the regional security environment became progressively fraught with challenges, Japan continued to strengthen its security cooperation with other Asian democracies, particularly India and Australia.

In Australia, the Turnbull government's trepidation about the increasingly complex and challenging regional security environment was reflected in its burgeoning defence budget, which facilitated investment in important military hardware, including 12 new submarines. Like its counterparts in Southeast Asia, the Australian government remained concerned about the threat from terrorists linked to the Islamic State, also known as ISIS or ISIL, in the Middle East. But it appeared to see the principal longer-term threats to the region as emanating from East Asia, particularly China's challenge to the region's 'rules-based order'. Canberra sought to maintain equable, constructive relations with Beijing, not least for economic reasons. Yet it displayed growing anxiety about the prospect that China would use its expanding, multidimensional influence to intimidate states in its region. Part of Canberra's response was to attempt to strengthen defence and security relations with its Asian partners such as India, Japan and Singapore. As was the case for other countries in the region disturbed by the changing balance of power, Australia viewed the uncertainty generated by the advent of the Trump administration as an incentive to pursue intra-regional collaboration.

China's preparations for the 19th Party Congress

The CCP's 200-strong Central Committee held its Sixth Plenum in late October 2016, marking the start of a one-year countdown to China's leadership reshuffle at the 19th Party Congress, at which five out of seven members of the Politburo Standing Committee were expected to retire. Xi, the CCP's general secretary, delivered a speech at the plenum focusing on supervision within the party and preparations for the congress amid a 'complex international and domestic situation'. However, his primary message was that the leadership would intensify the relentless anti-corruption drive he had launched in 2012.

The plenum confirmed the expulsion of Wang Min and Niu Zhizhong, party secretary of Liaoning province and deputy commander of the People's Armed Police respectively (ironically, Wang had been a strong advocate of the anti-corruption campaign). The communiqué produced at the conclusion of the plenum placed considerable emphasis on Xi's role as the party's 'core leader', a label previously reserved for Mao Zedong, Deng Xiaoping and Jiang Zemin (but not Xi's immediate predecessor, Hu Jintao). In March 2017, at the annual meeting of the National People's Congress (NPC), China's legislative body, Xi was repeatedly referred to as being 'at the core' of the party leadership. The return of this terminology suggested that he had strengthened his control of internal party rules, allowing him to directly appoint his successor. This prompted speculation that Xi would breach party custom to reappoint his ally Wang Qishan as head of the Central Commission for Discipline Inspection, which oversees the anti-corruption drive.

There were rumours that Xi would exploit a ten-year cycle that allows CCP general secretaries to place members of their patronage networks among the next generation of leaders, as a means to retain behind-the-scenes factional influence in retirement. Although Xi had promoted some of his allies, he also appointed technocrats lacking factional loyalties to senior positions in the party. There was also growing evidence that he was relying on Wang's Central Commission for Discipline Inspection to nurture new leaders of China's provinces and central government. This trend created widespread belief that the anti-corruption campaign was a mechanism to purge the party and bolster his power base.

Indeed, the 15 February 2017 edition of influential state magazine *Qiushi* featured a rare acknowledgement of the existence of factional rivalry within the party. The issue provided details on the party plenum that were omitted from its official communiqué, including Xi's comments on political conspiracies fomented by disgraced leaders he had removed from power. Among the figures he named were Zhou Yongkang, Ling Jihua and Xu Caihou, formerly head of the Ministry of Public Security, Hu's chief of staff and deputy chairman of the Central Military Commission respectively. Xi further reinforced his position in February, appointing He Lifeng, a former colleague in the Fujian provincial government, as chief of the powerful National Development and Reform Commission. He also appointed other former associates to lead China's commerce and justice ministries.

The anti-corruption campaign showed no sign of abating: there were reports of the arrest, imprisonment or expulsion from the party of senior figures almost every week. The investigations extended to officials who had retired or fled abroad. In November 2016, Yang Xiuzhu, former deputy director of the construction department in the coastal province of Zhejiang and China's most-wanted fugitive for economic crimes, surrendered to the Chinese police after 13 years in hiding abroad. The Supreme People's Court revealed in March 2017 that 164 suspects from 37 countries had been repatriated since 2014, when Beijing launched *Operation Sky Net,* its initiative to pursue foreign-based targets of the anti-corruption campaign.

Investigations into members of the Central Commission for Discipline Inspection reflected the intensity of the campaign. It came to light in April 2017 that Zhang Huawei, former head of a central inspection group, had been accused of a 'serious violation of party discipline'. The following month, the Supreme People's Court revealed that the judicial system had tried 45,000 graft cases implicating 63,000 people, including 35 provincial or ministerial officials, and 240 prefectural officials.

Xi's authoritarianism also affected wider Chinese society, with the government launching a crackdown on human-rights activists such as Jiang Tianyong, a Christian lawyer who was arrested in November 2016. The party also demanded loyalty from China's universities and colleges; in January, it dispatched inspectors to monitor institutions' compliance. The same month, the government introduced a law that required all foreign non-governmental organisations to apply for official approval from the police, banning them from activities deemed harmful to the 'national, social and public interest'.

Ethnic tension continued to rise in Xinjiang, a northwestern autonomous region home to around eight million largely Muslim Uighurs. Following the appointment of Chen Quanguo as Xinjiang party secretary in August 2016, the authorities engaged in a heavy-handed response to growing jihadist and separatist violence there. Chen introduced a community-monitoring system that he had used with some success in neighbouring Tibet. However, there was an increase in violence in the region in the first quarter of 2017, with 19 deaths in four reported incidents.

The harsh measures Chen introduced included the confiscation of Uighurs' passports and other travel restrictions. Some prefectures required the registration of all sharp objects and the installation of GPS trackers in vehicles. In March, Xinjiang introduced legislation banning long beards and women's headscarves on public transportation, and forbidding parents from giving their children religious names. On 27 February, Chen ordered a mass rally in Urumqi involving 10,000 paramilitary personnel, the fourth such event in 2017. Addressing Xinjiang's delegation to the NPC in March, Xi called for a (rhetorical) 'great wall of iron' in Xinjiang to safeguard national unity, ethnic solidarity and social stability. He described the region as an important 'security barrier' and a hub for the Belt and Road Initiative.

At a meeting in March, the 'two sessions' – China's rubber-stamp legislative body, the NPC, and its quasi-upper house, the Chinese People's Political Consultative Conference – focused on the implementation of the 13th Five-Year Plan (2016–20), emphasising innovation strategy, poverty reduction and environmental protection. The two sessions noted that China experienced GDP growth of 6.7% in 2016, its lowest in three decades, and targeted an average annual growth rate of 6.5% until 2020. The NPC also called for a push for globalisation with 'Chinese wisdom' and a successful Belt and Road Forum.

At the NPC, Xi called for supply-side structural reform, particularly in agriculture, and for cutting overcapacity in the wider economy. He also stressed that China would further liberalise its economy by promoting trade and opening its markets to foreign investors. At the NPC's opening session, Premier Li Keqiang used his annual work report to stress that meeting the growth target would help stabilise markets and facilitate the economy's structural adjustments. Li stated that the government intended to create more than 11m jobs in 2017, up from 10m the previous year. Despite ongoing debate on the issue within the party and among prominent commentators, he reiterated in March that China would at some point open its services, manufacturing and mining sectors to foreign investment.

In his role as chairman of the Central Military Commission, Xi declared in September 2016 that the number of PLA troops would be cut from 2.3m to 2m, calling for the military to be 'smaller but stronger'. He also announced that five theatre commands would replace China's seven military regions. The Central Military Commission's four general-staff departments would be reconstituted into 15 new functional departments. Xi appointed Mayor of Beijing Cai Qi, a close associate, to end the PLA's involvement in businesses, something that it had failed to do for nearly 20 years.

At the NPC, Vice-Foreign Minister Fu Ying announced that Chinese defence spending would rise to 1.3% of GDP in 2017. Premier Li said that China would strengthen its maritime forces, air defences and border controls to protect its sovereignty and security, while enhancing defence-technology innovation and 'military–civilian integration' – a term widely interpreted as referring to civilian defence contracting.

On 16 May, the NPC published a draft bill that would grant wide-ranging new powers to China's intelligence agencies, enhancing their ability to conduct domestic surveillance. Receiving little coverage in state media outlets, the measure seemed to come in response to recent counter-intelligence failures, such as the reported penetration of the Ministry of State Security by CIA agents.

In anticipation of Hong Kong's 26 March election of a new chief executive and the 20th anniversary of its return to China, Premier Li used his NPC speech to dismiss the idea that the territory could become independent. He pledged to fully implement the 'one country, two systems' approach to the special administrative region in compliance with its basic law. The day before the election, hundreds of residents of Hong Kong protested against Beijing's apparent attempts to influence its outcome. In late March, Li confirmed the election of pro-Beijing candidate Carrie Lam as the fifth chief executive of Hong Kong, a role that she would take up on 1 July.

Ambitions of global leadership

China continued to face major political and security challenges on its periphery, including the Arbitral Tribunal's ruling on the South China Sea, provocations by the North Korean regime and an upsurge in the conflict involving ethnic armed groups in Myanmar (which prompted China to mobilise troops near its southern border with the country in March 2017). Beijing's skilful diplomacy was evident in its efforts to host the G20 summit in September 2016, a bilateral summit with the US in April and the Belt and Road Forum, an event that focused on the defining foreign-policy initiative of Xi's first five-year tenure. Meanwhile, Beijing continued to promulgate its vision of regional and global order, maintaining a carefully choreographed narrative across the military, diplomatic and economic spheres. This narrative stemmed from Xi's proclamation of a 'new type of major-power relationship' at the Sunnylands bilateral summit with then US president Barack Obama in June 2013, as well as from the three principles declared at the May 2014 Conference on Interaction and Confidence-Building Measures in Asia summit: no conflict or confrontation, mutual respect and mutually beneficial cooperation.

Alarmed by what it viewed as a drift towards unilateralism and protectionism following the United Kingdom's vote to leave the

European Union and Trump's election as US president, Beijing exploited every opportunity to promote an inclusive approach to globalisation. The G20 summit, the first to be hosted by China, was widely regarded as a boost to Xi's influence abroad. The event culminated in Beijing's and the Obama administration's ratification of the COP-21 agreement on climate change, while its joint communiqué emphasised the importance of international trade and investment, opposition to protectionism and the defence of globalisation from populist attack. Xi continued to promote globalisation during a tour of Latin America in November, calling on attendees of the APEC Economic Leaders' Summit in Lima to support a global economy experiencing a sluggish recovery. Ning Gaoning, co-chairman of the APEC Business Advisory Council, used the summit to dismiss Trump's pledge to introduce a 40% tariff on Chinese imports as unrealistic, advocating resolve in the face of the anti-globalisation movement.

The alacrity with which Xi accepted an invitation to deliver the opening address at the World Economic Forum Davos summit in January 2017 stemmed as much from the absence of US leadership as the need to promote globalisation. Xi's speech served not only to rebut Trump's condemnation of China during the US election campaign but also to foreshadow the vision he would put forward at the Belt and Road Forum. At the Boao Forum for Asia, held in Hainan on 25 March, Vice-Premier Zhang Gaoli asserted that 'big nations' should not damage stability or the strategic balance for selfish gain. Calling for strategic cooperation and mutual trust, he said that major powers should also respect one another's core interests, a thinly veiled reference to friction between the US, its allies and China over Beijing's territorial claims.

Despite turbulence in the Sino-US relationship at the outset of the Trump presidency, the Mar-a-Lago bilateral summit on 6 April proved successful for China, with the countries' presidents agreeing to pursue bilateral relations from a 'new starting point'. Trump's pre-inauguration telephone conversation with Tsai Ing-wen, the independence-minded president of Taiwan, initially created unease in Beijing. But, to Beijing's relief, once in office Trump endorsed the One China policy, while US

Secretary of State Rex Tillerson effectively repeated Beijing's foreign-policy mantra of 'no conflict, no confrontation, mutual respect, and win–win cooperation'.

President Tsai's conversation with Trump and continued refusal to endorse the 1992 Consensus – a tacit agreement between the CCP and Taiwan's Kuomintang Party that there is only one China – prompted Beijing to develop its ties with the Taiwanese opposition. Chinese state media hailed talks in November between Xi and a delegation led by Kuomintang Party head Hung Hsiu-chu, during which both sides reiterated the 1992 Consensus. Beijing launched a campaign to reduce the number of countries that formally recognised Taiwan and sought to isolate it in international forums. As a consequence, São Tomé and Principe severed its diplomatic relations with Taipei in December, and Panama followed suit in mid-June, reducing the number of states that recognised Taiwan to 20.

At the Mar-a-Lago summit, Xi stressed that there were 'a thousand reasons to make the China–US relationship a success and not a single reason to break it'. He invited Trump to pay a state visit to China in 2017 and encouraged close bilateral contact through high-level cooperation mechanisms, including diplomatic, security and economic dialogues.

Washington and Beijing also made some progress in establishing new means of defence and security engagement. After North Korea conducted missile tests on the eve of the summit, the sides agreed to cooperate in stabilising the Korean Peninsula. They created a new strategic security dialogue designed to raise the level at which US and Chinese defence officials engaged with one another, and a new dialogue between their chiefs of joint staff.

Xi and Trump formulated a 100-day plan for talks aimed at resolving disagreements over trade. In May 2017, Beijing agreed to allow US beef exports to enter China directly and initiated the process of admitting US electronic-payment firms to the Chinese market. In return, the US authorised imports of Chinese poultry products and exports of liquefied natural gas to China, while giving Chinese banks greater access to the US market. However, despite this early progress, many economists predicted that the US–China economic dialogue would encounter difficulties on market access, transparency and the free flow of goods. Nonetheless, China was reassured by intensive rounds of negotiations between the sides, and by Washington's decision to appoint a senior official as head of the US delegation at the Belt and Road Forum.

The summit was one of the largest international events to be held in Beijing in several years, involving almost 30 heads of state and government, along with thousands of other delegates. Evoking the ancient Silk Road, Xi had launched the Belt and Road Initiative to improve interconnectivity across Asia, Europe and Africa, creating links between major cities, promoting development and pursuing a variety of infrastructure projects. He stated that China had invested US$14.5 billion in the undertaking in 2016, and more than US$60bn since its inception in 2013. According to Xi, 68 countries and international organisations had signed Belt and Road Initiative cooperation agreements with China, and a list of more than 270 summit objectives had been recorded.

Some observers viewed the Belt and Road Forum as an attempt to energise an initiative that lacked clearly defined strategic purpose, dispel suggestions that political interference would accompany Chinese economic investment and counter claims that China was attempting to offload excess industrial capacity on the developing world. Beijing declared that it would provide an additional US$14.5bn to the Silk Road Fund and another 380bn yuan (US$56bn) in loans related to the project. Furthermore, Xi announced that the Belt and Road Forum was designed to incentivise China's financial sector to establish foreign-based Chinese-currency funds worth 300bn yuan (US$45bn). Emphasising inclusivity and global participation, he welcomed cooperation with the World Bank, the New Development Bank and the Chinese-led Asian Infrastructure Investment Bank (AIIB) in underwriting the initiative.

Japan's expanding security role

Throughout the year to mid-2017, the government of Japanese Prime Minister Shinzo Abe continued to carve out a more assertive security role for Japan in the Asia-Pacific and further afield, under a foreign policy it termed 'proactive pacifism'. In pursuit of this agenda, Abe appointed Tomomi Inada – widely seen as a hawkish conservative with revisionist views on Japan's wartime history – as minister of defence in August 2016.

Having gained ten seats in an election held the previous month, Abe's Liberal Democratic Party (LDP) and Komeito, its coalition partner, established a dominant position in the upper house of the Diet. As a consequence, Abe was well positioned to seek re-election as LDP leader in September 2017. Were he to succeed and stay in office until 2020, he would become Japan's longest-serving prime minister.

However, two scandals damaged Abe's popularity, casting doubt on his political future. In June 2017, as one of these scandals escalated, he announced that the LDP would step up its efforts to revise Article 9 of Japan's constitution, which renounces war. The party aimed to submit an amendment recognising the JSDF as the country's armed forces to the Diet by the end of the year. The draft bill had the potential to pave the way for further reform, including more comprehensive constitutional revision, but, if successful, would almost certainly draw criticism from South Korea and China.

Japan's National Security Council continued to formulate strategy for, and coordinate, overseas JSDF missions conducted under two pieces of legislation: the March 2016 International Peace Support Law and the Legislation for Peace and Security. In June 2017, the helicopter carrier *Izumo* (the country's largest vessel) escorted a US supply ship after its departure from Yokosuka port, the first such deployment of a Japanese warship alongside a US Navy vessel. Moreover, the *Izumo*, along with the destroyer *Sazanami*, proceeded to join the US carrier strike group led by the USS *Ronald Reagan* in the South China Sea for a bilateral exercise, another first for a Japanese warship. In November 2016, the Japan Ground Self-Defense Force (JGSDF) deployed a new contingent to assist the United Nations Mission in South Sudan (UNMISS). Although Japanese troops had first deployed to the country in a non-combat role five years earlier, under new Japanese legislation the contingent was permitted to use force in assisting UN troops who had come under attack. However, the Japanese government, citing the deteriorating security condition in South Sudan, announced in March 2017 that the contingent would be recalled the following May.

North Korea continued to pose the most significant security threat to Japan. In August 2016, for the first time since 1998, Pyongyang launched a *Nodong* single-stage medium-range ballistic missile (MRBM) into Japan's exclusive economic zone (EEZ), eliciting an official protest from Tokyo. In March 2017, North Korea launched four extended-range *Scud* missiles, three of which landed in Japan's EEZ. In May, Pyongyang launched a new type of precision-guided *Scud* with terminal manoeuvrability into Japan's claimed EEZ off the coast of the disputed Dokdo/Takeshima Islands. The intensified pace of North Korean missile tests spurred Japan to take a range of precautionary measures, increasing its preparedness for a retaliatory strike and energising diplomatic efforts to moderate Pyongyang's aggressive behaviour. The Abe government continued to emphasise ballistic-missile defence as the cornerstone of Japan's strategy to counter the threat from North Korea.

Abe's government considered but did not issue an open-ended intercept order that directed the JSDF to shoot down any North Korean test projectiles threatening Japanese territory. To reinforce existing *Patriot* PAC-3 systems and *Aegis*-equipped guided-missile destroyers, Tokyo began considering procurement of a THAAD battery from the US and an *Aegis Ashore* installation featuring Standard Missile-3 Block IIA interceptors.

Moreover, in early 2017, Japan began to conduct its first civilian-evacuation drills in preparation for a potential North Korean ballistic-missile attack. In February, the Japan Ministry of Defense's Acquisition, Technology and Logistics Agency, in coordination with the US Missile Defense Agency, conducted a successful interception of an MRBM-class target using the SM-3 Block IIA – the first test of its kind involving that interceptor. (A second intercept test of the SM-3 Block IIA failed in June 2017, but a subsequent US investigation attributed the failure to human error during the test.)

Due to the threat from North Korea, Japanese defence officials revisited the possibility of buying BGM-109 *Tomahawk* land-attack cruise missiles. Were they to do so, this would be Japan's first post-1945 acquisition of an overtly offensive military system, a move that might require constitutional revision and would likely face considerable domestic political and legal opposition.

Tokyo's diplomatic efforts in Northeast Asia had mixed results. By early 2017, relations between Japan and South Korea had become frosty, reflecting mutual dissatisfaction with the implementation of a December 2015 agreement on the so-called 'comfort women' issue (involving reparations for Japanese forces' sexual enslavement of Korean women during the Second World War). Both governments had described the deal as 'final and irreversible' when it was struck, but the subsequent intervention of South Korean civil-society groups undermined Seoul's commitment to implement it, spurring Tokyo to recall the Japanese ambassador to South Korea in January 2017. Although the envoy returned three months later, the dispute was likely to remain an obstacle to cooperation between Washington's two allies in Northeast Asia despite the growing North Korean threat.

Japan also continued to be concerned about China's behaviour, particularly in the East China Sea. The People's Liberation Army Navy (PLAN) and the China Coast Guard increased their patrols within Japan's claimed 12-nautical-mile territorial sea and contiguous zone near the Senkaku/Diaoyu Islands, which are administered by Japan but claimed by both China and Taiwan. The East China Sea became the scene of increasingly frequent stand-offs between the Japanese authorities and China's navy, law-enforcement and even civilian vessels. In August 2016, seven China Coast Guard ships, accompanied by 230 fishing boats, entered the 12nm territorial sea of the Senkakus/Diaoyus. Beijing employed the same tactics it had used in the South China Sea – including in the seizure of Scarborough Shoal from the Philippines in 2012 and the disagreement with Vietnam over the Haiyang Shiyou 981 oil rig two years later. Tokyo claimed that Chinese vessels conducted more than 30 incursions into the waters near the Senkakus/Diaoyus in

2016, many of them in the lead-up to the ruling by the Arbitral Tribunal at The Hague in July 2016. Beijing's unilateral development of infrastructure for exploiting natural resources in the East China Sea, in contravention of a 2008 bilateral agreement on joint resource development, created anxiety in Tokyo. Japan alleged that China had established 16 gas-exploration rigs in the western half of the sea. In August 2016, the Japanese Ministry of Foreign Affairs said that Japan had detected radar equipment on a Chinese gas platform near disputed waters.

Amid this tension, Japan asserted itself as an interested party in the dispute in the South China Sea, facilitated by the Abe government's reinterpretation of the constitution to allow for collective self-defence. The Japanese Ministry of Foreign Affairs called on Beijing and Manila to respect the ruling by the Arbitral Tribunal as 'final and legally binding on the parties to the dispute'. It added that 'Japan strongly expects that the parties' compliance with this award will eventually lead to the peaceful settlement of disputes in the South China Sea.'

Speaking in Washington in September 2016, Defense Minister Inada clarified Tokyo's plans in the South China Sea, outlining objectives that it would pursue in conjunction with the US. She stated that the Japan Maritime Self-Defense Force (JMSDF) would 'increase its engagement' in the South China Sea by conducting 'joint training cruises with the US Navy' and 'bilateral and multilateral exercises with regional navies', and would provide 'capacity building assistance to coastal nations' in the area. China's envoy to Japan had reportedly told Tokyo that Beijing would treat Japanese participation in US-led freedom-of-navigation operations (FONOPs) in the South China Sea as a 'red line'. While Japan did not participate in such operations, it maintained a regular JMSDF presence there, deploying the *Izumo* to the South China Sea in June 2017 (the ship subsequently travelled on to the Indian Ocean). Moreover, Inada declared, 'I strongly support the US Navy's freedom-of-navigation operations, which go a long way to upholding the rules-based international maritime order'.

Intent on strengthening the maritime law-enforcement capacity of friendly Southeast Asian countries facing an assertive China, Japan worked to develop its security relationship with the Philippines and Vietnam. In October 2016, President Duterte visited Japan, where he and Abe signed an agreement under which Tokyo would provide Manila with two additional patrol vessels. In March 2017, the Japanese government loaned two TC-90 maritime-patrol aircraft to the Philippines to help the country monitor its EEZ more effectively. Tokyo planned to eventually lease out five such aircraft to Manila. In June 2017, during a port call by the *Izumo* to Subic Bay, Duterte became the first foreign head of state to tour the ship. In July 2016, a Japan Coast Guard vessel visited Da Nang, the first time that one of Japan's vessels had travelled to Vietnam since September 2015, when the countries signed a memorandum on coastguard cooperation. Following up on its commitments to assist in capacity-building in the South China Sea, in June 2017 Japan dispatched coastguard vessel *Echigo* to train Vietnamese law-enforcement officers in an exercise designed to combat illegal fishing. Japan also provided the Vietnam Coast Guard cutter used in the drill.

Japan sustained its engagement with Russia on their dispute over the Kuril Islands/Northern Territories, following the resumption of high-level diplomatic contact between the sides at a bilateral summit in Sochi in May 2016. Although Russian President Vladimir Putin's visit to Tokyo in December resulted in no breakthroughs on the matter, Japan expanded the size and scope of its Russia-related economic initiatives. With Abe having attended the Eastern Economic Forum in Vladivostok three months prior, the sides used Putin's visit to announce a range of economic-cooperation agreements on energy, infrastructure and investment. In August 2016, the Japanese government created the new role of minister for economic cooperation with Russia, a position taken up by Hiroshige Seko, the newly appointed minister of economy, trade and industry.

Adjustments in strategy and defence-export initiatives

Trump's election forced Japan to adjust its strategic outlook. During the US election campaign, Abe had met with Hillary Clinton, Trump's opponent, on the assumption that she would become the next US president. After Trump won, Abe rushed to New York to meet the then-president-elect and repair any damage from his mistake, an effort that appeared to pay off in February, when he became one of the first world leaders to be invited to the White House by the new administration. Although the US–Japan alliance comfortably survived the political transition in Washington, Abe's government was incentivised to hedge against the strategic uncertainty engendered by Trump's presidency, as a means to preserve the regional security architecture and the rules-based order in the Asia-Pacific. As a consequence, what former US defence secretary Ashton Carter called a 'principled security network' appeared to persist in the region, with Tokyo taking the lead in promoting coordination among like-minded Asian powers. As part of the process, Japan maintained its high-level interactions, and attempted to align its strategy, with India and Australia, the Asia-Pacific democracies with which it had most in common. At a meeting in January 2017, Abe and Australian Prime Minister Malcolm Turnbull agreed to boost defence cooperation between their countries, signing a military logistical-support deal. Three months later, Japan and Australia convened the seventh meeting between their foreign and defence ministers. The meeting's closing statement reaffirmed support for a 'free and open rules-based order' in the Asia-Pacific and for the first time the parties 'reaffirmed their intention to further develop trilateral cooperation and coordination among Japan, Australia and India'.

Indian Prime Minister Narendra Modi visited Japan in November 2016, marking the tenth consecutive annual prime-ministerial summit between India and Japan since the countries signed their global strategic partnership in 2006, during Abe's first term. Abe and Modi affirmed their commitment to 'a balanced, open, inclusive, stable, transparent and rules-based economic, political and security architecture in the Indo-Pacific region', including 'freedom of navigation and over flight' in the region's maritime commons.

Japan's defence industry continued to benefit from major orders for new JSDF equipment. Most significantly, Mitsubishi Heavy Industries and Lockheed Martin jointly announced in June 2017 that the Japanese firm would assemble the F-35A Joint Strike Fighter in Japan for the Japanese Air Self-Defense Force. However, despite lifting its self-imposed ban on defence exports in 2014, the Japanese government failed to conclude any significant defence contracts in the year to mid-2017. The leading contender for Japan's first major overseas sale of defence equipment was India's potential purchase of 12 ShinMaywa US-2 amphibious search-and-rescue aircraft. That agreement remained under negotiation and was not concluded during Abe's meeting with Modi in November.

By mid-2017, Japan's defence-export efforts remained largely aspirational, and Japanese defence firms were turning their attention to South and Southeast Asian countries. Japan entered into negotiations with New Zealand to export the P-1 maritime-patrol aircraft and a Mitsubishi–Kawasaki consortium received a request for information to participate in the competition to build India's Project 75-I air-independent propulsion, diesel-electric submarine. Many analysts continued to ascribe Japan's difficulties in entering the crowded global defence market to its relative inexperience with the complex bidding processes and negotiations long familiar to its competitors.

Escalating instability on the Korean Peninsula

The security environment on the Korean Peninsula deteriorated further in the year to mid-2017, as the Democratic People's Republic of Korea (DPRK) continued to enhance its ballistic-missile capability and conducted its fifth nuclear test. Pyongyang's principal aim appeared to be not to threaten South Korea and Japan with its missiles but rather to develop the capacity to strike the continental US with a nuclear weapon. Despite international condemnation of the North Korean regime and US attempts to coerce it, policymakers in concerned countries appeared to lack good options for dealing with the crisis. Political transitions in the US and South Korea complicated alliance relationships in the region, hindering attempts to formulate a unified response to the threat. Against a background of high-profile North Korean cyber attacks, assassinations and human-rights abuses, there seemed to be little prospect of a timely, peaceful resolution to the crisis.

North Korea conducted its second nuclear test of 2016 – and its fifth ever – in September at the Punggye-ri facility in the east of the country. Norwegian seismologists calculated the yield of the device used in the test to be around 20 kilotons, larger than that of any deployed in its previous efforts. As with Pyongyang's fourth nuclear test eight months earlier, the larger yield was thought to indicate the inclusion of nuclear-fusion fuel such as tritium or deuterium, which is absent from a standard fission weapon. Although such 'boosted' devices are not as powerful as thermonuclear weapons, they could aid the process of miniaturisation, facilitating attempts to marry a nuclear warhead with a missile. Although the size of North Korea's stockpile of fissile material remained unclear, reports that the country was continuing operations at its Yongbyon nuclear facility suggested that it had access to a growing quantity of plutonium. There was scant publicly available information on the country's reserves of highly enriched uranium.

Despite the apparent progress of its nuclear programme, North Korea's rapid advances in the development of ballistic-missile systems were the primary cause for concern among major powers. The mixture of missile technologies Pyongyang displayed seemed to confirm that it was focused on developing a long-range missile capable of targeting the continental US. The rate of testing indicated that North Korean technicians were working to a predetermined, objective-based schedule rather than merely testing systems on symbolic dates for political effect. Although it experienced several failures in the effort, the DPRK conducted 20 missile tests involving a range of systems in the year to mid-2017. These systems included *Scud*-C and extended-range *Scud*s – which may have been used to improve operational readiness, and have signalled an aim to overwhelm missile-defence systems in Northeast Asia – as well as longer-range weapons. The emergence of the submarine-launched ballistic missile *Bukkeuseong*-1 and its evolution into the solid-fuel, land-based *Bukkeuseong*-2 was significant due to the systems' high mobility and the speed with which they could be prepared for launch. Increased testing of the *Musudan* intermediate-range ballistic missile, also known as the *Hwasong*-10, pointed toward North Korea's longer-range ambitions. Pyongyang revealed a system named the *Hwasong*-12 during a military parade in April 2017, and reportedly conducted a successful test of the weapon several weeks later. The missile caused more anxiety for the US than other systems because of its potential range and re-entry-vehicle capabilities, which could potentially deliver a 650-kilogram warhead to a target 4,000 kilometres away. Several *Hwasong*-12s were test-launched at lofted trajectories, thereby avoiding provocative overflight of neighbouring countries that might heighten the risk of miscalculation and conflict. The steeper angle of launch also provided for a higher re-entry speed, testing key elements of the missile's capabilities.

The *Hwasong*-12 is a single-stage, liquid-fuel system with a range greater than that of the *Musudan* but shorter than that of the KN-08, a rumoured intercontinental ballistic missile (ICBM), and its derivative, the KN-14. In a Senate hearing in May 2017, US Deputy Assistant Secretary of Defense Robert Soofer stated that 'North Korea is poised to conduct its first ICBM flight test in 2017'. This assessment echoed Kim Jong-un's declaration in his 2017 New Year address that 'ICBM rocket test launch preparation is in its last stage'. Indeed, the US Intelligence Community had for some time expected North Korea to test an ICBM, stating in 2014 that despite a lack of testing, the country had 'taken initial steps towards' fielding a system capable of delivering a nuclear payload to the continental US.

Alongside its determined development of missiles, North Korea also drew increasing attention and criticism for its alleged use of cyber capabilities. Due to reported connections between Pyongyang and an online group named 'Lazarus', British and US officials attributed the WannaCry ransomware attacks – which began in May 2017 and infected more than 300,000 computers globally – to North Korea.

Cyber operations provided Pyongyang with a means to finance its nuclear and ballistic-missile programmes while under wide-ranging international sanctions. Such undertakings tended to be complex and were often carried out via third countries, with funds transferred through international payment systems to be laundered using a variety of businesses in other states. As this layered approach created barriers to detection and prevention, North Korea employed similar money-laundering methods to evade sanctions. Attempts by academics and non-governmental organisations to map the country's illicit networks continued to identify numerous intermediaries and front companies around the world charged with trading goods, services and funds on behalf of the North Korean leadership.

In response to Pyongyang's illicit military-procurement operations, as well as provocations such as the fifth nuclear test, the UN Security Council adopted Resolution 2321 in November 2016. Designed to close loopholes in existing provisions, the measure focused on North Korea's exports of products such as coal, the majority of which went to China, its largest trading partner. The resolution restricted the value and volume of Chinese coal imports from North Korea, after which Beijing announced in February 2017 that it would suspend all coal imports from North Korea for the remainder of the year. However, there remained reasons to doubt the effectiveness of sanctions on North Korea. In its 2017 annual report, the UN Panel of Experts on North Korea described the implementation of multilateral sanctions as 'insufficient and highly inconsistent'. As multilateral sanctions became more complicated, implementation further stretched already limited resources. This problem was exacerbated by a lack of political will in key regions, especially Africa and Southeast Asia.

Rising pressure on Pyongyang

The Obama administration had viewed multilateral sanctions as an important element of a strategy to force North Korea to resume negotiations on its nuclear and missile programmes. Under Trump, there was a sense that this patience would be replaced with greater urgency, due to both the new president's rhetoric and the growing North Korean missile threat. As president-elect, Trump tweeted that a North Korean ICBM 'won't happen', raising expectations that the US would engage in military action against Pyongyang. Yet despite limited attempts at coercive diplomacy – including the deployment of submarines, long-range bombers and a carrier strike group led by the USS *Carl Vinson* near the Korean Peninsula – Washington's North Korea policy appeared to remain largely unchanged. Seoul was concerned by Trump's initial lack of commitment to US security guarantees but was later reassured by US Secretary of Defense James Mattis, who during a visit to the Republic of Korea (ROK) in February promised that 'we stand firmly, 100 percent, shoulder to shoulder with you'. In May, Mattis expressed his preference for resolving the crisis through diplomatic means, adding: 'it would be a catastrophic war if this turns into a combat'.

With military action seen as a last resort and sanctions deemed ineffective, Trump commissioned a policy review in March. The following month, the process concluded without generating any significant new options. As a consequence, Washington broadened its sanctions on North Korea in June, targeting companies and individuals that allegedly supported its weapons programmes, including two Russian firms. The UN also expanded its list of sanctioned entities, while the EU introduced new restrictions on North Korea. By mid-2017, none of these measures appeared to have had a marked impact on Pyongyang's missile programme or its willingness to engage in diplomacy.

Recognising China's importance to resolving the crisis on the Korean Peninsula, Trump used his April 2017 meeting with President Xi to request that Beijing increase economic pressure on Pyongyang (the Chinese president reportedly asked for 100 days in which to address the problem). By agreeing to broader multilateral sanctions, China appeared to demonstrate its credentials as a responsible international actor. Yet it was unclear how stringently Beijing would apply the new punitive measures, as it seemed unwilling to use its uniquely powerful influence on Pyongyang in a manner that would risk regime collapse.

Moreover, this influence appeared to be waning. Aside from their trade relationship, China had few options to demonstrate its displeasure with North Korea's provocative behaviour. By destabilising the Asia-Pacific security environment, Pyongyang became more of a burden for Beijing. As a consequence, Chinese Foreign Minister Wang Yi proposed in April a deal under which Pyongyang would halt its nuclear and missile tests in exchange for the suspension of the annual US–ROK military exercises, a particular source of concern among the North Korean leadership (it was unclear whether North Korea had been consulted prior to the announcement). Wang described the US and North Korea as 'two accelerating trains coming toward each other, and neither side is willing to give way'. His proposal was rejected outright by the US and the ROK. Chinese Ambassador to the US Cui Tiankai subsequently claimed that his country had 'done its utmost' to find a solution, explaining that 'while the US worries about the DPRK nuclear ambition, the DPRK justifies it by the US threat to its survival. Suspicion is mutual and runs deep. Both sides are locked in a chicken-or-egg dilemma, and neither intends to take the first step.'

The assassination of Kim Jong-nam, Kim Jong-un's elder half-brother, in Kuala Lumpur airport in February 2017 emphasised Pyongyang's disregard for international law. The killing caused a diplomatic stand-off between Malaysia and North Korea, not least because it had been carried out using the nerve agent VX, a highly toxic, banned chemical weapon that is difficult to produce without state support. By ordering the use of such a substance on foreign soil, Kim Jong-un signalled his willingness to go to great lengths to protect his regime from perceived external threats. The incident also raised concern about the extent of North Korea's biological- and chemical-weapons programmes, which had theretofore been largely overshadowed by its development of missiles and nuclear arms.

The murder of Kim Jong-nam made it more difficult for Asian states to ignore North Korea's behaviour. Southeast Asian governments had generally opted to avoid direct criticism of the regime, believing that diplomatic engagement was the only way to resolve the tension on the Korean Peninsula. However, their condemnation of Pyongyang became more explicit in the wake of the assassination, further isolating North Korea. Malaysia restricted visa-free travel for North Koreans and shuttered companies linked to Pyongyang. The Trump administration emphasised the importance of engaging with regional actors on the issue, inviting the leaders of the Philippines and Thailand to the White House partly to garner their support in implementing sanctions on the DPRK.

The US and its allies also highlighted North Korea's human-rights abuses with the aim of pressuring Pyongyang. The passage of UN Security Council Resolution 2345 in March strengthened the UN's efforts to assess and develop strategies to respond to such abuses by enhancing the role of the UN Office of the High Commissioner for Human Rights in Seoul. Following the measure, the office would receive additional support to plan for the eventual prosecution of North Korean leaders and officials who were responsible for human-rights violations. Nonetheless, the move was unlikely to have a significant impact on the Kim regime in the short term – as Tomás Ojea Quintana, UN human-rights special rapporteur for the DPRK, recognised in March, stating that there were no 'quick fixes or instant solutions' to the situation. The DPRK's continuing human-rights abuses received additional international exposure in June, following the death of US citizen Otto Warmbier. The 22-year-old had recently been released from North Korean custody in a coma after being detained 17 months earlier for stealing a poster on a tourist visit. The circumstances surrounding his death were unclear, but he was assumed to have been tortured by the DPRK authorities.

Abrupt political transition in Seoul

Domestic politics in South Korea added a further layer of complexity to the situation on the Korean Peninsula. President Park Geun-hye was impeached in December 2016 for providing Choi Soon-sil, a close friend, with access to classified information that allowed her to interfere in state affairs and accrue unlawful financial benefits. Mass demonstrations took place in Seoul calling for Park's prosecution, before South Korea's Constitutional Court confirmed her removal from office in

March, triggering presidential elections. The early frontrunner in the contest was liberal candidate Moon Jae-in, who went on to win comfortably. Elected with a mandate to improve relations between Seoul and Pyongyang, Moon faced an intractable challenge in balancing domestic political objectives with the concerns of the US, China and Japan.

A priority on Moon's agenda remained the controversial THAAD system that was hurriedly deployed to South Korea in the lead-up to the presidential elections, following several years of prevarication on the issue. The move generated persistent opposition from Beijing, which claimed that the system's AN/TPY-2 X-Band radar had sufficient range to track Chinese missiles. This capability, Beijing argued, undermined strategic stability between the US and China. As the technical aspects of this argument remained questionable, it appeared that China was actually concerned by the increase in US ballistic-missile-defence assets in the region – a fear also shared by Russia – and increasingly close military cooperation between the US and South Korea. Beijing's opposition to the THAAD deployment manifested in unofficial trade restrictions and embargoes on South Korea, leading to a significant reduction in Chinese tourist visits in the ROK and boycotts of Korean brand Lotte in China (the THAAD battery was located on a golf course in Seongju owned by the Lotte Group). Anxiety about the deployment also provoked local demonstrations in South Korea, due to questions regarding its effectiveness and fears that the area was more likely to be targeted by the North Korean military.

As the THAAD dispute continued, North Korea's ongoing missile tests drove President Moon to admit in May 2017 that he would not immediately open a dialogue with Pyongyang. It was instead 'a time to heighten sanctions and pressure', he said, following a phone conversation with Japanese Prime Minister Abe. During the presidency of Park Geun-hye, relations between Japan and South Korea had improved, as reflected in their November 2016 signing of a military-intelligence agreement under which they would share sensitive information on the North Korean missile and nuclear threat. The deal proceeded despite opposition within the ROK, where memories of Japanese colonial rule over South Korea still provoke unease and distrust. Pyongyang played on this fear in its response to the declaration of the agreement, criticising Seoul for having exposed the Korean Peninsula to invasion. In November 2016, Chinese Foreign Ministry spokesperson Geng Shuang reacted negatively to the 'Cold War mentality' of closer ROK–Japan cooperation, citing concerns that it would 'aggravate antagonism and confrontation'. However, the prospects for continuing improvement in Japan–South Korea relations were reduced by South Koreans' resurgent dismay about a December 2015 deal on Japanese wartime reparations. Therefore, it was possible that the Moon administration would revisit the issue, a decision that would be popular in South Korea.

President Moon was forced to evaluate a multitude of domestic and international relationships and responsibilities at a time of increasing regional tension. Any decision to reverse the THAAD deployment would be perceived as deference to Chinese demands that devalued the US–ROK alliance. Yet a decision to maintain the deployment would all but guarantee continued Chinese opposition and hostility, as Beijing had invested too much political capital in its opposition to the move to back down. North Korea would continue to exploit such disputes, undermining any attempts to unify the positions of the US, China, the ROK and Japan. Moon also faced a conundrum in attempting to engage with Pyongyang diplomatically when Kim Jong-un appeared to be content in isolation. And it was unclear what Moon could plausibly offer in exchange for a freeze on missile development, let alone the denuclearisation of the Korean Peninsula. As the security situation deteriorated, patience was likely to wear thin on all sides, if less so in China. Although the prospect of military action remained remote, North Korea's advance towards a nuclear-capable ICBM was met with intensifying anxiety among Asian leaders and members of the new US administration.

Relative calm in the South China Sea

A series of unexpected political developments contributed to a marked decline in tension in the South China Sea in the year to mid-2017. In contrast to the previous five years, the parties to the territorial and maritime-boundaries dispute there only engaged in minor confrontations.

Although the Arbitral Tribunal at The Hague rejected most of China's jurisdictional claims in the South China Sea in July 2016, the new administration in Manila led by President Duterte chose to de-emphasise the ruling and to focus instead on repairing relations and strengthening economic ties with Beijing. In response, China refrained from potentially provocative actions to flout the ruling and punish the Philippines, and in October lifted a blockade that had prevented Philippine citizens from fishing near Scarborough Shoal since 2012 – a major source of friction between the countries.

Trump's unexpected victory in the US presidential elections also affected the dispute in the South China Sea. Despite global concerns that he would trigger a trade war with China and push back against Beijing's assertiveness in the sea, the tone of Sino-US relations improved due to the apparent rapport between Trump and Xi. Moreover, the growing crisis over North Korea's nuclear and ballistic-missile programmes heightened the new US administration's need to cooperate with Beijing. In January and February 2017, the White House rejected several requests from the US Pacific Command to conduct FONOPs in the South China Sea – operations of the kind that the Obama administration had used to target Chinese-occupied features, angering Beijing. However, in May and July the US Navy conducted FONOPs at Mischief Reef, in the Spratlys, and Triton Island, in the Paracels.

Some Southeast Asian countries seemed to show increasing deference towards Beijing, perhaps in reaction to China's economic blandishments, the expanding capabilities of its military (especially the PLAN) and concern that Trump would weaken US security and trade commitments in the Asia-Pacific. Improving relations between ASEAN and China led to progress in their negotiations on establishing a Code of Conduct for the South China Sea. Accordingly, many observers saw the dispute in the South China Sea as shifting in China's favour.

However, despite the reduction in tension, the main drivers of the disagreement – nationalism, competition over resources and geopolitical rivalry – remained essentially unchanged. None of the states directly involved in the dispute compromised on its jurisdictional claims, while major stakeholders such as the US and Japan maintained their positions. Moreover, efforts by ASEAN and China to establish an effective conflict-management regime had yet to yield substantive results. As a consequence, it was possible that the dispute would intensify once again.

Issued three and a half years after the Philippines initiated proceedings, the Arbitral Tribunal's ruling was far more sweeping and clear-cut than expected in repudiating Beijing's territorial claims in the South China Sea. Although the court did not declare China's 'nine-dash line' (the demarcation of its claims encompassing most of the sea) to be illegal per se, it ruled that what the country called its 'historic rights' to living and non-living resources within the line were incompatible with the 1982 United Nations Convention on the Law of the Sea (UNCLOS). The court also found that China had violated the Philippines' sovereign rights in its 200nm EEZ by undertaking reclamation work at Mischief Reef and harassing Philippine fishing boats and survey vessels. It castigated Beijing for having conducted extensive reclamation activities that caused irreparable damage to the marine ecosystem. In a surprise decision, the court ruled that the Spratlys included no islands capable of sustaining human life, and thus had no EEZ; rather, they were either rocks, entitled to a 12nm territorial sea, or semi-submerged or submerged features that did not generate any maritime jurisdictional zones. Having refused to participate in the case, China described the ruling as 'null and void'. Chinese officials questioned the competence and integrity of the judges on the court, while media outlets controlled by Beijing denounced the ruling as a political conspiracy instigated by the US and Japan. Taiwan, whose claims mirror those of China, also rejected the court's judgment.

The ruling was a victory not only for the Philippines but also other Southeast Asian claimants, as it established that China could not legally claim ownership of resources where the nine-dash line overlapped with their EEZs. Nonetheless, ASEAN states' reactions to the ruling were generally muted due to their reluctance to antagonise

China. Vietnam came closest to calling on both parties to abide by the ruling when it noted that the verdict was binding for both China and the Philippines. Both Malaysia and Singapore stated that all parties should 'fully respect legal and diplomatic processes'. Indonesia urged the disputants to 'exercise self-restraint' and respect international law. Thailand, Myanmar and Laos stressed the importance of implementing the 2002 ASEAN–China Declaration on the Conduct of Parties in the South China Sea and of expediting talks on the Code of Conduct.

The US, Japan and Australia called on both parties to abide by the ruling. However, due to internal divisions, the EU merely acknowledged the ruling. In a sign of growing coordination between Beijing and Moscow on issues that affected their core interests, President Putin stated in September 2016 that he supported China's rejection of the ruling. Russia was alone among major powers in adopting this position.

Limited deference to Chinese power

Duterte's unwillingness to support the arbitration process partly stemmed from his belief that it needlessly provoked China, given that the country would almost certainly fail to comply with the ruling. After the ruling was issued, he held to his promise not to 'taunt' Beijing on the decision: the Philippines initially welcomed the ruling and stated that it would issue a more detailed response later.

This detailed response never came. Instead, Duterte put the ruling to one side, proposed bilateral talks with China on the dispute and in October travelled to Beijing. There, Duterte reportedly reached an understanding with Xi that led China to lift its blockade of Scarborough Shoal. During Duterte's visit, China also promised to provide US$24bn in economic support to the Philippines, which included funding for several major infrastructure projects. Reduced tension between Manila and Beijing led to increased interaction between the Philippine and Chinese coastguards, visits to the Philippines by PLAN ships and the May 2017 inaugural meeting of a bilateral consultative mechanism to address South China Sea issues – all of which would have been unthinkable under Duterte's predecessor. Senior Chinese officials lavished praise on Duterte for not only moving to repair relations with China but also for the positive impact of his policy on broader ASEAN–China relations. For instance, at a press conference in March, Foreign Minister Wang enthused that 'the turnaround in China–Philippine relations has scattered the dark clouds over China–ASEAN relations' and lowered tension in the South China Sea 'significantly'.

Yet Manila was still concerned about China's approach to the sea, particularly its continuing militarisation of artificial islands; the deployment of survey ships to Benham Rise (an area east of Luzon and outside the nine-dash line in which the UN recognised the Philippines' sovereign rights); and – according to comments from a Chinese provincial official later denied by Beijing – ambitions to establish a research station on Scarborough Shoal. Indeed, China continued to develop the infrastructure on its seven man-made islands in the Spratlys. As shown by a variety of reports often supported by detailed satellite imagery, Beijing's work on runways, aircraft hangars, multistorey buildings, lighthouses and radar facilities there neared completion. Despite Xi's reassurances in September 2015 that China would not militarise the dispute in the South China Sea, satellite imagery revealed that the country had installed anti-aircraft and anti-missile systems on the largest of its artificial features on Subi, Mischief and Fiery Cross reefs (although runways on the reefs appeared to be complete, by mid-2017 China had yet to deploy combat aircraft there). Chinese officials continued to claim that the infrastructural development in the sea was mainly for civilian purposes, and that any military equipment there was only intended for self-defence. The transformation of the seven expanded features into operational bases significantly enhanced China's ability to project and sustain military power into the heart of maritime Southeast Asia.

Although Duterte brushed aside these developments and lamented that the Philippines was unable to prevent Beijing from doing as it wished in the South China Sea, the country's national-security establishment, including defence minister Delfin Lorenzana and senior officers in the Armed Forces of the Philippines, expressed greater anxiety over the matter. In April, Duterte responded to their concerns by ordering an upgrade of military infrastructure on Philippines-controlled islets in the sea.

A significant recalibration of Manila's foreign policy also helped smooth its relations with Beijing, while discomfiting Washington. After taking office, Duterte pledged to pursue an 'independent foreign policy' designed to lessen his country's supposed dependence on the US, repair its relations with China and strengthen its ties to what he called 'non-traditional' partners such as Russia, Japan and India. According to Jose Santiago Sta. Romana, Philippine ambassador to China, the policy aimed to find the 'geopolitical sweet spot' between China and the US that would best protect the national interest. Duterte was dismissive of the US–Philippine alliance and openly questioned Washington's commitment to Philippine security. He spoke of 'separating' from the US, expelling US forces from the southern Philippines, ending purchases of US arms, terminating joint US–Philippine military exercises and abrogating a 2014 agreement that facilitated the rotational deployment of US forces to the country. However, although the US and the Philippines scaled down their military exercises, the alliance relationship remained largely unaltered, as demonstrated by the presence of US special-forces advisers, and the transfer of military equipment to the Armed Forces of the Philippines, during the Marawi crisis. Therefore, Duterte's strategy appeared to centre on de-emphasis of the South China Sea dispute, efforts to capture Chinese economic largesse and sustainment of the US–Philippine alliance. It was unclear whether the strategy would prove successful.

The relationship between Hanoi and Beijing also continued to recover following the 2014 stand-off when China moved its Haiyang Shiyou 981 oil platform into waters near the Paracel Islands. The sides engaged in several visits involving senior leaders who pledged to maintain stability, manage disputes and enhance cooperation. Nonetheless, despite the generally positive trend in relations, Vietnam remained wary of China's presence in the South China Sea and continued to strengthen its position there by undertaking limited infrastructural development on the atolls under its control. Hanoi also objected to activities such as Chinese civilian cruises to the Paracels and Beijing's imposition of a fishing ban in northern areas of the South China Sea during May–August. In June–July, bilateral relations became tense again when China allegedly threatened to use force against Vietnam unless it suspended drilling in its EEZ in an area that overlapped with the nine-dash line. Vietnam reportedly complied, at least temporarily.

In keeping with past practice, Malaysia de-emphasised the dispute in the South China Sea but maintained its claims to sovereignty and jurisdiction over some features there. In March 2017, Foreign Minister Anifah Aman stated in parliament that as Malaysia did not recognise China's nine-dash line, there were no overlapping claims between the countries. Brunei, also a claimant (if a minor one), maintained its customary silence over the dispute.

Although it had no claim to sovereignty over any features in the Spratlys, Indonesia remained a party to the dispute because China's nine-dash line overlaps with the EEZ of the Natuna Islands. Incursions by Chinese fishing trawlers into Indonesia's EEZ – which Beijing refers to as its 'traditional fishing grounds', a concept unrecognised by UNCLOS – resulted in several tense encounters between Indonesian and Chinese coastguard vessels. Jakarta responded by strengthening its military presence on and around the Natunas; staging several high-profile air and naval exercises nearby; promoting the economic development of the islands; and renaming the waters that surround them the 'North Natuna Sea'.

The broader South China Sea dispute contributed to strained relations between China and non-claimant state Singapore, which Beijing accused of tacitly supporting the Arbitral Tribunal ruling. Singapore replied that while it was neutral in the dispute, its national interest demanded that international law and freedom of navigation be upheld in the sea.

Contrasting responses from ASEAN and Washington

In the year to mid-2017, China and ASEAN achieved a modicum of progress in their two-decade effort to manage – but not resolve – the South

China Sea dispute. However, this progress was more an effect than a cause of reduced tension between the sides. In August 2016, ASEAN and Chinese officials approved guidelines to establish diplomatic hotlines for use during maritime emergencies, and agreed to apply the Code for Unplanned Encounters at Sea to the South China Sea. Signed in 2014 by members of the Western Pacific Naval Symposium, the agreement was designed to prevent dangerous incidents through communications and manoeuvring protocols. However, the agreement was non-binding and did not apply to the coastguard vessels involved in the majority of tense stand-offs in the South China Sea in the preceding five years. Furthermore, the agreement had already been adopted by China and all ASEAN member states except Myanmar – whose navy does not operate in the South China Sea – and landlocked Laos.

Following the Arbitral Tribunal's ruling, Chinese Foreign Minister Wang echoed a long-standing call by ASEAN to expedite talks on the Code of Conduct, which had made only limited progress since commencing in 2013. In September 2016, they pledged to issue a framework agreement by mid-2017. After several rounds of talks in Guiyang the following May, Southeast Asian and Chinese officials agreed on a draft framework for the Code of Conduct that was expected to be approved at a meeting of their foreign ministers in August. Although the text of the draft framework was not publicly available, reportedly the agreement would not be legally binding, despite some ASEAN countries' hopes to the contrary. It was widely believed that the sides could take several years to reach a final agreement on the Code of Conduct.

In contrast to previous years, ASEAN was able to maintain a unified stand on the South China Sea. Despite having close political and economic ties to China, Laos proved relatively adept in its role as ASEAN chair for 2016, balancing the interests of claimant and non-claimant states while forging a consensus among the organisation's ten members. The Philippines took over the chair from Laos in January, and in keeping with President Duterte's strategy ensured that the South China Sea dispute had an inconspicuous place on ASEAN's agenda. Unlike ASEAN statements issued in previous years, the final communiqué of the organisation's 30th summit, held in Manila in April 2017, omitted references to land-reclamation activities in the South China Sea and the militarisation of the dispute there, downgrading the 'serious concerns' expressed by some members in previous years over recent developments to 'concerns'. The call for disagreements to be resolved with 'full respect for legal and diplomatic process' was only a vague reference to the ruling on the dispute. Duterte dismissed claims that the Philippines had watered down the statement under pressure from Beijing, saying that he wanted to avoid causing 'trouble' with China and that ASEAN was in no position to pressure Beijing in any case. While the statement was welcomed by China, it did little to enhance ASEAN's credibility.

The new US administration initially adopted far more combative rhetoric on the South China Sea. Although the dispute there barely rated a mention during the US presidential elections, subsequent comments from senior officials in the Trump administration indicated that Washington might favour a tough policy on China's actions in the maritime domain. In his 11 January confirmation hearing, secretary of state-designate Tillerson suggested that the US should physically prevent China from accessing its artificial islands in the Spratlys, provoking fears of a military crisis. White House spokesman Sean Spicer stated that if the artificial islands were in international waters rather than 'China proper', the US would 'defend international interests from being taken over by one country'. Stephen Bannon, Trump's nominal chief strategist, reportedly predicted that there would be a major war between the US and China in the South China Sea within a decade.

Nonetheless, the Trump administration quickly toned down its hawkish approach, partly to assuage concern about conflict among Asian states and partly to assist in the effort to enlist Beijing's cooperation in efforts to deal with North Korea's accelerating nuclear and ballistic-missile programmes. These considerations lay behind the White House's refusal to conduct FONOPs in early 2017. Tillerson clarified his earlier comments by stating that the US might blockade China's artificial islands only during a military crisis. And while Secretary of

Defense Mattis criticised China's 'increasingly confrontational' actions in the South China Sea, he said that the US favoured diplomacy over 'dramatic military moves'. The dispute was only mentioned in passing when President Trump met President Xi at the Mar-a-Lago summit.

But by May 2017, the Trump administration appeared to have hardened its approach to the South China Sea once again – possibly because it was disappointed in Beijing's inability or unwillingness to rein in Pyongyang. On 24 May, the US Navy destroyer USS *Dewey* conducted a FONOP near Mischief Reef designed to repudiate China's claim to a 12nm territorial sea around the feature. Beijing complained about the operation, accusing the US of undermining stability in the South China Sea. Two days after the FONOP, two Chinese jet fighters flew within a few hundred feet of a US surveillance aircraft over the South China Sea, highlighting the risks of an accidental clash between the US and Chinese armed forces. As the FONOP occurred two weeks before the 16th IISS Shangri-La Dialogue in Singapore, there was speculation that it was timed to buttress Mattis's plenary address at the event, in which he attempted to reassure Asian countries of Washington's 'enduring commitment' to the Asia-Pacific. In comments aimed at China, he reiterated US opposition to the militarisation of the South China Sea and 'unilateral, coercive changes to the status quo'. Speaking in New Zealand a few days later, Tillerson again described the militarisation of China's artificial islands as a threat to regional stability. On 2 July, the USS *Stethem* conducted a FONOP at Triton Island, indicating that the Trump administration had decided to increase the frequency of such operations in the South China Sea. China described the FONOP as a 'serious political and military provocation' and a violation of its sovereignty. Thus, by mid-year, renewed Sino-Vietnamese and US–China tensions in the South China Sea suggested that the 12-month lull was at an end.

Australia's increasingly fraught security environment

The government of Prime Minister Turnbull narrowly escaped defeat in early elections held on 2 July 2016, securing a one-seat majority.

Despite this sobering result, the ruling coalition – comprising the National Party and Turnbull's Liberal Party – continued to suffer from disputes between him and the right wing of his party, led by his predecessor Tony Abbott. Turnbull remained politically vulnerable due to public awareness of the divide within his party, the increased difficulty of passing legislation and the need constantly to compromise with Abbott's faction on key issues such as climate change and taxation.

The coalition's approval ratings steadily declined in the year to mid-2017, increasing pressure on the prime minister. By March 2017, its ratings trailed those of the opposition Labor Party by ten percentage points. The same month, major resistance from his backbenchers forced the prime minister to withdraw the ratification of an extradition treaty with China from the parliament's voting agenda at the last minute. This sparked a renewed public feud between Liberal factions, highlighting the negative effect of political volatility on the government's attempts to formulate foreign policy. Hopes that the new budget announced in May 2017 – which included an A$6.2bn (US$4.9bn) levy on banks – would reverse the trend proved unfounded. In June, Turnbull experienced renewed resistance from right-wing Liberals – this time over Australia's energy policy.

As a consequence, the prime minister was forced to invest significant effort in maintaining domestic political stability just as Australia faced rising uncertainty in the regional and global security environment. The new budget reflected this perception of risk, increasing defence funding to A$34.6bn (US$26.3bn) for 2017–18 from AS$32.3bn (US$24.7bn) the previous year. It also maintained the government's commitment to increase defence funding to 2% of GDP by 2020–21, to enable Australia's largest increase in defence capability since 1945 over following decades, as outlined in the 2016 Defence White Paper. Although it was unclear whether the government would maintain the funding levels required to fulfil the White Paper's ambitious agenda, Australia continued to make a significant investment in defence capabilities. A major step in the effort came in September 2016, when Canberra signed its first contract with French company DCNS for the licence construction of up to 12 *Shortfin Barracuda* submarines.

Australia maintained the deployment of around 780 military personnel on *Operation OKRA*, its mission to combat ISIS in Syria and Iraq. The deployment included an Air Task Group charged with conducting strikes and other missions; a Special Operations Task Group to provide military advice and assistance to the Iraqi security forces; and Task Group Taji, a combined Australia–New Zealand military-training force based near Baghdad. In May 2017, Minister for Defence Marise Payne also announced the deployment of an additional 30 troops to Afghanistan, bringing the Australian military's total strength there to 300 personnel.

Canberra also became increasingly concerned about the potential threat posed by terrorists returning to Australia from the Middle East and the increasing influence of ISIS in Southeast Asia. Duncan Lewis, director of the Australian Security Intelligence Organisation, warned in March that Australian tourists and expatriates were at growing risk of terrorism in countries such as Indonesia, Malaysia and the Philippines. Minister for Foreign Affairs Julie Bishop also warned about the prospect of militants establishing an Islamist 'caliphate' in the southern Philippines. In view of these potential threats, the budget increased funding for the Australian Secret Intelligence Service and the Australian Signals Directorate by A$75m (US$59m), and allocated an additional A$321m (US$254m) in counter-terrorism funding to Australian Federal Police over four years.

The Turnbull government also remained concerned about growing tensions in East Asia. Canberra regarded North Korea's accelerating nuclear activities and ballistic-missile tests as a major source of regional instability. Calling the regime in Pyongyang a 'reckless and dangerous threat', Turnbull in April 2017 sided with the US and its allies by stating that the onus was on China to exert greater pressure on the DPRK. A month earlier, Minister for Defence Industry Christopher Pyne had foreshadowed a seemingly imminent announcement on what he called a 'very expensive' missile-defence system; commentators speculated that North Korea's recent missile tests had inspired the Australian government to develop a missile-defence capability. However, during the period under consideration, no announcement was made.

China's growing assertiveness and challenge to the rules-based order in the Asia-Pacific created evident anxiety in Canberra. Australia has a strong interest in maintaining freedom of navigation and overflight, as well as the rule of law, in the South China Sea. Indeed, it was among the few countries to publicly call on China to respect the ruling of the Arbitral Tribunal, drawing an angry rebuke from Beijing.

Thus, Australia–China relations continued to be characterised by a mixture of tension and cooperation. For instance, during his visit to Canberra in March 2017, Premier Li told Turnbull that Beijing did not want to see Australia 'taking sides, as happened during the Cold War' and indicated that the country should pursue an independent foreign policy. Li and Turnbull signed trade and investment agreements, and announced an Australia–China High-Level Security Dialogue, which would focus on issues such as cyber security, transnational crime and counter-terrorism. However, Turnbull also reminded the Chinese premier that stability in the region depended on the 'rules-based order', an indirect reference to China's island-building activities in the South China Sea. Australia also refused to join China's Belt and Road Initiative. During his keynote address at the 16th IISS Shangri-La Dialogue, Turnbull warned against a 'coercive China' that would prompt regional countries to 'look to counterweight Beijing's power by bolstering alliances and partnerships, between themselves and especially with the United States'. Meanwhile, Beijing intensified its efforts to influence Australian public opinion through major donations to politicians and support for China-linked research institutions at universities, which had been going on for several years. Following Australian media reports on the extent of Chinese attempts to influence politicians, spy on Australians and intimidate academics and students who were critical of Beijing, in June 2017 the prime minister ordered a major inquiry into Australia's espionage and foreign-interference laws.

Yet while providing verbal support to US Navy FONOPs within 12nm of disputed features in the South China Sea, Canberra refrained from joining in these missions or conducting its own. Despite calls from the opposition to do so, the government argued that such a move would only escalate tension. The issue of possible FONOPs created considerable domestic debate within the Australian strategic-affairs community. Although some former political and military leaders supported the government's cautious approach, former defence secretary Dennis Richardson used his first speech after retiring in May 2017 to call for Australia to conduct a FONOP that would challenge China's claims to waters surrounding its artificial islands in the South China Sea. At the 2017 Shangri-La Dialogue, Payne only reiterated that Australian forces would continue to fly and sail in the South China Sea 'as they have for decades, consistent with the rights of freedom of navigation and freedom of overflight'.

Mixed success in strengthening international partnerships

As the 2016 Defence White Paper emphasised, the Turnbull government was committed to strengthening regional security and defence partnerships, especially those in Southeast Asia. Australia maintained a strong defence relationship with Singapore, but had only mixed success in improving that with Indonesia, its other key Southeast Asian partner. At the fourth dialogue between Australia's and Indonesia's foreign and defence ministers in October 2016, Indonesian Minister of Defense Ryamizard Ryacudu surprised many observers by declaring that Canberra and Jakarta had 'more or less agreed' to 'joint patrols' in the South China Sea. Yet in January 2017, Indonesia temporarily suspended all bilateral military cooperation after an incident at an Australian Army training facility that apparently caused serious offence to the Indonesian armed forces. It was not until Indonesian President Joko Widodo visited Sydney the following month that this cooperation was fully restored. During Widodo's visit, the sides stressed the importance of freedom of navigation and overflight in the South China Sea. Turnbull and Widodo also announced a Joint Declaration on Maritime Cooperation, which focused on areas such as maritime-border protection, as well as efforts to counter illegal fishing and transnational organised crime. However, Australia and Indonesia subsequently agreed no major defence initiatives, nor did they announce any progress towards joint patrols in the South China Sea. In early March, Bishop denied that Widodo had suggested 'joint patrols' with Australia in these waters during his visit.

Canberra also looked to strengthen its defence ties with India. The countries conducted their first bilateral special-forces exercise in October 2016, and planned to conduct another during the second half of 2017. In June 2017, the countries' navies held their second bilateral exercise off the coast of Western Australia, following their first joint naval exercise, in the Bay of Bengal, in 2015. During Prime Minister Turnbull's visit to India in April 2017, they announced that they would conduct their inaugural bilateral army exercise in 2018, and the first dialogue involving their foreign and defence ministers the same year. But despite Australia's stated interest in joining the India–US–Japan *Malabar* naval exercise, New Delhi blocked its bid to do so, allegedly out of concern about China's potential reaction.

The relationship between Canberra and Tokyo began to slowly recover, following Japan's disappointment in its failure to win the contract for building Australia's new class of submarines. This could be seen during Prime Minister Abe's January 2017 visit to Australia, as the countries signed an Acquisition and Cross-Servicing Agreement covering logistical support between their armed forces. Turnbull and Abe also set the target of concluding in 2017 an agreement on improving administrative, policy and legal procedures, which would facilitate joint operations and exercises. They also agreed to enhance cooperation in areas such as cyber security, as well as space and defence science and technology. Their joint statement described the situation in the South China Sea as being of 'serious concern to both leaders' and pledged to 'continue to work proactively, alongside the U.S. and other like-minded countries, including India, to maintain the rules-based international order'.

The Turnbull government also had to adapt to the new US administration. Trump's seeming lack of an Asia-Pacific strategy, unpredictability, enthusiasm for economic nationalism and apparent disregard for central pillars of the Western liberal order all caused concern in Canberra. Moreover, the relationship between Turnbull and Trump began poorly in February, when the US president reportedly cut short their phone conversation. The new US administration swiftly moved to cancel the Trans-Pacific Partnership, the economic centrepiece of the previous administration's 'rebalance' to the Asia-Pacific, and made clear that the White House would no longer use the term 'rebalance' (it suggested no alternative term for US strategy in the region).

As a consequence, Australia was left wondering about the content of the Trump administration's Asia strategy and indicated its frustration. In her IISS Fullerton Lecture in Singapore in mid-March 2017, Bishop sent an unusually strong message to Washington. Warning of China's growing threat to regional stability, she noted that many Asian countries were in a 'strategic holding pattern', waiting to see 'whether the United States and its security allies and partners can continue to play the robust and constructive role that they have for many decades in preserving the peace'. She also stated that 'if stability and prosperity are to continue, the United States must play an even greater role as the indispensable strategic power in the Indo-Pacific.' At the end of March, senior Australian government officials described the Trump administration's policy and its implications for Australia in even starker terms. In a remarkably frank public observation, Minister for Defence Industry Pyne said that the Trump administration was 'not business as usual' and that the Australian government had to 'rethink how that relationship will work'. Although Turnbull and Trump's first meeting in person, in New York in May 2017, was reportedly successful, Australia's doubts about the direction of the US under its new president did not subside. For instance, in his IISS Shangri-La Dialogue address, Turnbull noted the important role that the US played in Asia-Pacific stability but also stressed that Australia 'cannot rely on great powers to safeguard our interest'. In June, the first Australia–United States Ministerial Consultations under Trump failed to produce major new initiatives for the alliance. Nonetheless, the countries' military-to-military relationship continued to deepen at the working level. In December 2016, Canberra and Washington agreed on the temporary deployment of the most advanced US combat aircraft, the F-22 *Raptor*, to northern Australia; the following February, the first squadron of F-22s arrived at the Royal Australian Air Force base in Tindal, in the Northern Territories, for a bilateral exercise and training missions within the context of the bilateral Enhanced Air Cooperation initiative. The major bilateral *Exercise Talisman Saber*, involving more than 30,000 Australian and US troops, began in late June and would finish in late July.

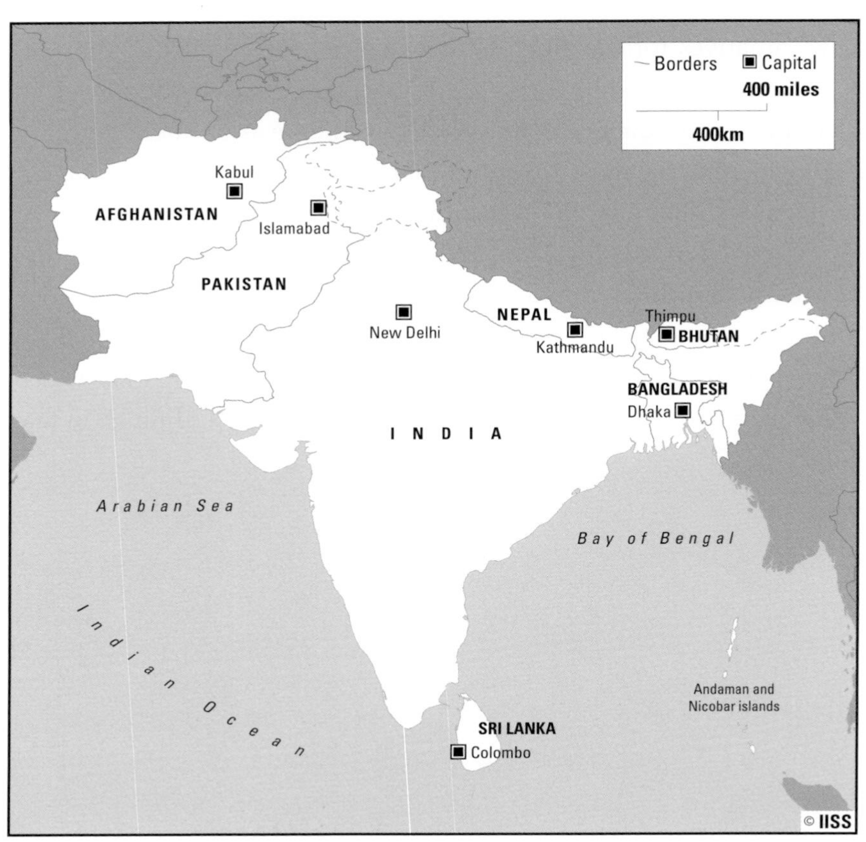
Borders
Capital
400 miles
400km
Kabul
AFGHANISTAN
Islamabad
PAKISTAN
New Delhi
NEPAL
Kathmandu
Thimpu
BHUTAN
BANGLADESH
Dhaka
I N D I A
Arabian Sea
Bay of Bengal
Indian Ocean
Andaman and
Nicobar islands
SRI LANKA
Colombo
© IISS

Chapter 5

South Asia and Afghanistan

India's economy experienced two major changes in the year to mid-2017. The first came on 8 November, when the government suddenly demonetised the country's 500- and 1,000-rupee notes; the second on 1 July, with its enactment of the Goods and Services Tax. The demonetisation, which affected 86% of all currency in circulation, was a bold but abrupt attempt to curb corruption by voiding so-called 'black money' (illegal or unaccounted-for currency exchanged outside the tax system). After New Delhi gave Indians just eight weeks to return their worthless banknotes, the resulting shortage of cash brought about countrywide hardship, especially in rural areas. Although the measure reportedly failed to collect a large amount of illegal cash – much of which was widely assumed to have been deposited in foreign bank accounts or exchanged for real estate, gold or jewellery – the tax base increased. The demonetisation did not decrease GDP growth by two percentage points or more, despite widespread speculation to the contrary. Instead, growth dipped from 7.9% in FY2015–16 to 7.2% in FY2016–17, and was projected to increase to 7.5% the following year. Thus, India continued to have the fastest-growing major economy in the world. The Goods and Services Tax, the most significant tax reform in the history of modern India, required amendment of the constitution. After parliament passed the law in August 2016, the government began preparing to transform the indirect tax system within India's US$2.4-trillion economy through the removal of internal tariff barriers and the replacement of 17 central, state and local taxes with a single tax. According to government officials, once implemented, the law would increase growth by an estimated one to two percentage points.

In March 2017, despite the negative effects of the demonetisation, the ruling Bharatiya Janata Party (BJP) won overwhelming victories in state elections in Uttar Pradesh, the country's most populous state, and Uttarakhand. Deft political manoeuvring enabled the BJP to gain control of both the Goa and Manipur provincial assemblies despite winning fewer seats than its main rival, the Indian National Congress. The BJP's only setback in the elections came in Punjab, where it lost control of the assembly to Congress.

India's expanding security and development role

Relations between India and Pakistan remained tense, with their forces regularly exchanging fire across the international border, as well as the Line of Control that divided the Kashmir region. The situation deteriorated on 8 July 2016, when the death of a young militant leader sparked months of large-scale civilian unrest in the Indian state of Jammu and Kashmir. On 18 September, Pakistan-based militants killed 19 Indian soldiers in an attack on an army base in Uri, near the Line of Control. The Indian government responded by calling off the South Asia Association for Regional Cooperation summit scheduled to be held in Islamabad (an event that could only proceed with the involvement of all eight members of the organisation), and by launching on 29 September a special-forces operation against militant camps across the Line of Control. New Delhi publicly acknowledged the operation, the first time that it had done so for a covert mission of this kind. But it provided no further details to the media, seeking to prevent escalation in light of Islamabad's vehement denial that the strike had taken place. Despite the continuing absence of an official dialogue between the countries, their national-security advisers spoke over the phone and met on at least one occasion – in Russia in May.

New Delhi's relationship with Beijing was threatened by a stand-off between their troops that began in June 2017, when Indian soldiers halted construction on a Chinese road project in a disputed border area known as Doka La, Donglang and Doklam in India, China and Bhutan respectively. Whereas India remained concerned about the project's impact on the Siliguri Corridor, the thin strip of land that connects its seven northeastern states to the rest of the country, China warned that there would be 'serious consequences' unless Indian troops withdrew prior to negotiations. By late July, neither side had backed down.

Amid growing tension with both China and Pakistan, India made considerable progress in formulating a new, proactive policy on the Indian Ocean. The policy provided significant economic-, transportation- and energy-development incentives to select South Asian coastal and island states; ensured that India would be among the first contributors to humanitarian and disaster-relief operations in its neighbourhood; expanded bilateral maritime-security and -defence cooperation with island states; facilitated a diplomatic and political push into the southwestern and eastern areas of the Indian Ocean; and generated opportunities to deepen cooperation with the new US administration on Indian Ocean security. Yet there remained significant challenges in creating a regional consensus on, and implementing, the policy.

India continued to pursue the objective of becoming what it called a 'leading' power in the Indian Ocean, instead of one that merely balanced between China and the United States there. New Delhi aimed to counter the expanding Chinese naval presence in the ocean, thereby protecting sea lines of communication that were important to its energy security and trade relationships. It also sought to offset the growing influence that Beijing had acquired in South Asia through sponsorship of the China–Pakistan Economic Corridor (CPEC), part of the Belt and Road Initiative. India was particularly concerned about the establishment of China's first overseas military base in Djibouti, and the increase in deployments of Chinese naval vessels in the Indian Ocean since 2014. Beijing's development of Gwadar port and the visit of a Chinese diesel-electric submarine to Karachi in May 2017, alongside resumed Chinese work on the Colombo port-city project, exacerbated this anxiety – as did the lease of the Chinese-financed and -built Hambantota port to Chinese companies for commercial and security operations.

Partly in response to Beijing's assertiveness, New Delhi further developed its role in four key regions in or near the Indian Ocean. In the Gulf, India moved from a relationship based on energy, trade and expatriates to one with political and security dimensions, covering maritime security, defence cooperation and counter-terrorism. This involved regular Indian naval-ship visits to Gulf ports and military exercises. India signed a memorandum of understanding on port management with Qatar in December, and another on joint anti-piracy training with the United Arab Emirates in January.

New Delhi provided economic and financial aid – including defence-related lines of credit – and undertook port and energy projects in states throughout South Asia, with the exception of Pakistan. During a visit to India in April 2017, Bangladeshi Prime Minister Sheikh Hasina identified 17 new infrastructure projects in her country that would be funded with a US$4.5-billion Indian line of credit (New Delhi had extended Dhaka two other lines of credit, collectively worth US$2.8bn, since 2010). These projects included upgrades of the ports of Chittagong, Mongla and Payra, as well as of airports in Bangladesh. New Delhi and Dhaka also signed 13 other agreements collectively involving US$9bn of Indian investment, most of them in the energy sector. India appeared willing to invest US$2bn in Sri Lanka over four years, according to India's commerce and industry minister. As well as developing the port, oil terminals and refinery at Trincomalee, in northeastern Sri Lanka, India worked with Japan to set up a liquefied-natural-gas plant and terminal on Sri Lanka's western coast, along with partnerships on transportation projects. India also agreed to provide Bangladesh and Sri Lanka with defence-related lines of credit worth US$500 million and US$100m respectively.

The Indian Navy had become the first responder for humanitarian and disaster-relief operations in Bangladesh, Sri Lanka and the

Maldives. The first Indian defence ministerial visit to Bangladesh took place in December 2016, while the sides deepened their security cooperation through naval, coastguard and counter-terrorism arrangements. The first India–Maldives defence-cooperation dialogue took place in July 2016. India, Sri Lanka and the Maldives maintained their trilateral maritime-security and intelligence-sharing initiatives, conducting their 13th trilateral coastguard exercise in October. In the Bay of Bengal, the Indian Navy carried out regular coordinated patrols with its counterparts from Myanmar, Thailand and Indonesia. The largest warship in the Sri Lankan navy will be an Indian-built offshore patrol vessel scheduled to be commissioned in August 2017.

Indian Prime Minister Narendra Modi significantly expanded his predecessor's policy of acting as a net security provider to Indian Ocean island states. The first Indian defence ministerial visit to Mauritius, the world's third-largest Hindu-majority state, took place in December 2016, while the new Mauritian prime minister made his first trip to India in May. The sides signed a maritime-security agreement the same month. India was building an airstrip and jetty on the Mauritian island of Agaléga for surveillance purposes, had provided helicopters to Mauritius and had extended a US$500m line of credit to the country for the purchase of additional Indian small patrol boats.

New Delhi has also provided consistent support to the Mauritian government in attempts to reassert its sovereignty over the British-controlled Chagos Islands, including Diego Garcia, the site of a US military base. On 22 June, India joined 93 other countries in voting in favour of a UN resolution that sought the advice of the International Court of Justice on the British occupation of the Chagos Islands.

India also launched a coastal-surveillance-radar project in the Seychelles, and was upgrading the jetty and airstrip on Assumption Island for surveillance purposes. Indian naval ships and aircraft regularly carried out joint surveillance, patrols and hydrographic surveys of the exclusive economic zones of Mauritius, the Seychelles and the Maldives.

As half of India's trade passed through the disputed areas of the South China Sea, the country maintained its diplomatic efforts to promote a rules-based order and freedom of navigation and overflight there. As a consequence, New Delhi supported the July 2016 ruling on the dispute in the sea by the Permanent Court of Arbitration at The Hague, which rejected almost all of China's territorial claims. Equally, the previous month, the Indian Navy had conducted another iteration of its trilateral *Malabar* exercise with the US and Japan close to the South China Sea, and carried out port calls in the area. Due to its concern about Chinese naval power, India provided Vietnam with patrol boats; a US$500m line of credit for defence spending; access to satellite data for monitoring its waters; and submarine and combat-aircraft training. In July 2017, Vietnam granted an Indian oil firm a two-year extension to explore an offshore oil block, part of which is in the South China Sea. Thus, the Modi government built on the confluence between its 'Act East' policy and the commitment to freedom of navigation and overflight evident in Washington's and Tokyo's strategies in the Indo-Pacific region.

To bolster its surveillance capabilities, India purchased 22 *Guardian* unarmed unmanned aerial vehicles (UAVs) from the US and began the rotational deployment of advanced, US-made P8-I *Poseidon* maritime-patrol aircraft and Israeli-made UAVs around the Andaman and Nicobar Islands, close to the Strait of Malacca. New Delhi also approved in May the construction of a missile-test facility on Rutland Island, in the southern Andamans, and was expected to reach an agreement with Tokyo under which Japan would build a power plant on the islands.

Developing partnerships in the Indian Ocean

Few states in South Asia shared India's concerns about growing Chinese influence and assertiveness in the region. India refused to attend the May 2017 Belt and Road Forum in Beijing because it regarded CPEC projects in Gilgit-Baltistan – which it claims as part of Jammu and Kashmir – as a violation of Indian sovereignty. In contrast, the leaders of

Pakistan and Sri Lanka participated in the event, as did ministers from Bangladesh, the Maldives and Afghanistan. They expected CPEC to create projects worth US$62bn in Pakistan, and the wider Belt and Road Initiative to generate US$22bn in soft loans and US$14bn in joint ventures in Bangladesh; US$5bn in investment in Sri Lanka; and hundreds of millions of dollars in loans for a new runway and a mile-long bridge connecting the airport to the capital in the Maldives. A Chinese container ship departed Gwadar port for the first time in November 2016. In another demonstration of its economic and defence-diplomatic power, China sold two refurbished diesel-electric submarines to Bangladesh the same month, and was constructing eight submarines for Pakistan.

India was unable to compete with Beijing's capacity to fund projects, even if the high interest rates on many Chinese loans created growing national debt. Nonetheless, New Delhi began to mount a challenge to China's infrastructure projects in South Asia by providing new economic-, port- and energy-development incentives intended to enhance regional connectivity. In May, India and Japan launched the Asia–Africa Growth Corridor to promote growth and investment in Africa. In its first phase, this maritime corridor would link Africa with India and other countries in South Asia, including Bangladesh. A major Japanese bank also agreed to finance Indo–Japanese joint ventures in Africa. New Delhi continued to seek Washington's help in developing an Indo-Pacific Economic Corridor that would link South Asia with Southeast Asia.

Neither Mauritius nor the Seychelles joined the maritime-security-cooperation agreement between India, Sri Lanka and the Maldives due to political differences between the Maldives and Mauritius. There was little prospect of bolstering the role of the 21-member Indian Ocean Rim Association in maritime-security cooperation, given India's preference for dealing with other South Asian states bilaterally rather than in multilateral forums – despite Indian officials' positive rhetoric on the matter. But India aimed to follow China in gaining observer status in the five-member Indian Ocean Commission. In parallel, the Indian Ocean Naval Symposium would continue working to strengthen maritime-security cooperation among the navies of the 35 coastal and island states in the Indian Ocean.

India's initiative to develop the Iranian port city of Chabahar, less than 100 kilometres west of Gwadar port, was likely to face setbacks due to US President Donald Trump's hostility towards Iran. Despite committing US$500m to Chabahar in May 2016 (following the removal of nuclear-related sanctions on Iran), by mid-2017 bureaucratic delays had prevented India from awarding any contracts for the supply of equipment for the project. An initial Indian loan of US$150m for the project had not been disbursed.

Thus, having formulated a proactive Indian Ocean policy, New Delhi was under pressure to implement its plans in the region (despite its poor record on policy implementation). After India raised the expectations of Indian Ocean coastal and island states by promising to fund and participate in large-scale port and energy projects, the onus was on the Indian bureaucratic establishment and armed forces to fulfil these commitments.

Although the Indian Navy had an advantage over its Chinese counterpart in the Indian Ocean due to proximity, the range of its ships and its access to port facilities in the region, India's ambitious warship-building programme continued to suffer from innumerable delays and attendant cost rises, including in its programmes to produce aircraft carriers and nuclear-armed ballistic-missile submarines.

New Delhi's proactive approach to the Indian Ocean provided opportunities to deepen maritime-security cooperation with the Trump administration. The first meeting between Modi and Trump, in Washington on 26 June, was dominated by counter-terrorism and trade. There, the Indian prime minister also met with US Secretary of Defense James Mattis, who complimented 'India's long-term efforts to promote stability in the Indian Ocean region'. Similarly, at the IISS Shangri-La Dialogue in Singapore earlier that month, Mattis had publicly stated that the United States' recognition of India as a 'major defence partner' was partly due to the latter's 'indispensable role in maintaining stability in the Indian Ocean region'.

Having developed an essentially transactional rather than strategic relationship with the Trump administration, India's assumption of new responsibilities in the Indian Ocean provided significant opportunities for US naval forces to deploy elsewhere. Its new and expanded roles included challenging Chinese political narratives and economic influence; acting as the first responder for humanitarian and disaster-relief operations in the neighbourhood; expanding bilateral maritime-security and defence cooperation with island states; and focusing its diplomatic efforts on the southwestern and eastern areas of the Indian Ocean to increase its influence and raise its profile there.

Eager to avoid antagonising China, India would almost certainly continue to reject formal invitations to join the US in joint patrols in the South China Sea and – at least in the short term – to include Australia in naval exercises conducted alongside the US and Japan. Nonetheless, Indian forces remained engaged in regular bilateral and trilateral naval exercises with strategic partners. In a signal to China, the 2017 iteration of the *Malabar* exercise, held in the Bay of Bengal during 10–17 July, saw India contribute nine ships, its largest-ever contingent, and all three navies deploy aircraft or helicopter carriers. By mid-2017, the Indian and Chinese navies had engaged in no joint exercises, but their warships had exchanged port calls.

Challenges to CPEC

Although CPEC gained importance in Pakistan's foreign policy in the year to mid-2017, implementation of the initiative became increasingly contingent on domestic political, economic and security factors. Fuelled by Chinese loans and equity agreements, CPEC centred on an ambitious agenda to build road, rail and other links from western China to the Arabian Sea, a route along which the port of Gwadar served as an important hub.

Simultaneously, this 'project of projects' aimed to invest two-thirds of the funds needed to boost Pakistan's energy-generation capacity by 15,000 megawatts to end chronic electricity shortages; enhance trade and industrial production with nine special economic zones; and stimulate international collaboration areas such as science and technology. In 2015–17, the value of CPEC initiatives had risen by more than one-quarter to an estimated US$56bn due to the addition of projects including, in 2017, an upgrade of the railway between Karachi and Lahore, expansion of Gwadar airport's logistics hub and various road schemes in Pakistan, worth US$8bn, US$300m and US$160m respectively.

As a consequence, Islamabad regarded CPEC as a unique opportunity to gain much-needed investment at below-market prices, supporting Pakistan's long-term efforts to achieve prosperity. Moreover, the vast management and engineering challenges involved in CPEC had the potential to leave Pakistan with a more skilled labour force, and to connect the country with Central Asia (via China), amid a long-running dispute with Kabul over the Transit Trade Agreement. Islamabad also hoped that CPEC would create an economic anchor for its political, security and military ties with Beijing. This consideration gained importance at a time of increased friction between Islamabad and Washington, which stemmed from the Pakistani security establishment's alleged support for terrorist groups and Trump's failure to publicly endorse CPEC (as his predecessor had). China hoped to improve connectivity with South Asia, and to spur economic development in its western province of Xinjiang.

However, by mid-2017 Pakistan and China had completed few CPEC projects. Nonetheless, then Pakistani prime minister Nawaz Sharif inaugurated in May 2017 the first 660-megawatt unit of a coal-fired power station in his home state of Punjab, built in a record 22 months. The second followed six weeks later. These initiatives were among 19 'early harvest projects' (as the government called them) in energy that, alongside a handful of others, were fast-tracked for completion by 2019. Work had started on power projects in Sindh's Port Qasim and Punjab, and on an upgrade of the Karakoram highway (to China) and Gwadar's free-trade zone. Work on a US$8bn Karachi–Peshawar rail upgrade was scheduled to begin by 2018. The most reliable measure of progress remained Chinese and Pakistani officials' increasing confidence in disclosing expenditure. By June, China had accounted for actual CPEC investment of US$18bn – an increase of US$4bn in six months – and Pakistan for US$2.2bn since 2014. In Balochistan, US$475m had been invested in roads. New routes were being tested: in November 2016, two weeks after they crossed into Pakistan, 100 Chinese trucked containers became the first commercial shipment to travel through the country's western region (north to south) to reach the port of Gwadar.

To avoid exacerbating Pakistan's economic divisions and public discontent, Islamabad needed to evenly distribute CPEC projects across the country. Indeed, opposition party Tehreek-e-Insaf, led by former cricketer Imran Khan, criticised the routes chosen for transport links under the initiative. Controlling the Khyber Pakhtunkhwa legislature, the party claimed that CPEC disproportionately benefited Punjab and Lahore, both states controlled by Sharif's Pakistan Muslim League–Nawaz (PML–N). Nonetheless, all four provincial chief ministers joined Sharif's delegation at the Belt and Road Forum.

The government also needed to maintain the appropriate level of confidentiality in implementing CPEC projects alongside ministerial-level committees in China and Pakistan. The transparency of the process was improved by the creation of CPEC institutions in Pakistan that fit within the country's existing legal framework. Ahsan Iqbal, minister of planning and a member of the PML–N, had overall responsibility for CPEC in Pakistan, while a dedicated senate committee continued to meet to discuss related issues. Nonetheless, the State Bank of Pakistan and other institutions called for greater transparency in May, when a leak to the Pakistani press revealed divergence in China's and Pakistan's plans for CPEC. Iqbal referred to the leaked Chinese document, which also covered agribusiness and tourism, as a 'live document' (implying that it was subject to change).

One acute unanswered question raised by CPEC concerned the capacity of Pakistan's economy to absorb sudden large-scale investment. Another related to the initiative's short-term impact on the country's trade deficit, amid reports of empty goods containers returning to China from Pakistan. At the same time, Pakistani opposition groups claimed that China tolerated corruption involving CPEC projects and that some citizens had received inadequate compensation for land expropriated under the venture.

Some Pakistanis were also concerned about the effects of the construction of two Chinese-designed civilian nuclear reactors; its December 2016 investment in the Pakistan Stock Exchange; and Shanghai Electric Power Company's US$1.8bn purchase of a stake in Pakistani energy firm K-Electric from a Middle Eastern investor the previous month. In early 2017, despite GDP growth of 5.7% the previous year, Pakistan came close to experiencing a balance-of payments crisis, which it reportedly avoided with US$1bn in additional Chinese loans.

Islamabad gambled that the long-term growth generated by CPEC would allow it to repay its burgeoning debts. The cost of servicing these debts was expected to rise until the early 2020s, even with reported concessionary interest rates of 2% for infrastructure and 6–7% for energy projects. Pakistan already had a significant debt burden. In 2015–16 the government budget ran a deficit of 4.6% of GDP, which was almost entirely due to debt servicing, as the primary balance showed a deficit of just 0.1% of GDP. Therefore, while CPEC promised to integrate Pakistan with Asia's largest economy, it also created fear that the country would suffer from greater structural dependency, sparking some domestic debate about how the undertaking fit the national interest. To dispel these fears, the government attempted to ensure that tendering rules allowed Pakistani businesses to bid for CPEC projects, among other measures. Contracts directly awarded to Chinese companies stoked apprehension that Pakistani industry would not benefit from CPEC (even if comparisons with the era of the British East India Company were overblown). Equally, following reports of plans to grant Chinese workers visa-free entry to Pakistan, Islamabad promised to tighten checks on visa applications and shorten the documents' period of validity.

Initiated in 2014, Pakistan's wide-ranging, army-led crackdown on terrorists who targeted the state produced security benefits that supported progress on CPEC. By late 2016, with General Qamar Javed Bajwa and Lieutenant-General Naveed Mukhtar in charge of the military and intelligence services respectively, the protection of workers involved in CPEC projects had become the security forces' top priority. Baloch nationalists – who had long objected to the initiative, arguing that it would have few benefits for them – continued to pose a threat to CPEC, killing ten labourers in Gwadar in May 2017. Pakistan and China were alarmed by the abduction and murder of two Chinese nationals in Quetta in June 2017. Khorasan Province (ISIS–KP) – the South Asian branch of the Islamic State, also known as ISIS or ISIL – claimed responsibility for the killing, one of several high-profile operations by the group in the year. Although the incident appeared to be unrelated to CPEC, it formed part of a string of killings of Chinese citizens: in November 2016, unknown assailants shot dead two Chinese engineers. The previous August, a suicide bomb exploded in Quetta, killing 70 people and prompting the Chinese press to express concern about the deliberate targeting of a lawyers' association.

The Chinese foreign ministry responded to the June 2017 killings with faint praise for Pakistan's authorities, stating, 'we acknowledge the positive efforts made by the Pakistani side … [and] commend the pledge … to take further effective measures to ensure the security of Chinese nationals and institutions in Pakistan'. Thus, it appeared that the incident would reinforce the Pakistani military's central role in securing CPEC projects – as was reportedly favoured by Beijing. This further raised the profile of the Frontier Works Organisation, a military unit that was headed by a three-star general and that in 2015 became the first Pakistani construction organisation to complete a CPEC road. A two-star general headed the 15,000-strong Special Security Division. Tasked with protecting CPEC projects, the force included nine army battalions and six civilian units; there were unconfirmed reports that these numbers could double. Sections of Pakistan's private-security sector with links to the military were involved in protecting CPEC projects.

The National Security Committee, chaired by Sharif, coordinated the security of CPEC projects. China and Pakistan played down the absence of a formal meeting between Sharif and Chinese President Xi Jinping at the Shanghai Cooperation Organisation summit in June, at which Pakistan and India acceded to the grouping. Nonetheless, CPEC featured in discussions between Chinese leaders and the Pakistani Chairman of the Joint Chiefs of Staff Committee in Beijing shortly thereafter, and in Bajwa's meeting with the Chinese foreign minister in Islamabad later in the month. In December 2016, the Pakistan Navy had inaugurated Taskforce-88, which was charged with protecting Gwadar against terrorists and to that end equipped with frigates and fast attack craft, as well as manned and unmanned aircraft. In June 2017, the Chinese military dismissed reports that China would build a naval base in Gwadar as 'pure speculation'.

As China and Pakistan progressively emphasised the links between CPEC and the Belt and Road Initiative, India stepped up its opposition to the former initiative on sovereignty grounds, concerned about the status of Gilgit-Baltistan. In turn, Pakistani civilian and military leaders publicly accused India's foreign-intelligence agency of attempting to destabilise Pakistan by establishing a safe haven for terrorists and saboteurs on Afghan soil, and by opposing CPEC diplomatically. India was particularly worried about the potential militarisation of Gwadar port, a perspective that dovetailed with a US Department of Defense report that referred to Pakistan in the context of China's ambitions to acquire overseas military bases. Although the Chinese ambassador to India publicly – but apparently unofficially – proposed in May 2017 that India could be included in CPEC, this was unlikely to occur given New Delhi's deep anxiety about the strategic implications of the initiative (one that, perhaps uniquely, made Indian strategists fear for Pakistan's sovereignty).

Following reports that Russia's intelligence chief had visited Gwadar in late 2016, Moscow denied involvement in negotiations on CPEC. Pakistani and Chinese officials repeatedly emphasised that CPEC was not designed to change Pakistan's security role in South Asia. While the majority of Pakistani leaders appeared to share this view, they faced increasing tension between their desire for greater prosperity and their aspiration to remain anchored westwards towards traditional allies and partners, as well as to avoid over-reliance on Beijing.

Intensifying competition in Afghanistan

Afghanistan's tortuous political and security environment became even more complex in the year to mid-2017. The intensification of rivalry and mistrust among major powers operating in the country led to shifts in alliances and hinted at an increasingly insecure future. Four main factors contributed to rising concern about instability within, and emanating from, Afghanistan: the activities of ISIS–KP; the resurgence of the Afghan Taliban; doubts about the US military's role in the country, not least its seemingly failing counter-insurgency campaign there; and infighting between political factions loyal to President Ashraf Ghani and Chief Executive Officer Abdullah Abdullah respectively. These factors created the sense among major regional powers that they could gain a decisive advantage in determining Afghanistan's fate. Moscow, Beijing and Tehran all publicly indicated that as they could no longer rely on Washington to stabilise Afghanistan, it was in their interest to play a larger role in the country.

Violence in Afghanistan became more widespread and more deadly, involving increasingly advanced weapons and tactics. On 21 April, Taliban suicide bombers dressed in military uniforms killed around 140 Afghan soldiers and policemen after storming Camp Shaheen, the headquarters of the Afghan Army's 209 Corps, near Mazar-e-Sharif. On 31 May, a truck bombing near the German Embassy in Kabul killed more than 150 people, the highest death toll of any attack in the capital since the 2001 US-led intervention. Afghan intelligence agencies attributed the attack to the Pakistan-backed Haqqani network. Meanwhile, the Taliban expanded its influence across the country; by mid-2017, the group held more territory than it had since 2001.

Despite incurring heavy losses, ISIS–KP remained a serious threat, appearing to evolve and change tactics in response to a government counter-offensive. The group claimed responsibility for the 8 March attack on the Sardar Daud Khan military hospital that killed more than 100 people. On 13 April, the US dropped a GBU-43B Massive Ordnance Air Blast – one of its largest non-nuclear bombs – on an ISIS–KP tunnel complex in the eastern province of Nangarhar. This was the first time that the weapon had been used in battle. According to Afghan officials, the strike killed more than 90 militants. However, the group retained control of pockets of territory in eastern Afghanistan. There were signs that it was focusing its recruitment efforts on major cities, attempting to establish small cells for planning and conducting assaults in urban centres.

Against this backdrop, the US director of national intelligence stated in May 2017 that the security situation in Afghanistan was likely to deteriorate even if the country received sustained international support. President Trump subsequently gave the US Department of Defense the authority to set troop levels in Afghanistan – part of a broader regional strategy designed to ensure that US forces there had the support 'they need to win', as Secretary of Defense Mattis framed it.

Kabul's chronically poor relations with Islamabad also deteriorated further. On 10 March, Afghanistan complained to the UN Security Council that Pakistan had violated its territorial integrity, including through encroachment into its airspace and cross-border artillery fire. Some Afghan officials even accused Pakistan of engaging in an 'undeclared war' against Afghanistan through sponsorship of the Taliban. The Afghan and US governments reiterated their concerns about militants benefiting from safe havens in Pakistan, a charge Islamabad consistently denied. Moreover, growing hostility between India and Pakistan exacerbated their rivalry in Afghanistan.

Russia, China and Iran used the presence of ISIS–KP in Afghanistan to develop their relationships with the Afghan Taliban. The countries began dialogues with the group's leaders, who reportedly assured them that the Taliban campaign would be limited to Afghanistan and would keep ISIS–KP away from their borders. As a consequence, several US officials publicly criticised Russia and Iran for undermining the Afghan government and its NATO allies, and for legitimising the Taliban. Several senior US military leaders also indicated that Moscow was providing arms and other material support to the Taliban. Moscow denied the charge, often citing two reasons for the unexpected shift in its approach towards the group: ensuring the security of Russian citizens and political offices in Afghanistan, and countering ISIS–KP. Zamir Kabulov, Russian presidential envoy to Afghanistan, described the Taliban's opposition to the foreign-military presence in Afghanistan as 'justified'. Russia also took the initiative in the Afghan peace process, hosting several meetings with major powers in Moscow and insisting that the conflict be solved through talks with all interested groups, including the Taliban (but excluding ISIS–KP). These meetings included a trilateral discussion between Russia, China and Pakistan on 27 December 2016, followed by a dialogue that also involved Pakistan, Afghanistan and Iran on 15 February and talks further expanded to include five Central Asian states on 14 April. The US was only invited to the April meeting but declined to attend, describing the purpose of the talks as 'unclear'. According to Western and Afghan officials, Russia had used the emergence of ISIS–KP in Afghanistan as a justification for increasing its involvement in the country. Moscow's outreach to the Afghan Taliban and Islamabad also concerned New Delhi, which suspected that Russia had abandoned its policy of supporting opponents of the group.

Beijing also became more actively engaged in Afghanistan. Unsettled by the US-led counter-insurgency campaign in the country, as well as the US military's wider role there, China offered in June 2017 to mediate in the Afghan peace process. Beijing appeared to want to focus on improving Afghanistan–Pakistan relations, dispatching its foreign minister to both Islamabad and Kabul to support a new crisis-management mechanism between the two countries. Furthermore, China, Pakistan and Afghanistan stated in the June meeting that the Quadrilateral Coordination Group (which also includes the US) should be revived to conduct peace talks, calling on the Taliban to engage with the reconciliation process.

Iran's growing rivalry with Saudi Arabia and the UAE also added to the complexity of the situation. Although the Taliban was widely believed to have long-standing links with Riyadh and Abu Dhabi, the scale and nature of Tehran's support for the group had escalated. In January, a bombing at a government guest house in southern Kandahar killed 13 people, including five Emirati officials and the UAE's ambassador to Afghanistan, Juma Mohammed Abdullah al-Kaabi. This was the first time that a Gulf Arab country had been targeted in this way in Afghanistan. However, the Taliban denied involvement in the incident, blaming it on local rivalry. The Afghan government subsequently asked Pakistan to hand over three suspects in the attack, only for Islamabad to deny that it knew of their whereabouts.

By mid-2017, the intensifying competition for influence in Afghanistan involved dozens of regional and international state and non-state actors. Critics of Moscow, Beijing and Tehran argued that their growing engagement with Afghanistan – including the Russian-led peace talks – was not intended to benefit the country in the long term but to serve short-term political objectives in their relationships with the US. Yet none of these actors had the capacity to impose its will on Afghanistan acting alone. As much of the chaos manifest in the country was rooted in the broader regional security environment, it appeared that any lasting resolution of the Afghan conflict would depend on multilateral consensus and cooperation.

Chapter 6

Sub-Saharan Africa

The countries of sub-Saharan Africa experienced a shift in some aspects of their security environment in the year to mid-2017. Funding constraints on several of the region's main powers led to an increased focus on multilateral responses to democratic failures and security threats such as insurgencies. Meanwhile, the election of Donald Trump as US president raised the prospect of a shift in Washington's engagement with the region. Judging by his rhetoric, the US was likely to prioritise security and stability over development and democracy, a stance that could lead to closer relations with sub-Saharan African states that had poor human-rights records. President Trump looked set to emphasise efforts to tackle Islamist extremism in sub-Saharan Africa, including those targeting Somalia-based militant group al-Shabaab (although the difficulty of securing reliable intelligence was likely to continue hampering such operations). Yet in some respects, by June 2017 the US president had yet to develop a coherent policy stance on African issues. Washington's disengagement from sub-Saharan Africa had the potential to facilitate further expansion by Beijing, whose already substantial network of strategic interests in the region continued to grow further, partly through the promotion of the Belt and Road Initiative. Meanwhile, the role of European states in the region remained uncertain. Although the election of Emmanuel

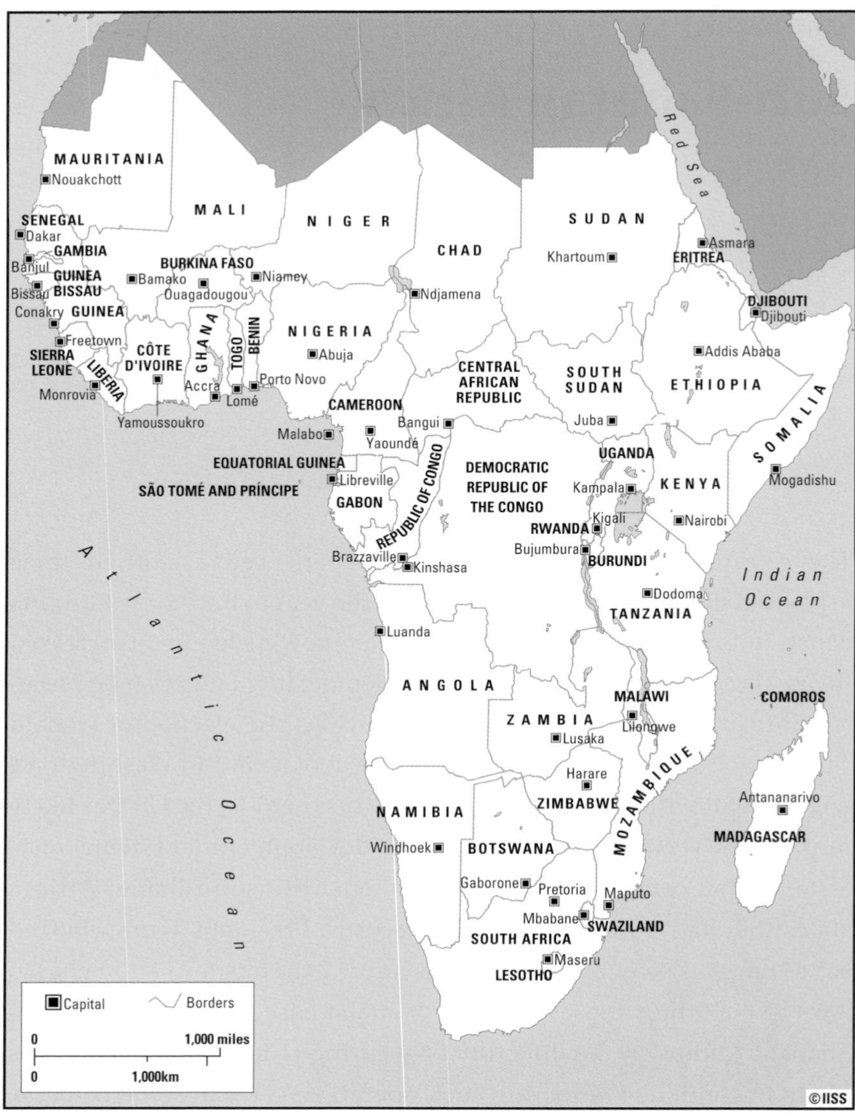

Macron as France's president suggested at least broad continuity in French relations with sub-Saharan Africa – or even increased French engagement with the region – there was a risk that rising domestic nationalism would lead some other European states to focus inwards.

This possibility led to renewed suggestions that sub-Saharan African states would play an enhanced role in regional security. There was considerable doubt about the will and capacity of several of the most influential countries among them to do so, as reflected in the second consecutive annual fall in military spending in the region. However, financial challenges underscored the opportunities for a more integrated approach. Indeed, the so-called G5 Sahel countries announced that they intended to create a joint force to combat terrorism and drug trafficking in the Sahel. Similarly, the Economic Community of West African States (ECOWAS) had marked success in enforcing a peaceful transfer of power in Gambia – an achievement that also indicated diminishing tolerance of autocrats in the region. Leaders accused of human-rights abuses potentially faced the prospect of trial by African institutions such as the Extraordinary African Chambers (EAC). Given African perceptions that global tribunals such as the International Criminal Court (ICC) had disproportionately targeted Africa, the EAC could be developed as a regional alternative – or adjunct – to the ICC.

Domestic turmoil preoccupied several key sub-Saharan African security powers, particularly Ethiopia. Oil-exporting states such as Angola and Nigeria experienced budgetary pressures arising from reduced state revenues, with both countries cutting their military spending in the year. Angola faced relatively few external or domestic threats; Nigeria made some progress against insurgent groups – assisted in part by splits within those groups – but continued to battle militant organisations such as Boko Haram and the Niger Delta Avengers. Funding constraints also continued to be a pre-eminent issue for the South African military, with local reports suggesting that the South African National Defence Force (SANDF) would cut a large number of jobs. Although the dismissal in early 2017 of a reformist finance minister may have eased pressure on the South African armed forces, there continued to be a mismatch between funding levels and the demands placed on the military.

Shifting US engagement

The US has only one official base in Africa, but operates as many as 50 smaller facilities across more than 20 states on the continent. Each of these facilities serves as a staging area for military operations and exercises. According to the Security Assistance Monitor, which tracks US foreign assistance globally, security assistance to sub-Saharan Africa dropped by almost 42%, to around US$671 million, between FY2015 and FY2016, but was projected to recover to US$873m in 2017. The region as a whole was projected to receive around 5.4% of total US security assistance, or less than one-third of the amount received by Egypt alone, in 2017. Nonetheless, the United States provided some sub-Saharan African countries with substantial assistance. Liberia, for example, received around US$33m in security assistance in FY2016. This partly reflected historical factors: Liberia was effectively founded by US citizens of African descent in the early nineteenth century, and Washington played a key role in the peacekeeping efforts that followed the country's 1999–2003 civil war. But it was also due to realities on the ground: while there is an international peacekeeping mandate in the country until March 2018, the UN Mission in Liberia, which has supported under-resourced local security services, has been withdrawn. Furthermore, Liberia's October 2017 legislative elections were expected to be divisive, prompting calls for additional security funding.

Angola also remained a key recipient of US aid, due to its strong military and perceived potential as a regional peacemaker. And Washington aimed to counter Chinese military influence there, especially after the country reportedly purchased Chinese-made assault guns and armoured personnel carriers in 2016. (Djibouti and several West or Central African states – including Cameroon, Chad and Senegal – also operate this type of assault gun.)

Washington's aid to the Central African Republic is intended to improve stability and security there by supporting President Faustin-Archange Touadéra's government, which was democratically elected in 2016. The country had experienced significant unrest and a severe humanitarian crisis since 2013, when a coup staged by Muslim Séléka rebels led to years of intercommunal violence. According to the UN Office for the Coordination of Humanitarian Affairs, the fighting in the Central African Republic has internally displaced around 425,000 people and forced 465,000 others to flee to neighbouring countries.

Almost 2.2m people, or nearly half the population, are in need of humanitarian aid. Given the country's position in a potentially volatile subregion – bordering Sudan and the Democratic Republic of the Congo, among other insecure states – US aid has played an important role in bolstering its security services.

The US also provided substantial support to East Africa and the Lake Chad region, where Benin, Cameroon, Chad and Niger have strengthened their military cooperation to contain activity by Nigerian-based insurgent group Boko Haram. However, top of the list in state terms is Somalia. The US has a long and not uniformly successful history of military intervention in Somalia. In the early 1990s, its peacekeeping mission there failed, culminating in the so-called '*Black Hawk* Down' incident, which eventually prompted its withdrawal from Somalia. But Washington has gradually re-engaged with the country over the past five years or so, notably via strikes using unmanned aerial vehicles. In March 2017, the US government designated Somalia a 'zone of active hostilities', giving local commanders greater authority to launch airstrikes and broadening the range of possible targets. The following month, the US military deployed soldiers – in non-combat roles – to Somalia for the first time since 1994. The newly deployed troops were tasked with training and equipping the Somali National Army (SNA), which would need greater support following the drawdown of Ethiopian troops in Somalia in October 2016 and, potentially, the withdrawal of the African Union Mission in Somalia (mooted to take place by the end of 2020). The troops added to the growing number of US military personnel in the region. Around 17% of all US commandos based overseas were stationed in continental Africa, up from just 1% in 2006. According to US Special Operations Command, there were 1,700 American special-operations personnel in 20 African states – the largest number in any region other than the Middle East.

These deployments in Somalia and elsewhere accorded with President Trump's campaign pledge to make the defeat of Islamist extremists the 'highest priority' of his administration, and his subsequent agreement to declare Somalia an 'area of active hostility'.

However, international efforts to tackle al-Shabaab have been constrained by the difficulty of securing reliable intelligence. And it remained unclear whether long-term security gains against Somalia's terrorist groups would be possible without a substantial expansion of the SNA. Moreover, strategic relations between sub-Saharan Africa and the US appeared to be in flux following Trump's inauguration. As of June 2017, Washington appeared to have no coherent strategy on the continent; indeed, the Trump administration had yet to appoint a head of the Bureau of African Affairs in the Department of State, and had few diplomatic contacts with sub-Saharan African heads of state. There was no indication that Africa was strategically significant to the Trump administration. Trump's 'skinny budget' proposal, released in March 2017, envisaged a 28% reduction in funding for the Department of State and the Agency for International Development – the government's main disbursers of foreign aid – in part to fund a sizeable increase in military expenditure. Equally, while broadly maintaining healthcare commitments (to HIV/AIDS and malaria, for example), the budget proposals would also entail the closure of several government agencies, including the US African Development Foundation, which invested more than US$50m in projects across 30 African states in 2016. Akinwumi Adesina, head of the African Development Bank (AfDB), warned that such cuts (which had yet to be approved by Congress) could turn the continent into 'a recruiting field for terrorists'.

Such an outcome would be inconsistent with Trump's pledges on Islamist terrorism, in pursuit of which he signed in January 2017 an executive order restricting entry to the US for refugees and nationals of seven Muslim-majority countries, including Somalia and Sudan. However, underscoring its lack of coherence on such issues, on 12 July the Trump administration postponed for a further three months the decision on whether to ease sanctions on Sudan, stating that it would take more time to assess whether the country had made progress in the required areas. In place since the late 1990s, these measures had significantly curtailed business and trade between Sudan and not only the US but also European and Gulf Arab states. According to the

US Department of the Treasury's Office of Foreign Assets Control, several factors led to the decision to provide sanctions relief: progress in US bilateral engagement with Sudan and positive developments in humanitarian-aid access; the announcement of government ceasefires in various conflict-prone Sudanese states; Khartoum's cooperation in resolving conflict in South Sudan; and, crucially, its work on counter-terrorism and efforts to tackle the Lord's Resistance Army (an armed group originating in Uganda).

The Trump administration's apparent decision not to re-impose sanctions on Sudan may have been an early sign that it was developing a more nuanced approach to tackling terrorist groups. The move may also have reflected a development of its position on Boko Haram. Prior to taking office, Trump's team questioned why the US was 'bothering' to tackle the Boko Haram insurgency. Nonetheless, the administration announced in April 2017 that it was proceeding with plans to sell up to 12 EMB-314 *Super Tucano* aircraft – which have reconnaissance and surveillance, as well as attack, capabilities – to Nigeria's air force to assist with the fight against the group. The deal, which could be worth up to US$600m, would be in line with the administration's aim of boosting employment among US defence-equipment manufacturers, as the aircraft would be partly produced by American firm Sierra Nevada Corporation. It would also be consistent with its de-emphasis of human-rights issues (or, critics argue, its wish to reverse the Obama administration's priorities). Trump's predecessor initially agreed to the sale of aircraft, but suspended the deal after a series of controversial incidents involving the Nigerian military, including its bombing of a refugee camp in January, which killed up to 170 civilians. (Similarly, the Trump administration stated in March that it intended to pursue the sale of around US$5 billion-worth of Lockheed Martin F-16 aircraft and related equipment to Bahrain, which the Obama administration had also held up due to human-rights concerns.) However, it was unclear whether Nigeria would be willing and able to pay the US$600m required for the aircraft and associated equipment, plus training and support costs. And President Muhammadu Buhari's regular absences from Nigeria for (undisclosed) medical reasons raised questions about the country's political stability, with the chief of army staff, Lieutenant-General Tukur Buratai, commenting in May that some politicians and soldiers might be plotting a coup. Although Nigeria has experienced only one peaceful transfer of power, in 2015, concerns about a successful putsch were probably misplaced given that democracy is relatively entrenched in Nigeria. Moreover, the country's armed forces are more professional than they were in 1966, 1975, 1983, 1985 and 1993, when they overthrew the civilian government. Nonetheless, there was a chance that the prospect of selling weapons to a potentially porous Nigerian military (another concern for the Obama administration) would prompt US legislators to check Trump's plans.

China's increasingly interventionist stance

A US retreat from sub-Saharan Africa could facilitate further expansion by China. Given the unpredictability of the Trump administration's foreign policy, it is unclear whether Washington would see this as a largely unconcerned move, a commercial challenge or an act of strategic aggression that sought to provide access to crucial natural resources and counter traditional Western influence. Regardless, there was little certainty that the US could halt such expansion even if it wished to do so.

Formal Sino-African relations are largely shaped by the Forum on China–Africa Cooperation. The sixth iteration of the forum, held in 2015, adopted the Johannesburg Action Plan, which committed the participants to security cooperation during 2016–18, including US$60m-worth of Chinese military assistance to the AU. Sino-African relations were dominated by China's continuing reorientation from a stated policy of non-interference to a more interventionist stance designed to protect its commercial interests, as well as the lives of the approximately 1m Chinese nationals based in Africa.

Notwithstanding the expected slowdown in Chinese economic growth over the next five years, and the Chinese authorities' stated aim of rebalancing the economy away from investment and towards consumption, Beijing remained keen to secure long-term strategic supplies of oil and minerals. This drove continued extractive-sector investments in states such as the Republic of Congo and the Democratic Republic of the Congo. In the former country, China announced in January that it would make a substantial investment in a special economic zone in the port city and oil-industry hub of Pointe-Noire. In the latter, China Molybdenum and Chinese private-equity firm BHR agreed the same month to buy a 24% stake in the giant Tenke Fungurume copper mine.

Chinese entities have also been increasingly involved in infrastructural investment under the Belt and Road Initiative, an effort designed to integrate and develop countries economically along ancient trading routes linking China to the world, mainly through the construction of physical infrastructure. At the inaugural Belt and Road Forum, held in May, Chinese President Xi Jinping promised additional loans and grants of around US$77.1bn for the initiative. Just two Sub-Saharan states, Ethiopia and Kenya, were invited to the forum. These countries are two of the largest recipients of Chinese foreign direct investment; East Africa continues to be the main focus of the Belt and Road Initiative on the continent. However, it is far from being the only focus. For example, the Zambian government signed in November 2016 a deal, worth nearly US$2.3bn, under which China Railway Construction will build a 389-kilometre railway running from Serenje, in Zambia's Central Province, to Chipata, near the Malawian border, where a link to Mchinji, in Malawi, was inaugurated in 2010. The new line will also connect to Mozambican rail systems, opening up other possible trade routes via Mozambique's Nacala and Beira ports. Meanwhile, in West Africa, President Buhari requested in April parliamentary approval to borrow US$5.85bn from China for rail projects. The three schemes – the Lagos–Ibadan segment of the project to modernise the Lagos–Kano railway, and the Kaduna–Kano and Lagos–Calabar railway projects – form part of the Buhari administration's medium-term Economic Recovery and Growth Plan, which prioritises efforts to address Nigeria's severe lack of infrastructure.

Experience suggests that such substantial infrastructure projects may rely largely on Chinese subcontractors and labour, leading to a steady expansion of the numbers of people operating in Africa under China's aegis. Even if Beijing does not ship in large volumes of Chinese workers – a practice that has created tension in several African states – the Chinese imperative to protect its growing network of strategic interests will remain. Having rescued its citizens from conflict in states such as Chad, Libya and Somalia, China is wary of financial losses and humanitarian emergencies. By late 2016, China had contributed more personnel to peacekeeping forces than any of the other four permanent members of the UN Security Council – deploying 2,600 people, or around 3% of the total – albeit far fewer than states such as Ethiopia, India and Pakistan. The vast majority of Chinese peacekeeping personnel are deployed to missions in Africa. For instance, in December 2016, China deployed the first 120 members of an additional 700-strong Chinese UN peacekeeping force in South Sudan, where two Chinese peacekeepers were killed in July 2016. It also maintained a substantial presence in Mali: in May 2017, it deployed 190 troops as part of its 395-strong peacekeeping force there. Beijing's construction of a naval base in Djibouti is also a statement of its intent to protect existing and prospective trade links, including the Maritime Silk Road connecting Asia with the Middle East, Africa and Europe. Although China insists that the Djibouti base is purely a support facility, reports in the Chinese media in 2014 suggested that more bases could follow in Dar es Salaam, Luanda, Mombasa, Walvis Bay and even Lagos.

Stable French policy and a push for regional self-reliance

The US was not alone in picking a new and largely untried head of state in the year to mid-2017. The French presidential election pitted two political outsiders against each other. A victory for Marine Le Pen, who adopted a Trump-style 'France first' policy, could have led to a substantial overhaul of France's security policy, with potentially serious implications for its close ties to states that were once its colonies. However, Macron's victory looked set to ensure that France adopted a more proactive stance. Although Macron has limited political experience, and prior to his election gave little insight into how he might approach his country's relations with sub-Saharan Africa, the fact that he made his first state trip outside Europe to Mali suggested that his priorities included promoting democracy and fighting Islamist militancy in the region. It also suggested that he would place Africa high on his agenda – a potentially significant move given that the French president has considerable powers in security and foreign policy.

Unlike Trump, Macron rapidly filled government positions with significant influence on Africa policy – and did so with candidates who suggested continuity, not least Jean-Yves Le Drian in the post of foreign minister. Having served as defence minister in the government of Macron's predecessor, Le Drian had faced criticism for his alleged militarisation of France's relations with its sub-Saharan African partners. He oversaw the reorganisation of France's security operations in the Central African Republic, Côte d'Ivoire and Mali, and supported the adoption of a more assertive approach to military and security issues within and outside the Francophone sphere of interests. To this end, Le Drian announced that 3,000–4,000 French troops would be stationed in West Africa to support regional counter-terrorism and other security programmes, as part of *Operation Barkhane*. Indeed, he continued to be regarded as the driving forcing behind France's counter-terrorism operations in West Africa. Furthermore, Franck Paris, appointed as Africa adviser to the new president, had promoted sub-Saharan African issues in European institutions.

Macron also sent a strong signal by choosing Mali as the destination of his first presidential trip outside of Europe, and by visiting troops deployed under *Operation Barkhane*. He also announced plans to visit Burkina Faso, Cameroon, Chad, Mauritania and Niger – the countries of the G5 Sahel – in November 2017 to attend a meeting on the fight against jihadist groups operating in the area. Another indication that France would at least maintain its commitment to the G5 Sahel came in June 2017, when Burkina Faso, Chad, Mali, Mauritania and Niger asked the European Union for US$56m to help establish a multinational force that would tackle Islamist militant groups.

Although Mali's government recaptured the north of the country from Islamist groups in 2013, jihadist attacks there and in neighbouring states remained a significant threat to stability. Major incidents of this kind included the killing of 22 members of the Nigerien security forces in a surprise attack on a refugee camp in Niger in October 2016; the killing of 12 Burkinabé soldiers in a December 2016 terrorist attack in Nassoumbou, in northern Burkina Faso; and a January 2017 suicide bombing at a security-forces base in Gao that killed 77 people, one of the most serious terrorist attacks in the region in recent years. Given the impact of this insecurity on broader regional issues such as food insecurity, migration and climate change, the presidents of the G5 Sahel states announced in February 2017 that the organisation would create a joint force to combat terrorism and drug trafficking in the Sahel.

The G5 Sahel heads of state added that, although their countries received support from UN peacekeepers and the soldiers involved in *Operation Barkhane*, they could not expect to rely 'only on foreign nations' to deploy troops to tackle the complex network of local and international terrorist groups operating in their region. Therefore, the five states agreed to form a joint force made up of special rapid-response units. Each of these units would comprise around 100 soldiers and be capable of countering fluid cross-border threats. The G5 hoped to reproduce the model of the Multinational Joint Task Force, a grouping of around 8,700 troops from Benin, Cameroon, Chad, Niger and Nigeria, which was deployed in late 2015 against Boko Haram. Although it proved unable to completely end Boko Haram's activities in the year to mid-2017, the force helped to contain the threat to specific areas (notably Nigeria's Sambisa forest and swamplands around Lake Chad). Boko Haram's weakening combat capability – more than 300 members of the group were killed in the final three months of 2016 alone – prompted it to shift tactics, conducting fewer attacks on the security forces and more on 'soft' targets, such as camps for internally displaced people.

However, the G5 Sahel force faced several difficulties, including that of operating in terrain favourable to highly mobile groups of jihadist fighters, as well as challenges related to financing, logistics and intelligence. Following the December 2016 attack in Burkina Faso, Pigrenona Zagré, chief of staff of the Burkinabé armed forces, admitted that the authorities were having difficulty obtaining intelligence about local security problems in the north of the country, and appealed to members of the public to provide them with information.

In this context, plans by the French Directorate of Cooperation of Security and Defence – a ministerial structure designed to develop international security and civil-protection collaboration – had significant potential. The organisation proposed the creation of a regional intelligence facility in the sub-Sahelian area, as well as the establishment, with French personnel, of a cyber-information platform designed to counter radicalisation and centres to bolster the operational preparedness of the Burkinabé and Nigerien militaries. All of these measures suggested that French counter-terrorism and peacekeeping initiatives in Western (and North) Africa would be maintained, and perhaps strengthened.

Continuing fall in African military spending

Many sub-Saharan African leaders feared that the Trump administration saw their region as strategically insignificant, and that European states – particularly major aid donors France, Germany and the United Kingdom, as well those important to migration policy, such as Italy – would turn inwards in response to rising domestic nationalism. As a consequence, these leaders renewed their calls for greater cooperation and integration within their region. However, this came at a time when several of the region's major players were under political or financial pressure, and as military spending in sub-Saharan Africa as a whole fell for the second consecutive year. This was the second annual decline after more than a decade of increases, with defence spending dropping from 1.27% of GDP in 2015 to 1.17% of GDP in 2016. Although there were considerable variations in national spending, oil-exporting countries in the region largely made the most stringent cuts, reflecting intense fiscal pressure arising from an international oil price that remained well below 2009–11 highs. Several of these states were particularly exposed to the low price due to their governments' failure to diversify the economy or reduce spending, thereby limiting fiscal buffers. Thus, the overall decline in sub-Saharan African military spending primarily stemmed from oil-exporting states Angola and South Sudan.

In Angola – sub-Saharan Africa's most militarised state – the government reduced the military budget from US$4.44bn in 2015 to US$2.78bn in 2016. If anything, the out-turn was likely to be lower, as the government struggled to reduce its fiscal deficit. Nonetheless, for several years Angola's military expenditure had been considerably higher than was justified by the external and domestic threats it faced. (Although a secessionist movement continued to operate in the province of Cabinda, it posed little threat to the central government and had not mounted a sustained terrorist campaign in recent years.) Instead, high defence spending reflected the Angolan government's desire to project power and an image as a regional peacemaker. Nonetheless, previously inflated military spending allowed Angola to absorb defence-budget cuts more easily than other oil-exporting countries in the region.

Perhaps the most notable cuts occurred in South Sudan, which reduced its security-sector spending by more than 50% between 2015 and 2016 despite the fact that it remained troubled by conflict throughout the period. Indeed, in December 2016, the United Nations' Commission on Human Rights in South Sudan warned that a 'steady process of ethnic cleansing' was under way in some parts of the country, and that it was 'standing on the brink of an all-out ethnic civil war, which could destabilise the entire region'. President Salva Kiir's dismissal of the army chief of staff, General Paul Malong Awan, in May 2017 did little to improve the country's prospects for stability. Although General Malong stated that he had no intention of staging a revolt against Kiir's government, several other senior officers had left the army in recent months, citing human-rights abuses and attempts to turn the military into a 'tribal army'. One of these officers, Thomas

Cirillo Swaka, announced that he had formed his own rebel group with the aim of forcing Kiir from office.

In this context, the decline in South Sudanese military spending was unexpected, but may have been in part an after-effect of sharp increases in such expenditure in preceding years. However, another factor in the reduction in spending (following inflation of more than 380%) was the fall in revenue from oil production. South Sudan is the most oil-dependent country in the world: the product accounts for almost all of the country's exports and around 60% of its GDP. However, production remained substantially lower than the maximum potential level in the year to mid-2017, with South Sudan earning US$852m in oil income, compared to US$3.2bn in the year to mid-2014. After deducting transit payments and the cost of transfers to neighbouring Sudan, net oil revenue was just US$353m, compared to US$2.33bn in the year to mid-2014. Therefore, although South Sudan reduced its military expenditure in absolute terms, the figure remained extremely high as a proportion of revenue. As a result, sectors such as health, education and infrastructure were significantly underfunded, with negative implications for future stability.

Côte d'Ivoire, Ghana, Guinea and Zambia also registered double-digit declines in defence spending. The export markets of Côte d'Ivoire and Ghana were affected by lower international commodity prices. However, political developments in the former country also underscored the potential risks of cutting expenditure on wages and benefits. In the first half of 2017, Côte d'Ivoire faced a series of mutinies, nominally over the government's failure to pay bonuses. The incidents also related to grievances over poor working conditions, rumours of corruption among high-ranking officers and the tension created by the integration into the army of former rebels from the 2002–07 and 2010–11 crisis periods. As the government remained reluctant to test the loyalty of the military – partly because the earlier crisis started as a mutiny in September 2002, before escalating into a civil war – it was expected to seek to pay off discontented soldiers. However, this was unsustainable in the long term given that unbudgeted social spending and low cocoa revenues had undermined government finances, and that overspending on military wages by other means would be unpopular with the electorate and the international community.

Meanwhile, several countries in the region increased their defence expenditure. For example, Botswana increased spending from US$404m in 2015 to US$486m in 2016 – one of the sharpest percentage rises in the world – as part of moves to modernise its military equipment. Botswana reportedly planned to purchase, inter alia, *Gripen* aircraft, T-50 and K2 *Black Panther* tanks, and *Piranha* armoured vehicles, despite its location in a peaceful subregion and lack of involvement in armed conflict.

In contrast, the defence budget of Nigeria – sub-Saharan Africa's largest producer of crude oil, and a state facing threats from a range of domestic insurgent groups – fell from US$1.95bn in 2015 to US$1.73bn in 2016. (Military expenditure had also become more politically sensitive since 2015, when President Buhari ordered the arrest of Nigeria's former national-security adviser for allegedly engaging in fraudulent arms dealings worth US$2bn.) Similarly, there was only a small increase in the Democratic Republic of the Congo's military expenditure, despite ongoing activity by M23 rebels in the east of the country and rising violence in the Kasai region, as well as growing political tension due to the postponement of presidential elections initially scheduled for November 2016. Mali's defence expenditure grew significantly in the year to mid-2017, albeit at a markedly lower rate than it had in the preceding year, amid chronic insecurity in the north and persistent terrorist threats from Islamist groups.

Intervention in Gambia

With government spending under pressure in many states, multinational regional organisations took on a greater role in the security sphere. In December 2016, after 22 years in power, Gambian President Yahya Jammeh lost a presidential election to Adama Barrow. The result was unexpected: although Jammeh officially received 72% of the popular vote in the 2011 presidential election, the result reflected not so much support for the president as the limits on free and fair elections in the country. In the run-up to the 2016 poll, the regime reportedly resorted to established tactics, arbitrarily detaining opponents, refusing to admit EU electoral observers and actively intervening in the vote to ensure victory. On polling day, the government blocked the internet and international telephone calls. However, faced with a unified opposition coalition (a rarity in Gambia) and an opponent who had never held public office, Jammeh secured only 39.6% of the vote, compared to 43.3% for Barrow. Even more surprisingly, Jammeh initially conceded victory to his opponent, only to file a complaint to the Supreme Court questioning the validity of the result (despite the fact that the independent electoral commission had confirmed the vote count).

There were signs that regional powers had tired of Jammeh's erratic policymaking – a particular source of concern for Senegal, which has a close relationship with Gambia. In contrast, Barrow had stated his desire to strengthen democratic norms and institutions by, inter alia, establishing an independent judiciary, protecting the freedom of the media and civil society, introducing a two-term limit on the presidency and reversing Jammeh's decision to withdraw from the ICC. Regional powers and the broader international community denounced Jammeh's refusal to step down and his promotion of almost 50 senior military personnel, in an apparent attempt to shore up support within the military. Perhaps because previous international sanctions had had little impact on the Gambian economy, the leaders of ECOWAS – who were acting as mediators between Barrow and Jammeh – quickly announced that they would deploy troops to Gambia if the latter refused to step down. The statement carried significant risks, particularly for Senegal. As the Gambian armed forces backed Jammeh, any military intervention threatened to trigger a violent conflict that would endanger civilians, as well as ECOWAS economies and regional stability. However, on 19 January – the date on which the new president was scheduled to take office – Gambian army chief Ousman Badjie declared that he would not order his troops to fight back against any ECOWAS intervention force. Unable to cling on to power without military support, Jammeh stepped down and left the country three days later.

This was the first time that ECOWAS had threatened a military intervention to uphold an election result in the absence of an ongoing conflict. (The organisation had intervened in civil conflicts in Sierra Leone and Liberia through the Economic Community of West African States Monitoring Group (ECOMOG), a multilateral armed force established in 1990.) By mid-2017, ECOWAS continued to engage in a mission in Guinea-Bissau, five years after being deployed there in the aftermath of a military coup. With a maximum of 20,000 armed-forces personnel at its disposal, ECOMOG's strength did not arise from troop numbers but rather its systematic response to crises in the region: seeking to involve all sides in negotiations and persuading regional leaders to engage in diplomacy, before moving to targeted intervention. In this way – and in contrast to many non-African forces – the organisation has acquired legitimacy among local politicians and populations.

The intervention in Gambia fit a broader trend: West Africa was becoming increasingly democratic – or at least less tolerant of dictators. Significantly, Jammeh had been the last remaining West African leader to have come to power in a coup, and after stepping down became the target of an investigation into his alleged involvement in murder and torture. Other West African politicians also faced growing public demand for accountability. This trend became more apparent in April 2017, when the Appeals Chamber of the EAC – a tribunal established under an agreement between the AU and Senegal to try violations of international law committed in Chad between June 1982 and December 1990 – upheld the life sentence handed down to former president Hissène Habré. Meanwhile, Blaise Compaoré, former president of Burkina Faso, awaited trial over his alleged role in the deaths of protesters during a 2014 uprising. In Guinea, Lieutenant Aboubacar Sidiki Diakité – a member of the junta that governed the country during 2008–09 – was expected to stand trial in 2017 for his alleged involvement in mass human-rights violations.

Habré's trial was particularly significant given that this was the first time an African institution had set up the arrangements for trying such a human-rights case. Previously, such cases had been brought before global tribunals such as the ICC, which has been heavily criticised by African leaders for allegedly disproportionately targeting them. Indeed, allegations that the ICC is a Western institution that fails to hold Western leaders to account prompted the AU to call in February 2017 for the mass withdrawal from the ICC. The resulting resolution is non-binding, and Nigeria and Senegal have said that they oppose such a withdrawal. However, Burundi and South Africa have both stated their intention to withdraw from the court (in South Africa's case, a High Court ruling that the government's notice of withdrawal was unconstitutional meant that the move would be delayed, if not necessarily blocked). Therefore, the EAC could be developed as a regional alternative – or adjunct – to the ICC, particularly as the latter court only has the authority to rule on crimes committed after 2002, when its founding statute came into effect. Thus, the EAC had the potential to address impunity among leaders in sub-Saharan Africa, but also to encourage dictators to cling on to power out of fear of potential prosecution after leaving office.

Unrest in Ethiopia

The prospect that African leaders would seek to extend their terms was of particular concern given that perceived democratic failures – in combination with economic decline – were major drivers of regional insecurity in the year to mid-2017. For example, there were street protests and violence in the Democratic Republic of the Congo in December 2016, as the official term of President Joseph Kabila expired with little sign of when new elections would be held. There was also sporadic unrest in Swaziland and Gabon, due to a lack of political liberalisation and violence linked to the August 2016 presidential elections respectively. Perhaps the most striking example was Ethiopia, which experienced anti-government protests more widespread and sustained than any since 1991, when the Ethiopian People's Revolutionary Democratic Front (EPRDF) came to power. The protests started in 2015 – initially over a perceived territorial encroachment by the capital city, Addis Ababa, into Oromo land – but only spread significantly the following year. Localised incidents ranging from the attempted arrest of community leaders to a fatal stampede in the Oromia region exacerbated long-standing resentment of the EPRDF. The protesters perceived the government, led by the Tigray People's Liberation Front, as having oppressed the Oromo and Amhara ethnic groups, who comprise around one-third and one-quarter of the Ethiopian population respectively. By the second half of 2016, there were signs that the government's opponents were making loosely coordinated efforts to attack businesses linked to the ruling party – including foreign-owned firms, which are often expected to enter the Ethiopian market in joint ventures with local entities (many of them affiliated with the EPRDF). In October, this factor, combined with government fears that protests would escalate into a wider uprising, prompted the authorities to impose a six-month state of emergency. The government extended the state of emergency in March 2017, albeit while ending measures such as powers granted to the security services to stop and search suspects, and to search homes without court authorisation. Although the government's response halted large-scale unrest, there was little sign that it had effectively addressed the perceptions of economic and political marginalisation that created ethnic tension. Thus, there was a risk of renewed protests and instability if the government rescinded the state of emergency.

The state of emergency crystallised growing Western concerns about the government's intolerance of criticism, and its tendency to blur the boundaries between internal political dissent and terrorism. Ethiopia's donors and partners continued to balance these concerns against a recognition of its strategic importance as a populous, Western-allied country near the Gulf of Aden, as well as fears that it would descend into what Prime Minister Hailemariam Desalegn called 'ethnic conflict' if the unrest continued. However, such a development remained relatively unlikely, not least because Ethiopia lacked rebel groups with the coordination and military capability to begin a civil war. Most of the groups that wished to overthrow the regime were based abroad – usually outside of sub-Saharan Africa – and they had few obvious sources of financing. There was a possibility that Eritrea might support groups that opposed Ethiopia's regime: the countries' border dispute led to a violent clash in June 2016, prompting Asmara to claim that Addis Ababa was 'contemplating full-scale war' against it. But any sustained backing for rebel groups would almost certainly work to Eritrea's detriment given Ethiopia's overwhelming military superiority.

US–Angola defence agreement

Despite coming under pressure from budget cuts, the Angolan authorities continued to seek a prominent role in efforts to tackle regional and global challenges. For example, Angola acted as the head of the International Conference of the Great Lakes Region for the second successive year (albeit while coming to the end of its term as a non-permanent member of the UN Security Council in December 2016). Such activity primarily involved diplomatic rather than security initiatives: the Angolan military was involved in relatively few external operations during the year to mid-2017. Nonetheless, in keeping with its regional and global aspirations, Angola signed several defence agreements with high-profile partners, including China and the US.

Angola and the US have long cooperated in the defence sector. In 2009 the US government declared that Angola was a 'strategic partner' – one of only three in Africa (along with Nigeria and South Africa). However, the focus of the partnership has tended to be 'soft' areas such as training, healthcare (including that to combat HIV/AIDS) and education. Yet, in May 2017, US Secretary of Defense James Mattis and João Lourenço – Angola's defence minister, and the favourite to become its next president – signed a new memorandum of understanding (MoU) designed to boost defence cooperation. According to Mattis, the MoU was a step towards 'strategic partnership' with Angola that would initially focus on increased training and information-sharing opportunities, with the eventual aim of strengthening military-technical cooperation and engaging in further joint exercises. Angola is already a regular participant in multi-country exercises such as *Obangame Express*, an effort conducted by US Naval Forces Africa in March 2017. Involving 16 states, the exercise was designed to improve cooperation in the fight against threats in the Gulf of Guinea.

The US appeared keen to improve such practical links, likely due to the perception that Angola is one of relatively few states in sub-Saharan Africa that can provide substantial troop and equipment support to international peacekeeping operations. The US also remained keen to counter Chinese and Russian military influence in Angola. Moscow maintains close military relations with Luanda that date back to the Soviet era (when the now-ruling People's Movement for the Liberation of Angola was overtly Marxist), and has continued to supply the country with materiel – such as the *Kamaz* troop carriers and refurbished attack helicopters transferred in August–September 2016. More (new) helicopters were due to be delivered the following year, and in May 2017 the sides discussed joint military-technical projects, as well as security for initiatives run by parastatals such as Russian diamond company Alrosa. Similarly, China supplied assault guns and armoured personnel carriers to Angola during the second half of 2016, and in May 2017 signed agreements to strengthen cooperation between the countries' military institutions. Potential areas of interest could include Cabinda, where there was an upsurge in clashes between the government and separatist group the Front for the Liberation of the Enclave of Cabinda. In August 2016, the organisation issued a warning to the Chinese government specifically, saying that the presence of Chinese citizens in Angola 'constitutes a provocation'.

Constraints on the Nigerian and South African armed forces

Nigeria's security policy continued to focus on insurgency, especially the eight-year fight against Boko Haram in the northeast of the country and areas around Lake Chad. There were some signs of progress in the effort, partly due to a split within the group – with one faction commanded by Abubakar Shekau, its long-time leader, and another by Abu Musab al-Barnawi, who was appointed as its leader by the Islamic State, also known as ISIS or ISIL, in 2016. The split seemed to have the potential to benefit the Nigerian government, as the factions sometimes targeted each other rather than the state. Although there was a sharp decline in fatalities caused by the conflict in 2016, Boko Haram persisted with attacks on civilians. For instance, suicide bombings conducted by the group in a village near Maiduguri in March 2017 killed four people and injured eight others. Such violence underscored the fact that while the Nigerian military had some success in driving Boko Haram out of its main bases in the Sambisa forest, it struggled to erode the group's ability to launch random acts of terrorism.

Abuja also came under pressure from the civil conflict in the oil-producing Niger Delta region. Perhaps recognising the need to minimise the threat from this second insurgency, the government combined military operations in the region with financial measures. In May 2017, the administration claimed to have nearly tripled, to US$180m, the budget for an amnesty programme for former militants in the Niger Delta. Abuja also pledged to open a maritime university, resume abandoned construction projects and integrate illegal oil refineries in the area. Nonetheless, the same month rebel groups broke a de facto ceasefire by attacking an oil pipeline near Warri, in Delta State; in early June, a 'coalition' of militants in the Niger Delta called on other rebel groups to attack expatriates employed in the energy industry there rather than pipeline infrastructure.

Signs of fissures within the military, reflected by Lieutenant-General Buratai's statement on a possible officer-led coup in May, added to the complexity of the challenge. The same was true of economic underperformance – in 2016 Nigeria experienced a recession for the first time since the early 1990s – and the sense of frailty within the government created by Buhari's absence due to ill health.

Funding continued to be a pre-eminent issue for the South African military, following statements by South Africa's treasury that the SANDF would need to cut spending on salaries by almost 3bn rand (US$230m) over three years. Local media outlets reported in December 2016 that the SANDF had started the process of cutting almost 16,000 jobs, initially focusing on contract workers. However, the SANDF denied these reports, with the military spokesman Siphiwe Dlamini stating, 'whether the budget is cut or not there will be no retrenchments in the National Defence Force'. Although it was unclear whether this pledge could be fulfilled, President Jacob Zuma's March 2017 decision to replace reformist finance minister Pravin Gordhan with loyalist Malusi Gigaba may have eased the pressure on the SANDF. Nonetheless, Minister of Defence and Military Veterans Nosiviwe Mapisa-Nqakula told parliament in May that more than 55bn rand (US$4.2bn) was needed to address the 'serious mismatch' between funding levels and the demands placed on the Department of Defence. With the 48bn rand (US$3.7bn) allocated to the defence budget for 2017–18 equivalent to roughly 1% of GDP, Mapisa-Nqakula stated that various strategies would be considered. These strategies included a 'comprehensive [Department of Defence] efficiency programme' and the 'leveraging of alternative defence revenue streams' by, inter alia, developing intellectual property and ensuring that the department was reimbursed for participating in UN peacekeeping missions. Despite the tension between the SANDF's international and domestic commitments (such as border protection), the force continued to contribute to peacekeeping efforts. For instance, Zuma announced in May that the SANDF's mission to the Democratic Republic of the Congo would be extended, with more than 1,300 of its personnel deployed to the country.

Strategic Geography 2017

US–Mexico economic interdependence

The election of Donald Trump as US president in November 2016 unsettled many of the United States' major economic partners, especially Mexico. His narrative of economic revival in the US focused on efforts to address large trade deficits, decades-long decline in manufacturing employment and what he presented as uncontrolled immigration across the southern border. Yet it remained to be seen whether his declared strategy – which included renegotiation of, or withdrawal from, the North American Free Trade Agreement, as well as severe immigration measures – would benefit his supporters in states with close economic ties to Mexico, or those employed in industries reliant on complex cross-border production chains.

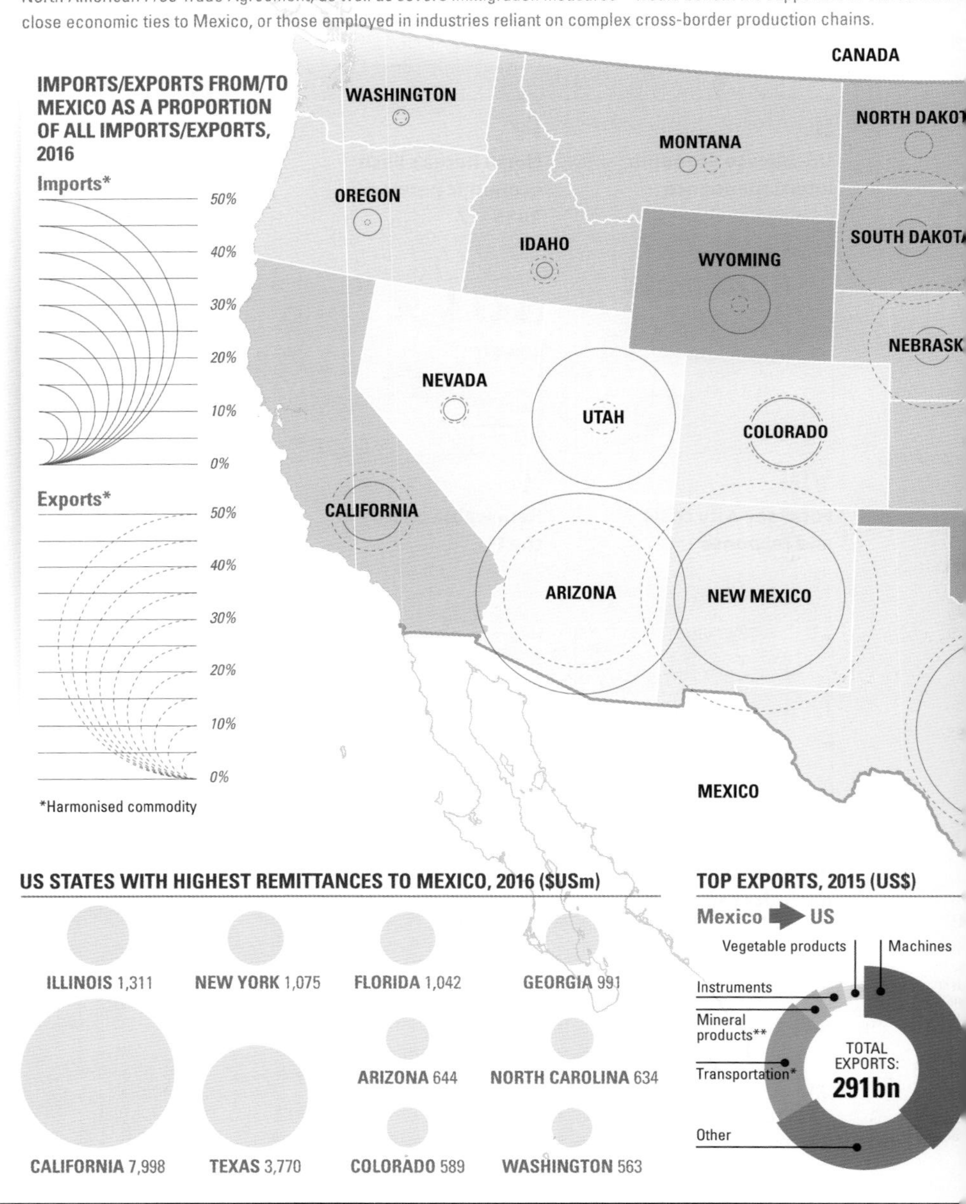

Sources: *New York Times*; US Census Bureau; Bank of Mexico; US Bureau of Economic Analysis; Observatory of Economic Complexity

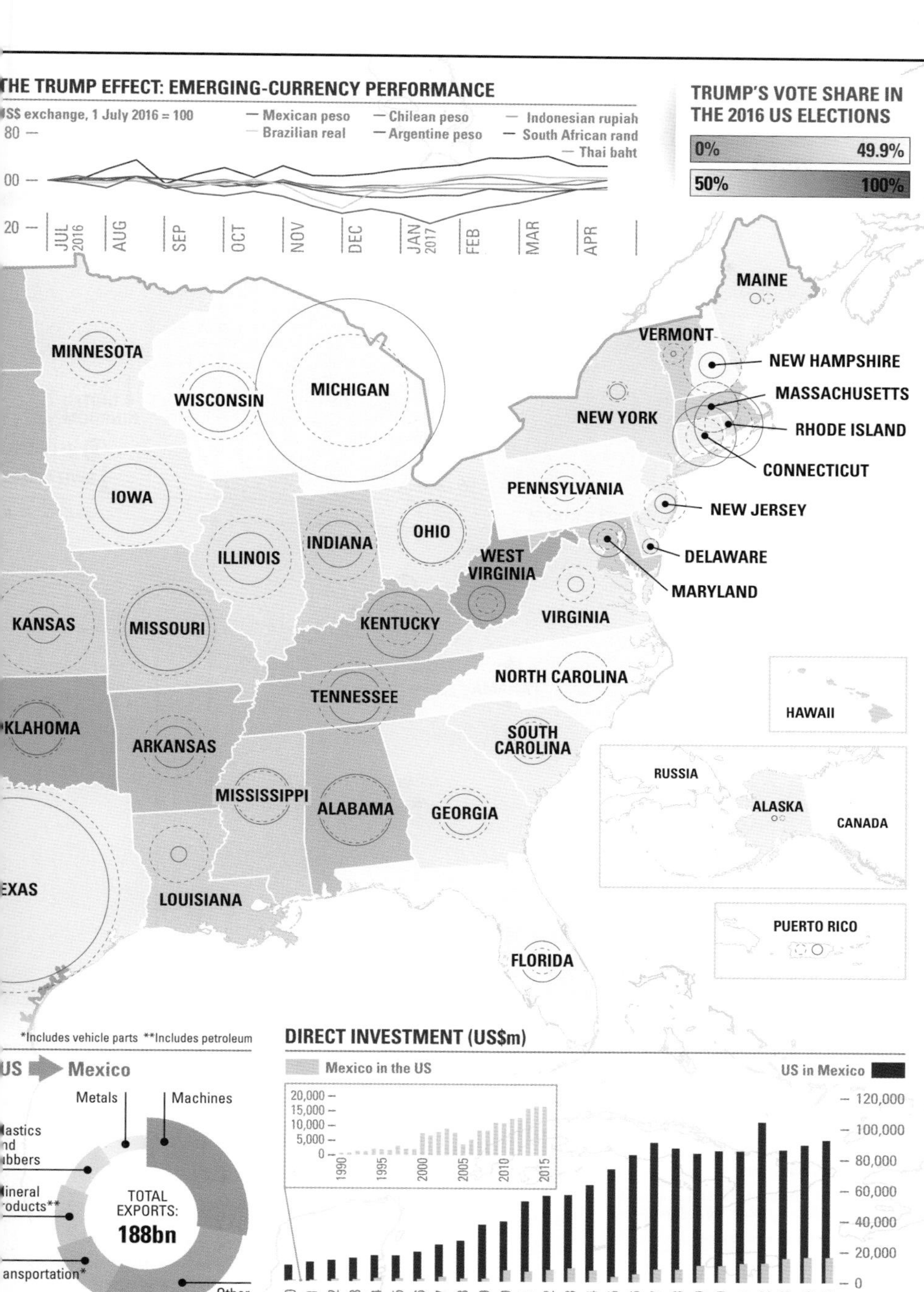

THE TRUMP EFFECT: EMERGING-CURRENCY PERFORMANCE
S$ exchange, 1 July 2016 = 100
Mexican peso
Brazilian real
Chilean peso
Argentine peso
Indonesian rupiah
South African rand
Thai baht
JUL 2016
AUG
SEP
OCT
NOV
DEC
JAN 2017
FEB
MAR
APR
TRUMP'S VOTE SHARE IN THE 2016 US ELECTIONS
0%
49.9%
50%
100%
MAINE
VERMONT
NEW HAMPSHIRE
MASSACHUSETTS
RHODE ISLAND
CONNECTICUT
NEW YORK
PENNSYLVANIA
NEW JERSEY
DELAWARE
MARYLAND
MINNESOTA
WISCONSIN
MICHIGAN
IOWA
ILLINOIS
INDIANA
OHIO
WEST VIRGINIA
VIRGINIA
KANSAS
MISSOURI
KENTUCKY
NORTH CAROLINA
TENNESSEE
KLAHOMA
ARKANSAS
SOUTH CAROLINA
MISSISSIPPI
ALABAMA
GEORGIA
EXAS
LOUISIANA
FLORIDA
HAWAII
RUSSIA
ALASKA
CANADA
PUERTO RICO
*Includes vehicle parts **Includes petroleum
US Mexico
Metals
Machines
lastics nd ubbers
lineral roducts**
TOTAL EXPORTS: 188bn
ansportation*
Other
DIRECT INVESTMENT (US$m)
Mexico in the US
US in Mexico
20,000
15,000
10,000
5,000
0
1990
1995
2000
2005
2010
2015
120,000
100,000
80,000
60,000
40,000
20,000
0
1990
1991
1992
1993
1994
1995
1996
1997
1998
1999
2000
2001
2002
2003
2004
2005
2006
2007
2008
2009
2010
2011
2012
2013
2014
2015

North Korea's illicit economic network, 2015–17

North Korea generates illicit income from the export of advanced, indigenously manufactured small arms to a variety of global buyers; remittances from foreign-based workers in the manufacturing and construction industries; and the trafficking of drugs, weapons and people across the world. The country maintains a network of front companies in at least a dozen major cities.

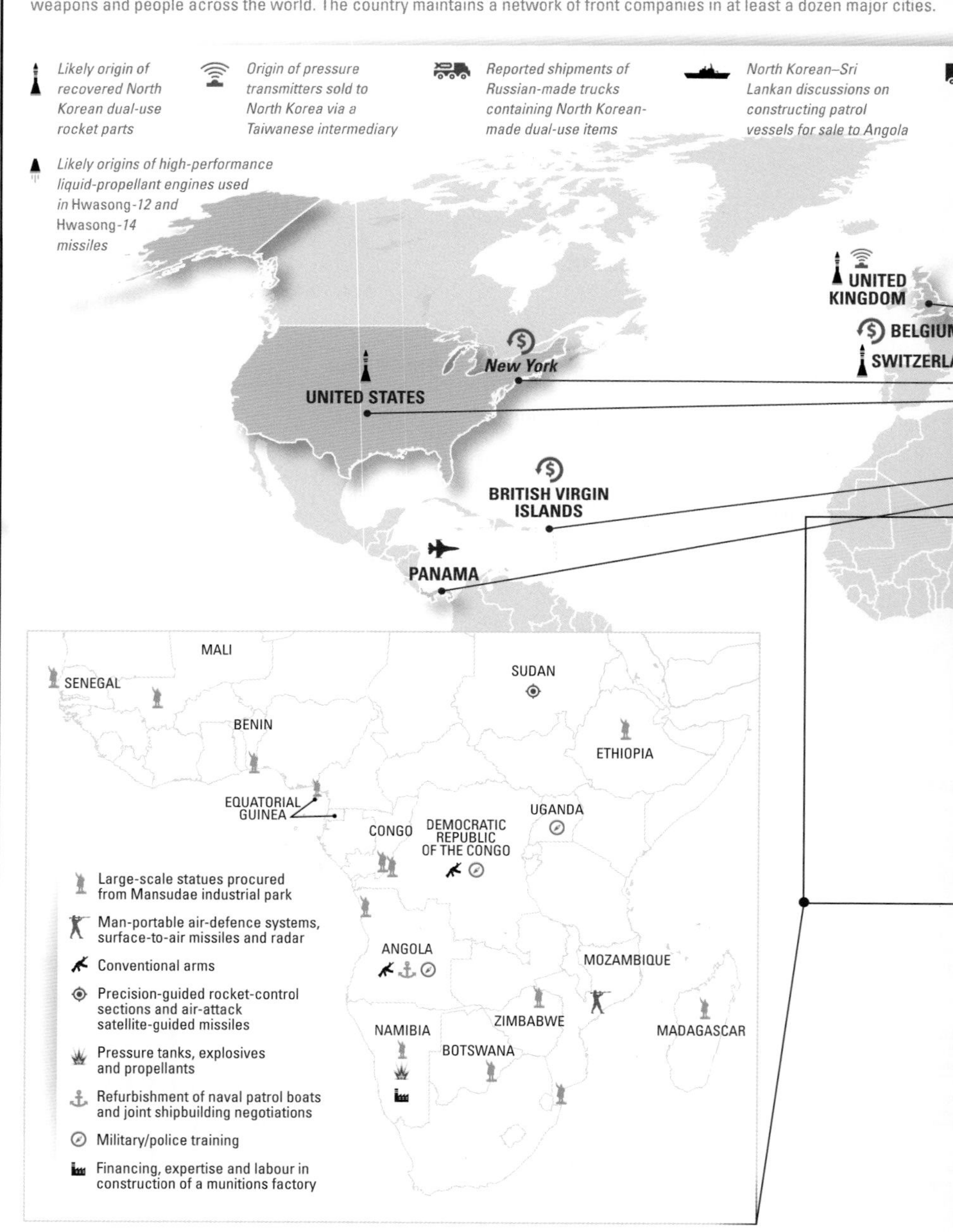

Sources: Final Report of Panel of Experts submitted pursuant to resolution 1874 (2009, S/2016/157, 24 February 2016; Final Report of Panel of Experts submitted pursuant to resolution (2009), S/2017/150, 27 February 2017

These firms are usually closely connected with the local North Korean embassy, which serves as an intermediary and holding entity for the procurement and transfer of foreign goods to the North, often through ports and other logistics facilities in China. Below are some examples of illicit North Korean trade.

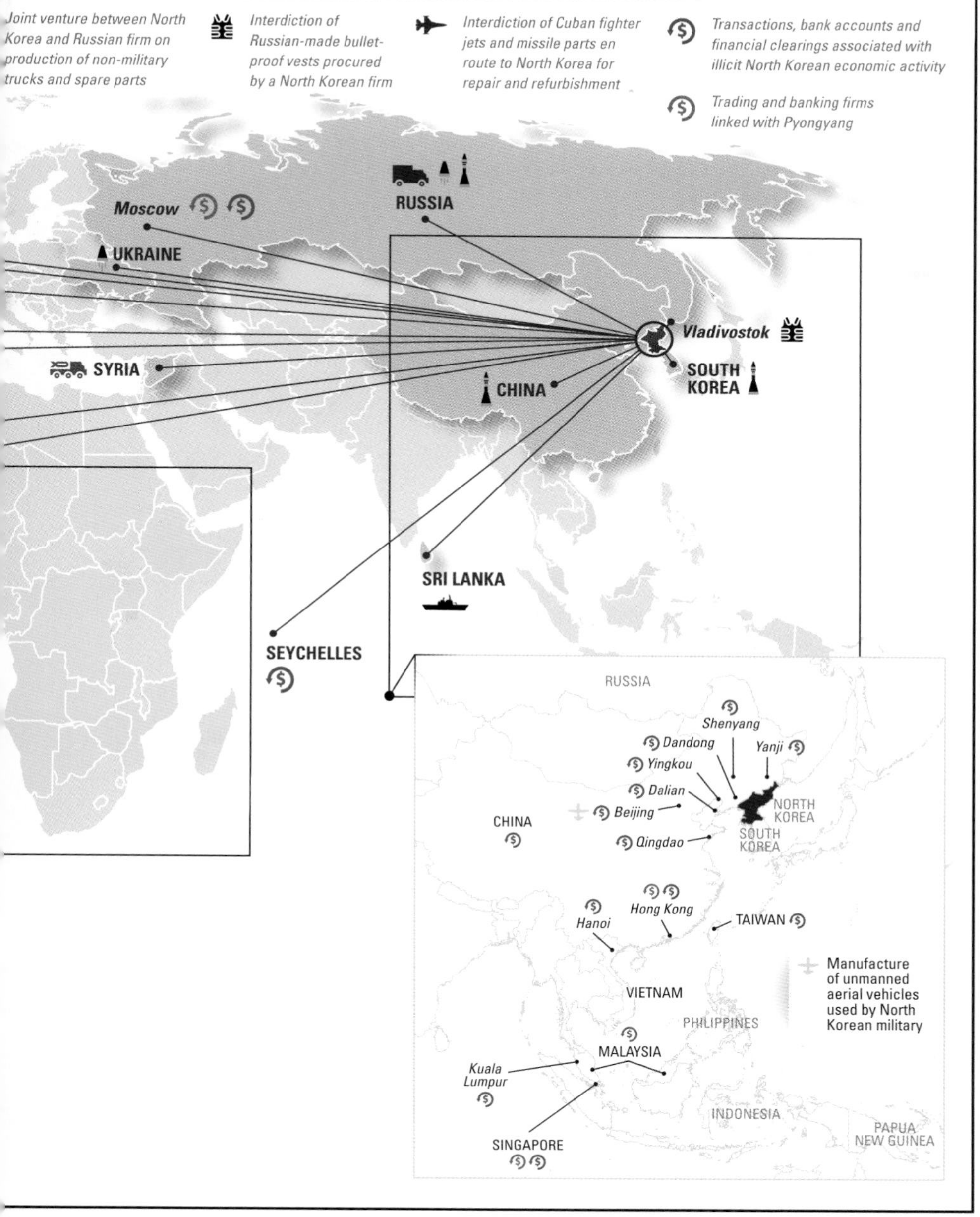

Iran's growing role in the Middle East and Southwest Asia

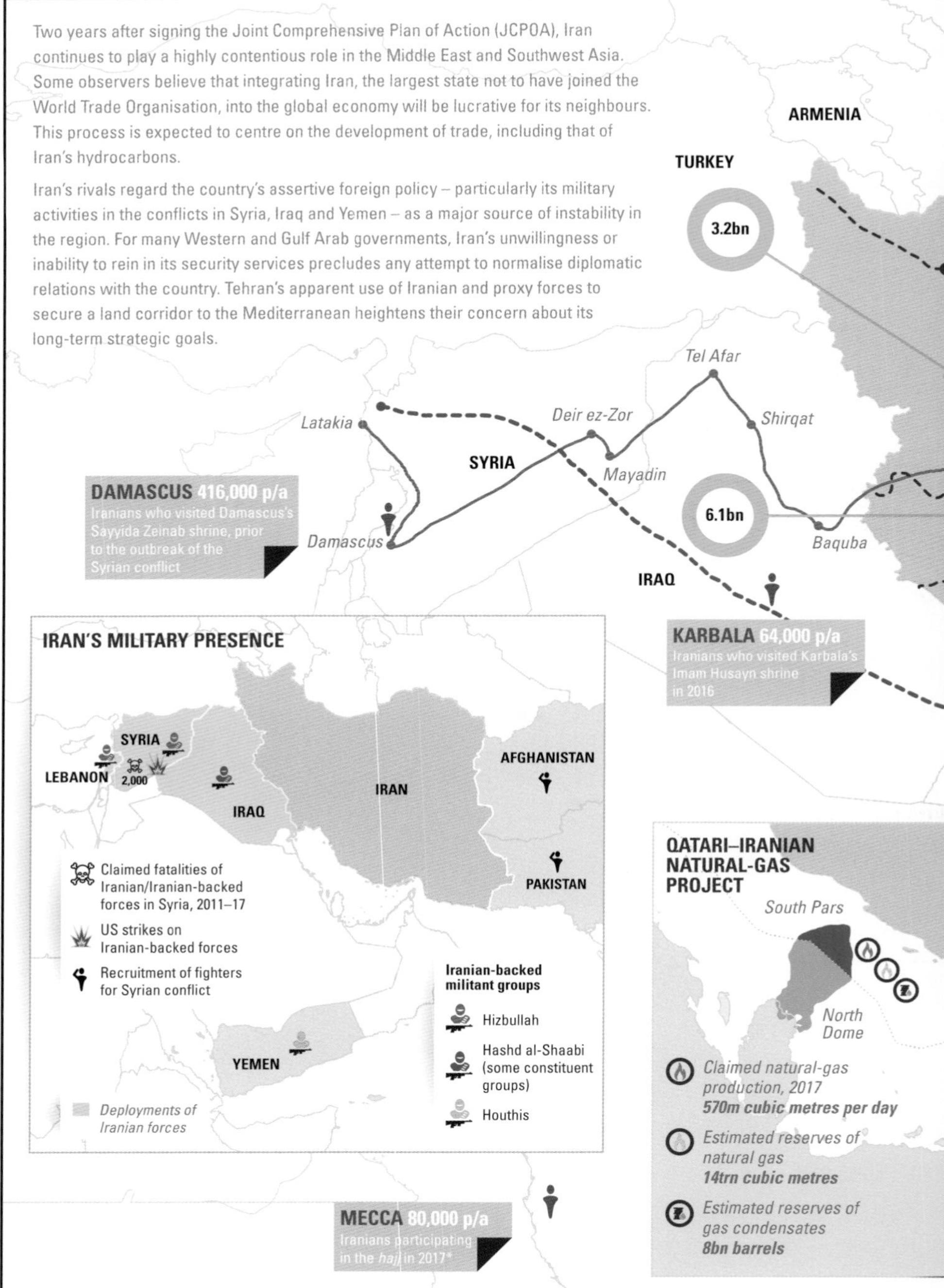

Two years after signing the Joint Comprehensive Plan of Action (JCPOA), Iran continues to play a highly contentious role in the Middle East and Southwest Asia. Some observers believe that integrating Iran, the largest state not to have joined the World Trade Organisation, into the global economy will be lucrative for its neighbours. This process is expected to centre on the development of trade, including that of Iran's hydrocarbons.
Iran's rivals regard the country's assertive foreign policy – particularly its military activities in the conflicts in Syria, Iraq and Yemen – as a major source of instability in the region. For many Western and Gulf Arab governments, Iran's unwillingness or inability to rein in its security services precludes any attempt to normalise diplomatic relations with the country. Tehran's apparent use of Iranian and proxy forces to secure a land corridor to the Mediterranean heightens their concern about its long-term strategic goals.
ARMENIA
TURKEY
3.2bn
Tel Afar
Latakia
Deir ez-Zor
Shirqat
SYRIA
Mayadin
DAMASCUS 416,000 p/a
Iranians who visited Damascus's Sayyida Zeinab shrine, prior to the outbreak of the Syrian conflict
6.1bn
Damascus
Baquba
IRAQ
KARBALA 64,000 p/a
Iranians who visited Karbala's Imam Husayn shrine in 2016
IRAN'S MILITARY PRESENCE
SYRIA
LEBANON
2,000
IRAQ
IRAN
AFGHANISTAN
PAKISTAN
YEMEN
Claimed fatalities of Iranian/Iranian-backed forces in Syria, 2011–17
US strikes on Iranian-backed forces
Recruitment of fighters for Syrian conflict
Iranian-backed militant groups
Hizbullah
Hashd al-Shaabi (some constituent groups)
Houthis
Deployments of Iranian forces
QATARI–IRANIAN NATURAL-GAS PROJECT
South Pars
North Dome
Claimed natural-gas production, 2017
570m cubic metres per day
Estimated reserves of natural gas
14trn cubic metres
Estimated reserves of gas condensates
8bn barrels
MECCA 80,000 p/a
Iranians participating in the hajj in 2017*

Sources: Islamic Republic of Iran Customs Administration; Tolo News; *Financial Tribune;* Iran News; PressTV; Reuters; Offshore Technology; *New York Times*; *Al-Monitor*; Iran Proje
IranWire; *Offshore Technology; Maritime Executive*

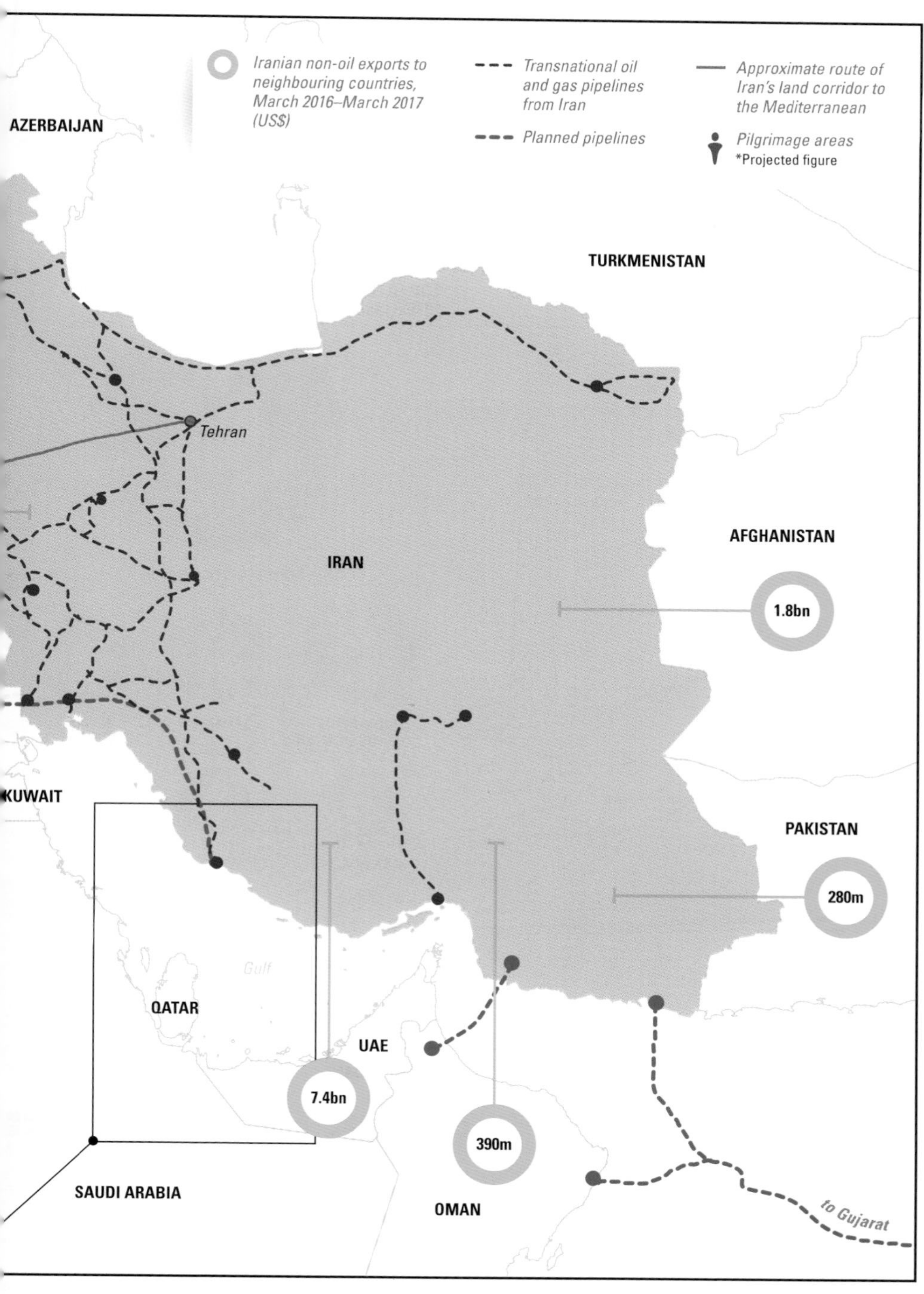
Iranian non-oil exports to neighbouring countries, March 2016–March 2017 (US$)
Transnational oil and gas pipelines from Iran
Approximate route of Iran's land corridor to the Mediterranean
Planned pipelines
Pilgrimage areas
*Projected figure
AZERBAIJAN
TURKMENISTAN
Tehran
IRAN
AFGHANISTAN
1.8bn
KUWAIT
PAKISTAN
280m
Gulf
QATAR
UAE
7.4bn
390m
SAUDI ARABIA
OMAN
to Gujarat

Food-security crisis and response

The estimated number of people experiencing severe food insecurity worldwide rose from 80 million in 2015 to 108m in 2016, largely due to the effects of conflict and El Niño events. The trend was particularly apparent in Africa and the Middle East, where ongoing violence displaced millions of people and poor growing conditions hampered agriculture. Although the 2016–17 crop harvest alleviated pressure in some regions, persistent instability and lower-than-average spring precipitation intensified food insecurity in others.

In February 2017, the United Nations declared a famine – in parts of South Sudan – for the first time since 2011. Somalia, Yemen and northern Nigeria also faced the possibility of famine in 2017. Although rich countries donated large quantities of food aid to the worst-affected countries, a range of state and non-state actors often obstructed deliveries of this aid. Few, if any, major powers appeared willing and able to address the political disputes behind much of the food insecurity in the Middle East and Africa.

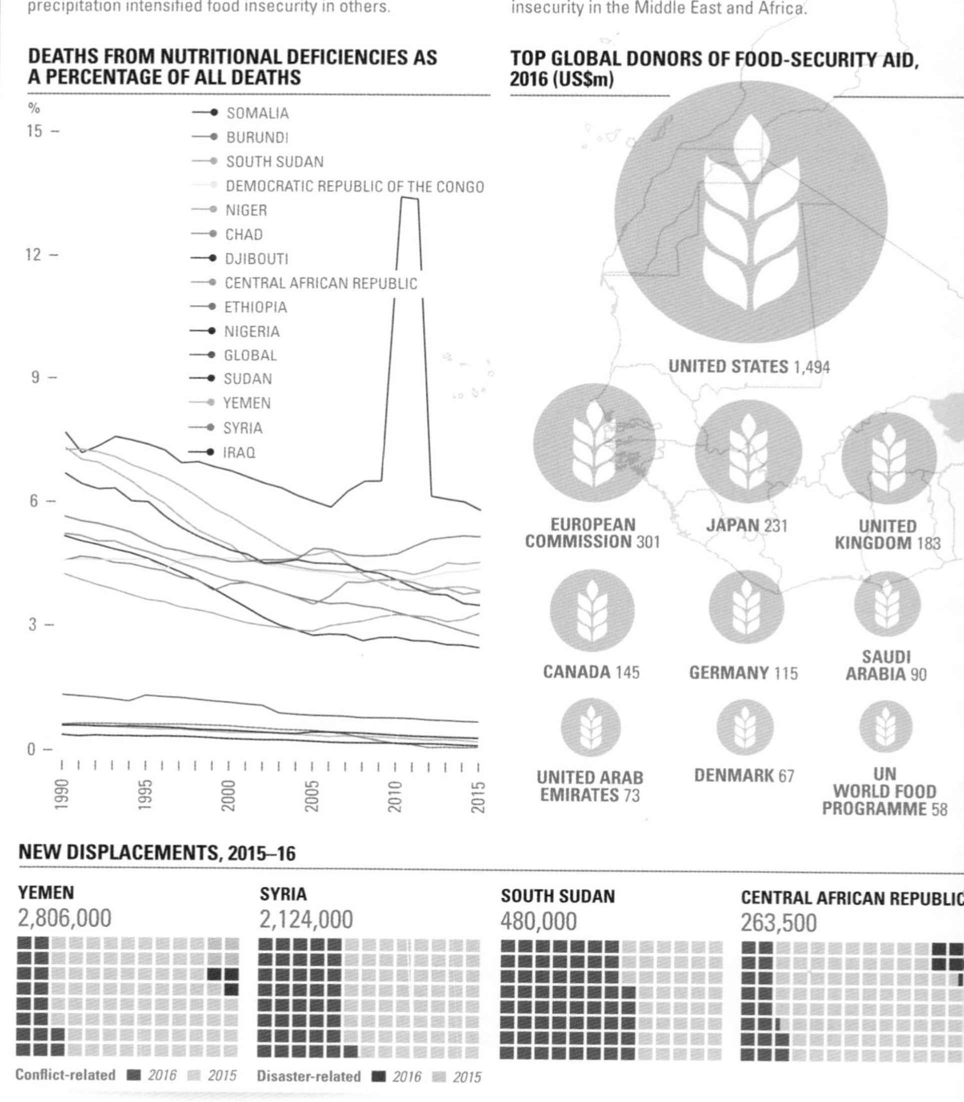

Sources: UN Food and Agriculture Organization; Food Security Information Network; Famine Early Warning Systems Network; Global Health Data Exchange; Financial Tracking Servi[ce]; Internal Displacement Monitoring Centre

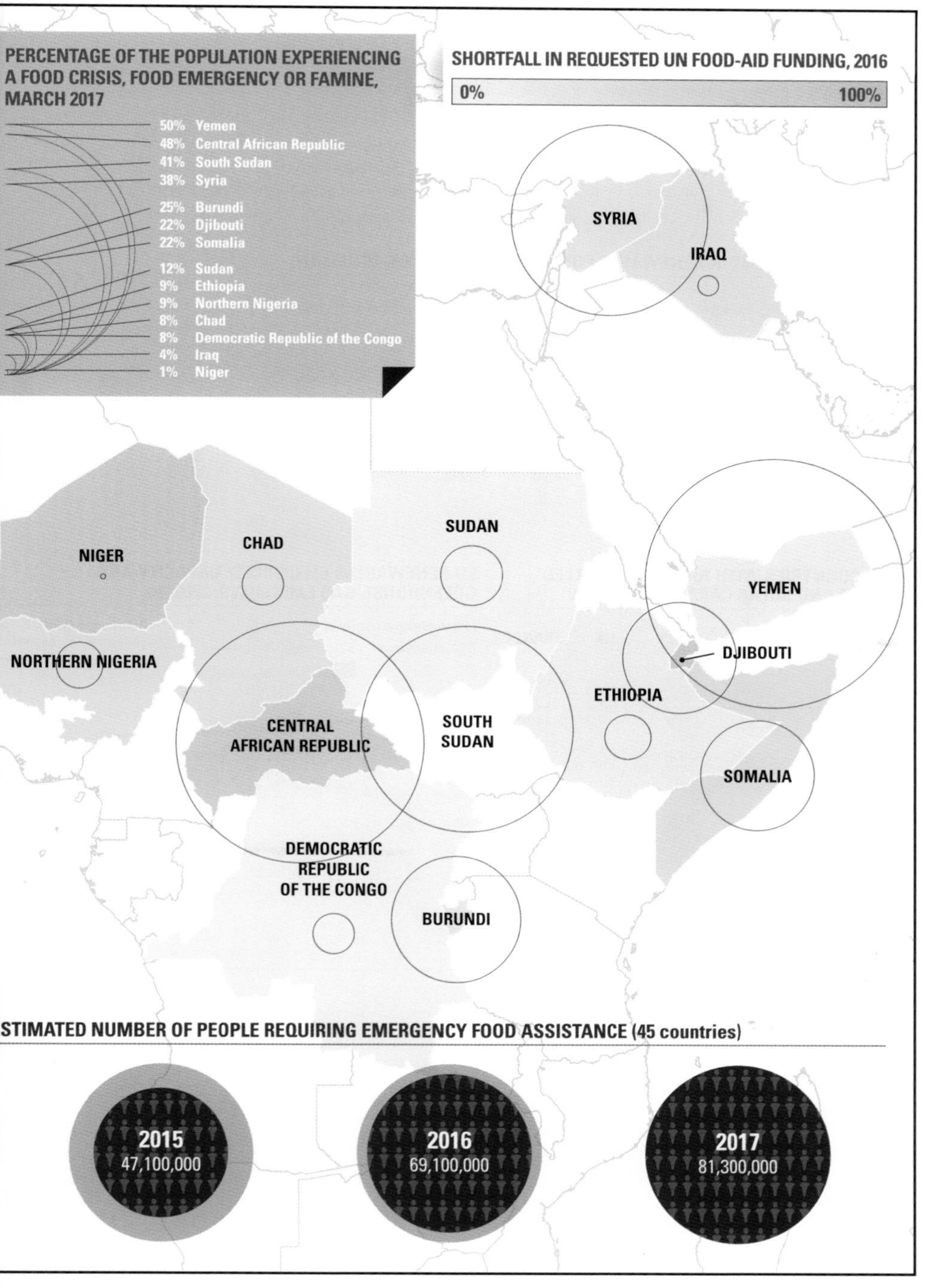
PERCENTAGE OF THE POPULATION EXPERIENCING A FOOD CRISIS, FOOD EMERGENCY OR FAMINE, MARCH 2017
50% Yemen
48% Central African Republic
41% South Sudan
38% Syria
25% Burundi
22% Djibouti
22% Somalia
12% Sudan
9% Ethiopia
9% Northern Nigeria
8% Chad
8% Democratic Republic of the Congo
4% Iraq
1% Niger
SHORTFALL IN REQUESTED UN FOOD-AID FUNDING, 2016
0%
100%
SYRIA
IRAQ
NIGER
CHAD
SUDAN
YEMEN
NORTHERN NIGERIA
DJIBOUTI
ETHIOPIA
CENTRAL AFRICAN REPUBLIC
SOUTH SUDAN
SOMALIA
DEMOCRATIC REPUBLIC OF THE CONGO
BURUNDI
ESTIMATED NUMBER OF PEOPLE REQUIRING EMERGENCY FOOD ASSISTANCE (45 countries)
2015
47,100,000
2016
69,100,000
2017
81,300,000

Renewable energy in the EU

By ratifying the COP-21 agreement in October 2016, the European Union reaffirmed its intent to limit the effects of climate change. Between 1990 and 2015, the EU28 reduced greenhouse-gas emissions by 22%, largely by replacing fossil fuels with renewable sources of energy. It is on track to meet its goal of ensuring that, by 2020, at least 30% of the electricity supply comes from renewables.

Some EU countries invested billions of euros in wind and solar energy, acquiring almost enough installed renewables capacity to meet peak demand. Indeed, in good conditions, these countries covered a huge share of their power needs with wind and solar energy. Yet average utilisation rates remained low, indicating a disconnect between the scale of the investment and its effects. Nonetheless, beyond its environmental impact, the shift towards renewables reduced the EU's reliance on energy imports, a potentially important consideration in an unstable political and security environment.

NEW INVESTMENT IN RENEWABLE POWER AND FUELS, 2006–15 (US$BN)

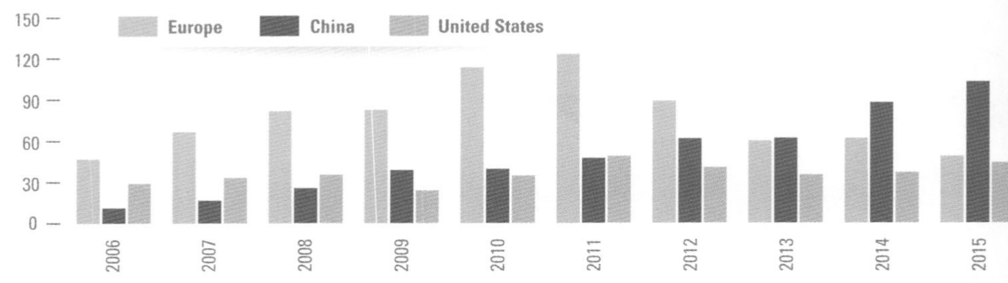

EU COUNTRIES WITH HIGHEST INSTALLED WIND AND SOLAR CAPACITY, 2015 (GW)

EU RENEWABLES ELECTRICITY CAPACITY AND GREENHOUSE-GAS EMISSIONS, 2006–15

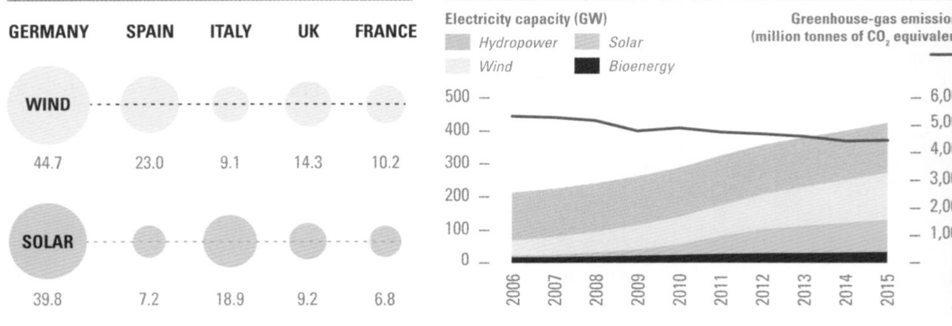

TEMPERATURE AND FLOODING CHANGES IN EUROPE

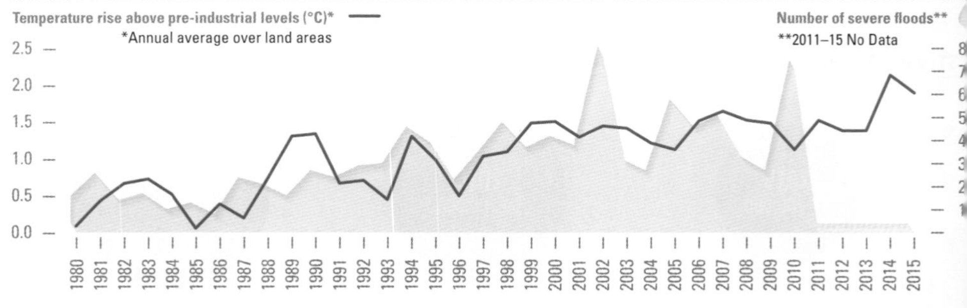

Sources: European Commission; International Renewable Energy Agency; US National Oceanic and Atmospheric Administration; European Environment Agency

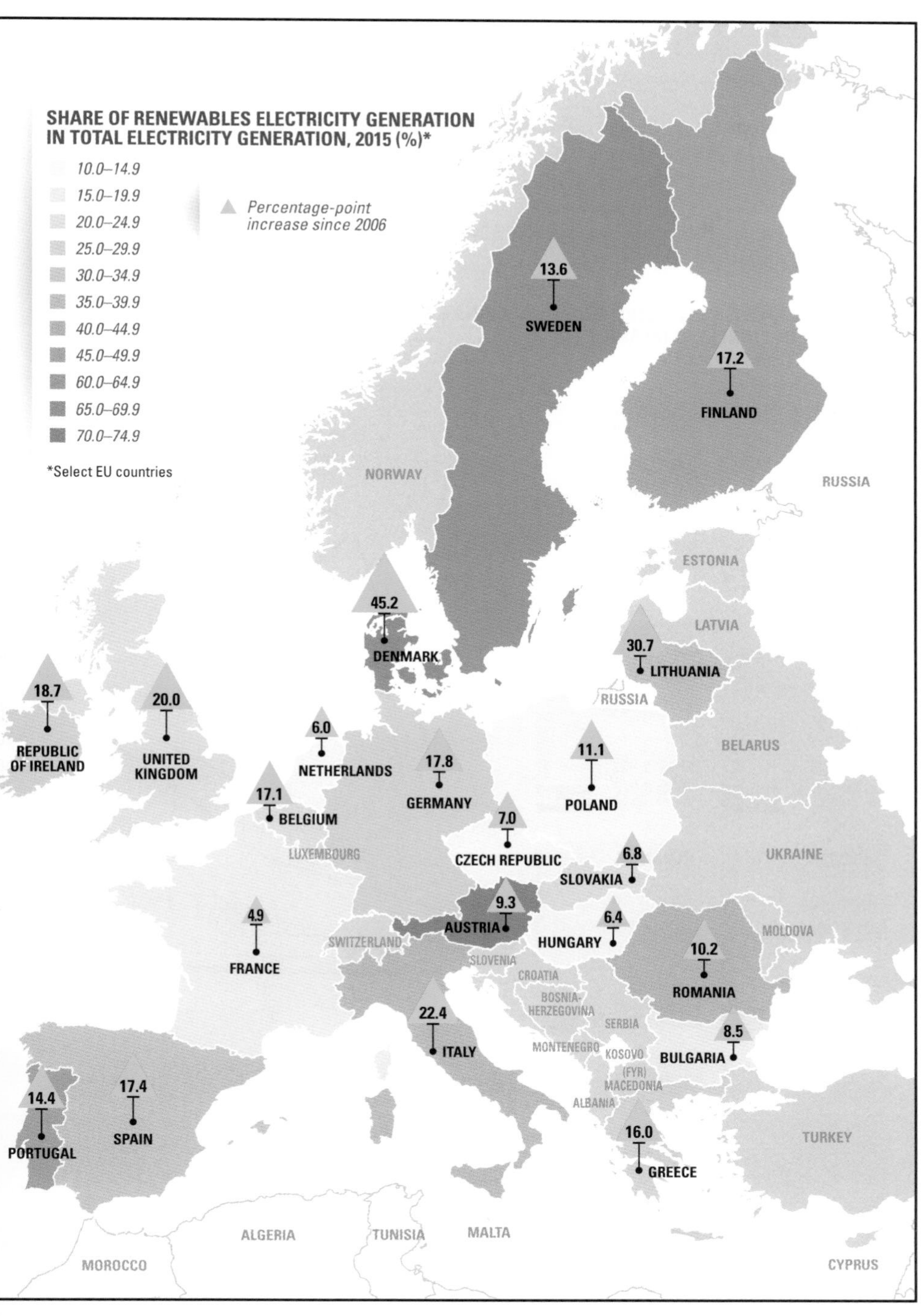
SHARE OF RENEWABLES ELECTRICITY GENERATION IN TOTAL ELECTRICITY GENERATION, 2015 (%)*
10.0–14.9
15.0–19.9
20.0–24.9
25.0–29.9
30.0–34.9
35.0–39.9
40.0–44.9
45.0–49.9
60.0–64.9
65.0–69.9
70.0–74.9
*Select EU countries
Percentage-point increase since 2006
13.6
SWEDEN
17.2
FINLAND
NORWAY
RUSSIA
ESTONIA
45.2
DENMARK
LATVIA
30.7
LITHUANIA
RUSSIA
18.7
REPUBLIC OF IRELAND
20.0
UNITED KINGDOM
6.0
NETHERLANDS
17.8
GERMANY
11.1
POLAND
BELARUS
17.1
BELGIUM
LUXEMBOURG
7.0
CZECH REPUBLIC
6.8
SLOVAKIA
UKRAINE
4.9
FRANCE
SWITZERLAND
9.3
AUSTRIA
6.4
HUNGARY
MOLDOVA
10.2
ROMANIA
SLOVENIA
CROATIA
BOSNIA-HERZEGOVINA
SERBIA
22.4
ITALY
MONTENEGRO
KOSOVO
8.5
BULGARIA
(FYR) MACEDONIA
ALBANIA
14.4
PORTUGAL
17.4
SPAIN
16.0
GREECE
TURKEY
ALGERIA
TUNISIA
MALTA
MOROCCO
CYPRUS

Chinese-funded infrastructure in East Africa

China has in recent years significantly increased its investment in East Africa, an area that includes several important waypoints on the country's Maritime Silk Road, part of the wider Belt and Road Initiative. Beijing has funded and built a series of rail networks and airports, along with a range of energy and water infrastructure, in the region. Four of the five largest Chinese-funded railways in Africa have been built in the east of the continent, while China has constructed its first overseas military base in Djibouti.

For Beijing, access to natural resources and emerging markets is crucial to boost decelerating, if still high, Chinese economic growth. For East African governments, Beijing offers a path to industrialisation and broader development. Yet mounting debt to China, as well as uncertainty about the local benefits of many projects, has drawn criticism from African civil society and several Western countries.

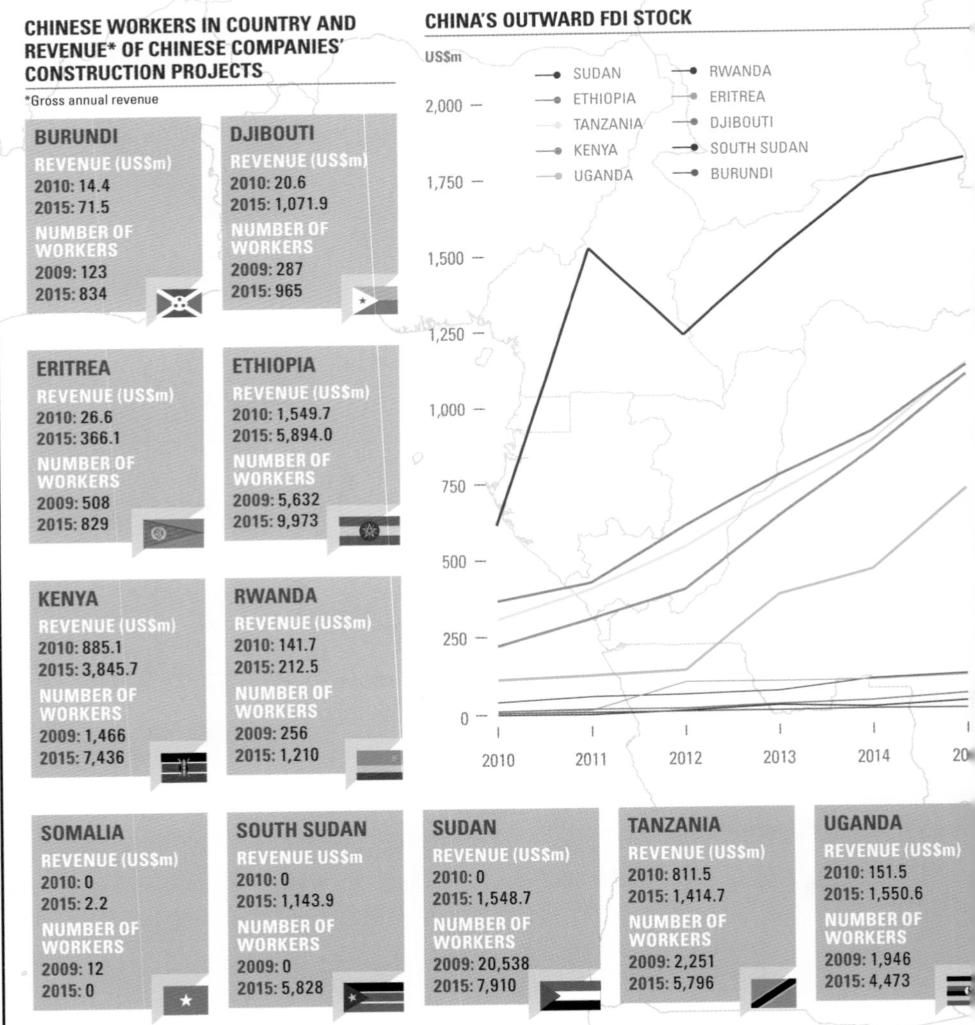

Sources: Tanzania Zambia Railway Authority; China Railway Eryuan Engineering Group; CNN; Johns Hopkins University; Sudan Railways; State Council of the People's Republic of Chin AidData; Reuters; *Horn Diplomat*; TanzaniaInvest; Ugandan Parliament; NBC; China Africa Research Initiative

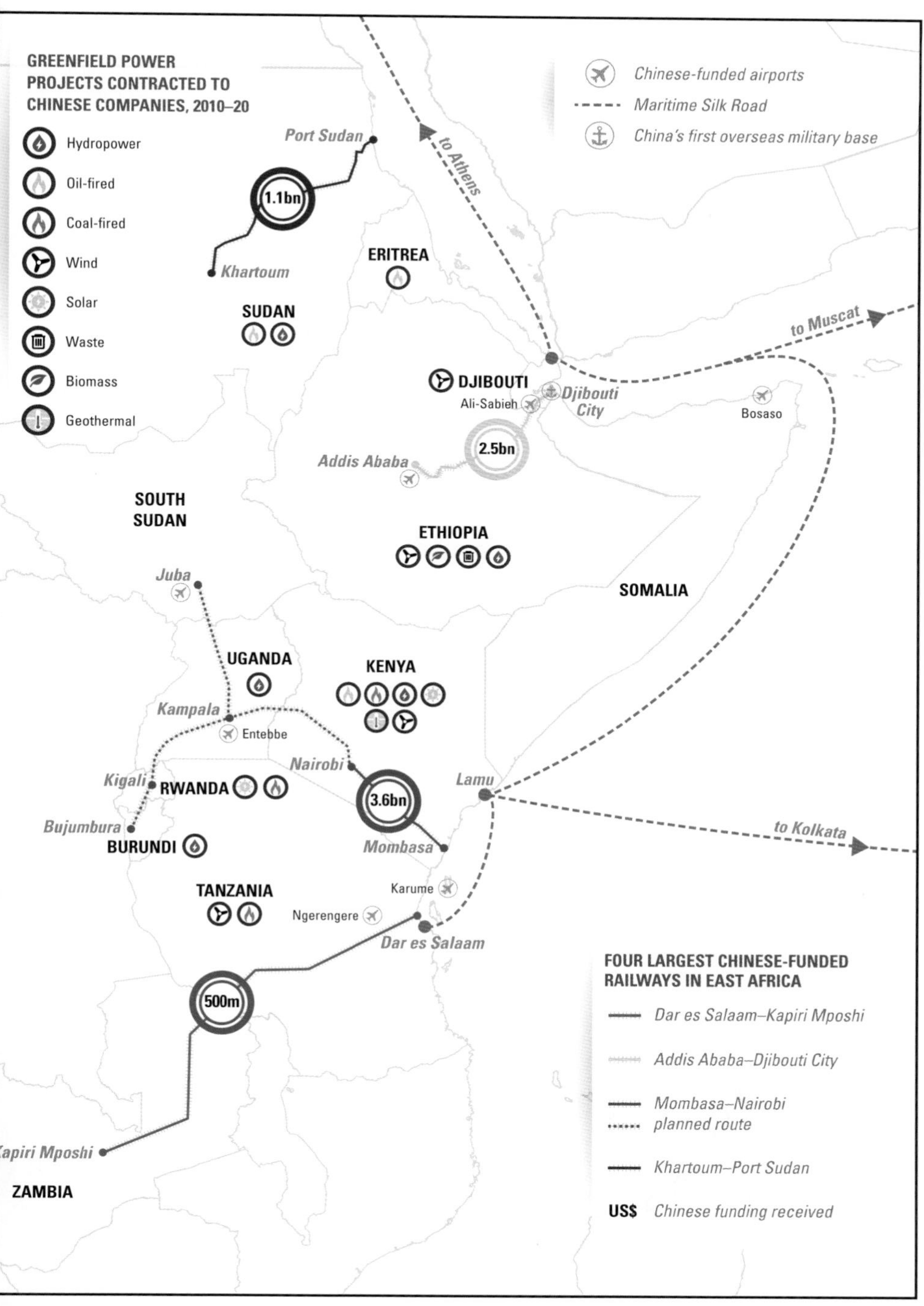

GREENFIELD POWER PROJECTS CONTRACTED TO CHINESE COMPANIES, 2010–20
Hydropower
Oil-fired
Coal-fired
Wind
Solar
Waste
Biomass
Geothermal
Chinese-funded airports
Maritime Silk Road
China's first overseas military base
Port Sudan
to Athens
1.1bn
Khartoum
ERITREA
SUDAN
to Muscat
DJIBOUTI
Djibouti City
Ali-Sabieh
Bosaso
2.5bn
Addis Ababa
SOUTH SUDAN
ETHIOPIA
SOMALIA
Juba
UGANDA
KENYA
Kampala
Entebbe
Nairobi
Kigali
RWANDA
Lamu
3.6bn
Bujumbura
BURUNDI
Mombasa
to Kolkata
TANZANIA
Karume
Ngerengere
Dar es Salaam
FOUR LARGEST CHINESE-FUNDED RAILWAYS IN EAST AFRICA
500m
Dar es Salaam–Kapiri Mposhi
Addis Ababa–Djibouti City
Mombasa–Nairobi
planned route
Kapiri Mposhi
Khartoum–Port Sudan
ZAMBIA
US$ Chinese funding received

Philippines' counter-narcotics campaign

In June 2016, Philippine President Rodrigo Duterte launched a nationwide 'war on drugs' that led police officers and vigilantes to carry out thousands of extrajudicial killings. The campaign drew sharp criticism from the United Nations, the United States and the European Union. Duterte appeared to suspend the initiative in January the following year, when the murder of a South Korean citizen at the Philippine National Police Headquarters in Quezon City – allegedly carried out by officers from the Anti-Illegal Drugs Group – sparked anger in Seoul. He resumed the campaign the following March.

The president's approach to counter-narcotics demonstrated the challenges of enforcing the rule of law in one area (drug production, sale and use) by undermining it in another (due process), and of applying the forceful anti-crime tactics he adopted as mayor of Davao City to a country of more than 100 million people. The campaign's focus on low-level distributors and users seemingly did little to constrain the transnational trafficking networks behind the Philippines' methamphetamine crisis. In October 2016, as part of its rapprochement with the Philippines under Duterte, China pledged US$15m to Manila's drug-rehabilitation and law-enforcement efforts. But it remained unclear to what extent Beijing would address Chinese criminal groups' dominant role in the Philippines' methamphetamine trade.

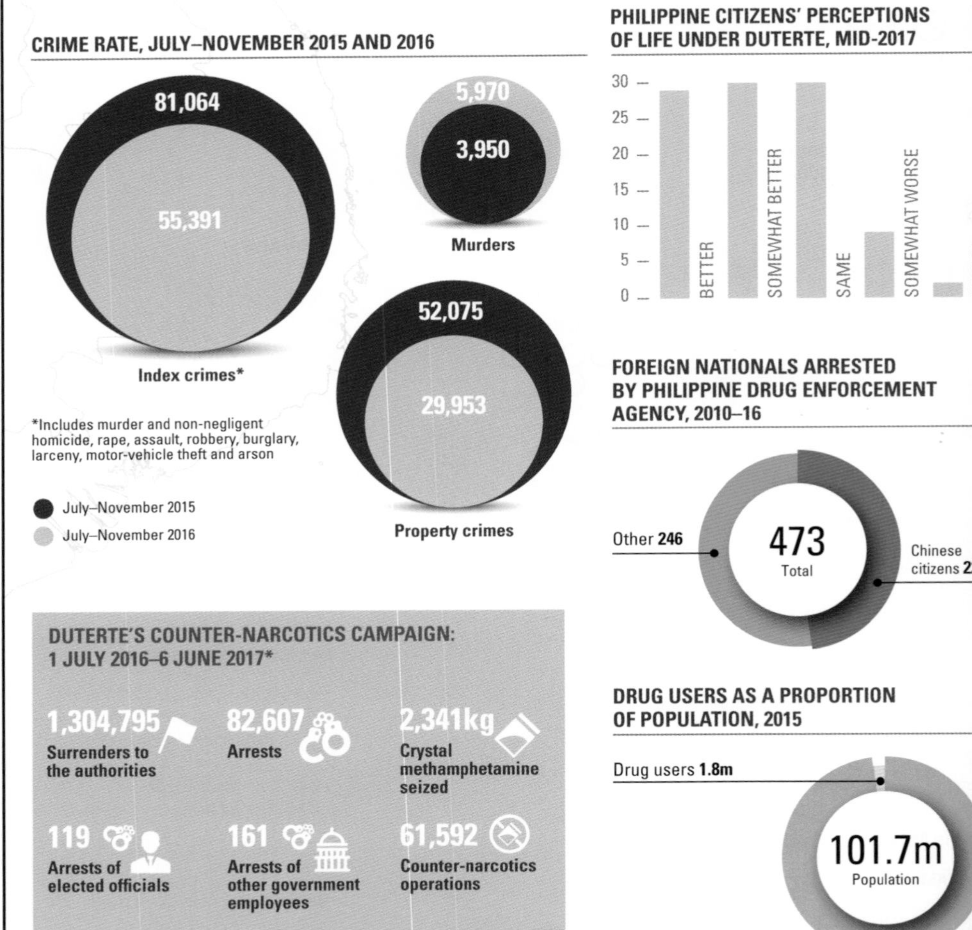

Sources: Philippine Center for Investigative Journalism; UN Office on Drugs and Crime; IISS; Philippine Drug Enforcement Agency; DW; GMA Network; *Philippine Star*, Philippine D Enforcement Agency; Dangerous Drugs Board; World Bank; *Financial Times*

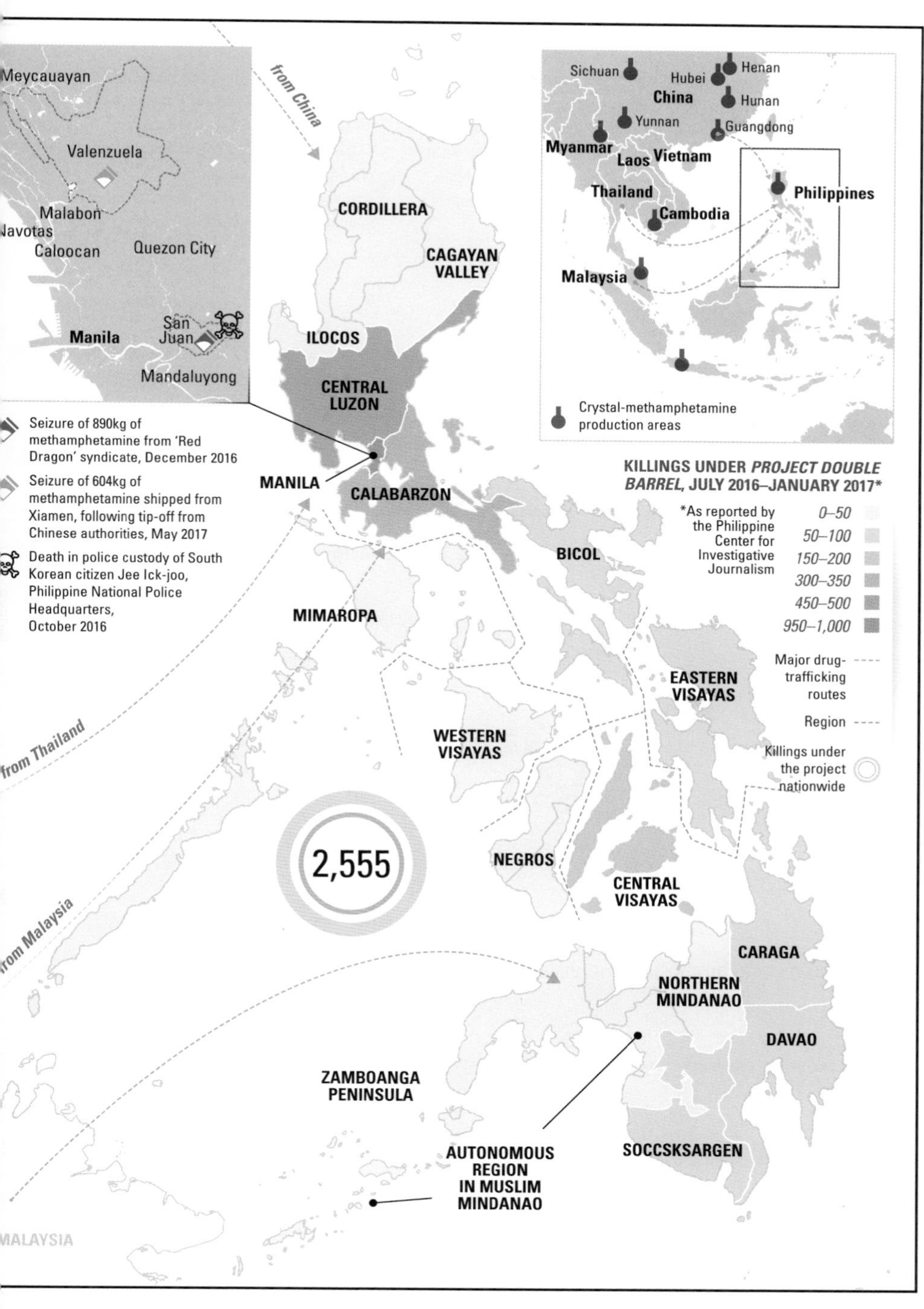

Meycauayan
Valenzuela
Malabon
Navotas
Caloocan
Quezon City
Manila
San Juan
Mandaluyong
from China
from Thailand
from Malaysia
Sichuan
Hubei
Henan
China
Hunan
Yunnan
Guangdong
Myanmar
Laos
Vietnam
Thailand
Philippines
Cambodia
Malaysia
Crystal-methamphetamine production areas
CORDILLERA
CAGAYAN VALLEY
ILOCOS
CENTRAL LUZON
MANILA
CALABARZON
BICOL
MIMAROPA
EASTERN VISAYAS
WESTERN VISAYAS
NEGROS
CENTRAL VISAYAS
2,555
CARAGA
NORTHERN MINDANAO
DAVAO
ZAMBOANGA PENINSULA
SOCCSKSARGEN
AUTONOMOUS REGION IN MUSLIM MINDANAO
MALAYSIA
Seizure of 890kg of methamphetamine from 'Red Dragon' syndicate, December 2016
Seizure of 604kg of methamphetamine shipped from Xiamen, following tip-off from Chinese authorities, May 2017
Death in police custody of South Korean citizen Jee Ick-joo, Philippine National Police Headquarters, October 2016
KILLINGS UNDER *PROJECT DOUBLE BARREL*, JULY 2016–JANUARY 2017*
*As reported by the Philippine Center for Investigative Journalism
0–50
50–100
150–200
300–350
450–500
950–1,000
Major drug-trafficking routes
Region
Killings under the project nationwide

Constitutional change and conflict in Turkey

On the night of 15–16 July 2016, a group of mid-ranking military officers tried and failed to overthrow the Turkish government. The incident prompted President Recep Tayyip Erdogan to declare a state of emergency that has persisted ever since, significantly reducing the checks and balances on the power of his Justice and Development Party (AKP). The government purged thousands of Turks allegedly affiliated with influential US-based cleric Fethullah Gülen, whom Erdogan accused of orchestrating the coup attempt.

On 16 April 2017, as the military crackdown against militant group the Kurdistan Workers' Party (PKK) continued in the southeast, Erdogan won a referendu on changing 18 articles of the country's constitution. The victory promised to empower the office of the president, moving Turkey towards one-man rule and perhaps fatally damaging its aspirations for membership of the European Union.

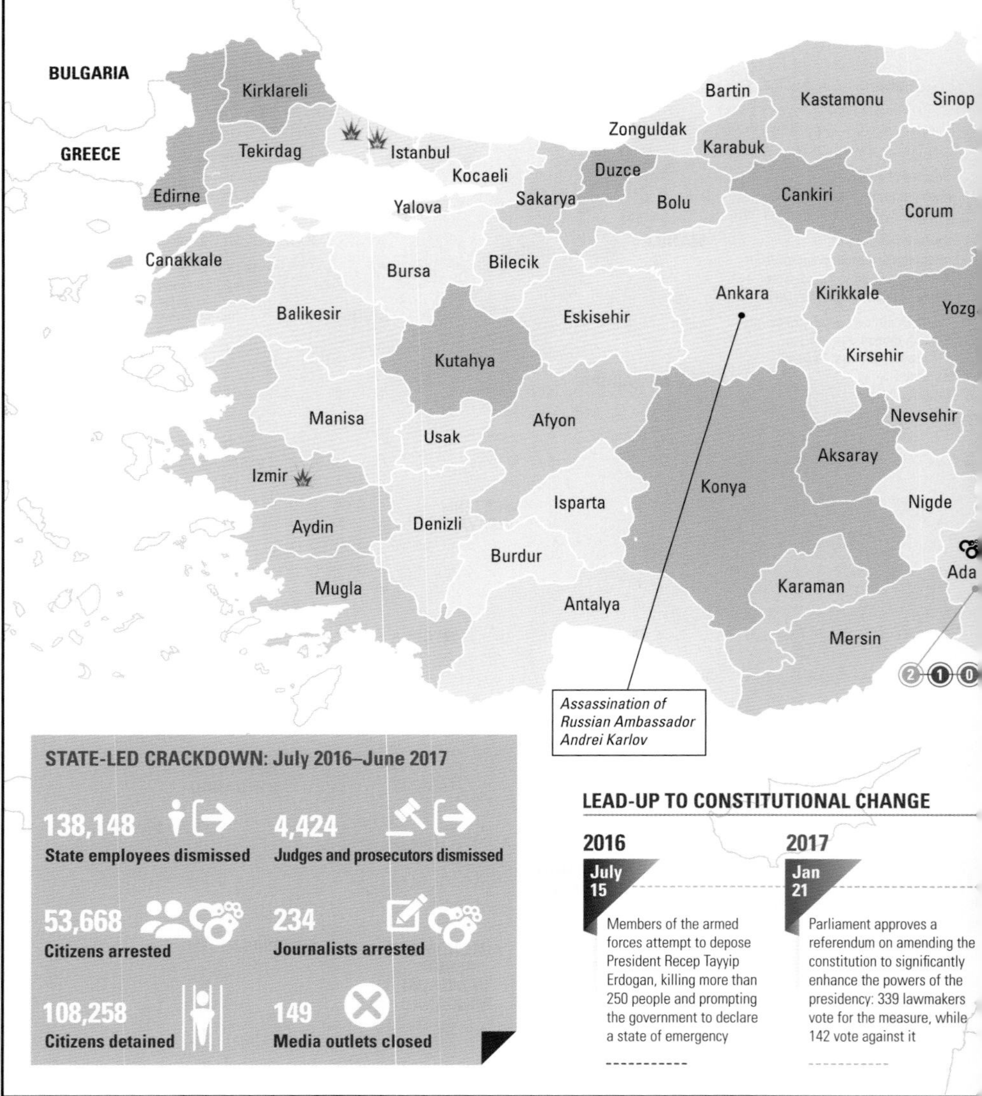

Sources: Turkish Electoral Board; IISS Armed Conflict Database, International Crisis Group; PEN International; Stockholm Center for Freedom; Turkey Purge

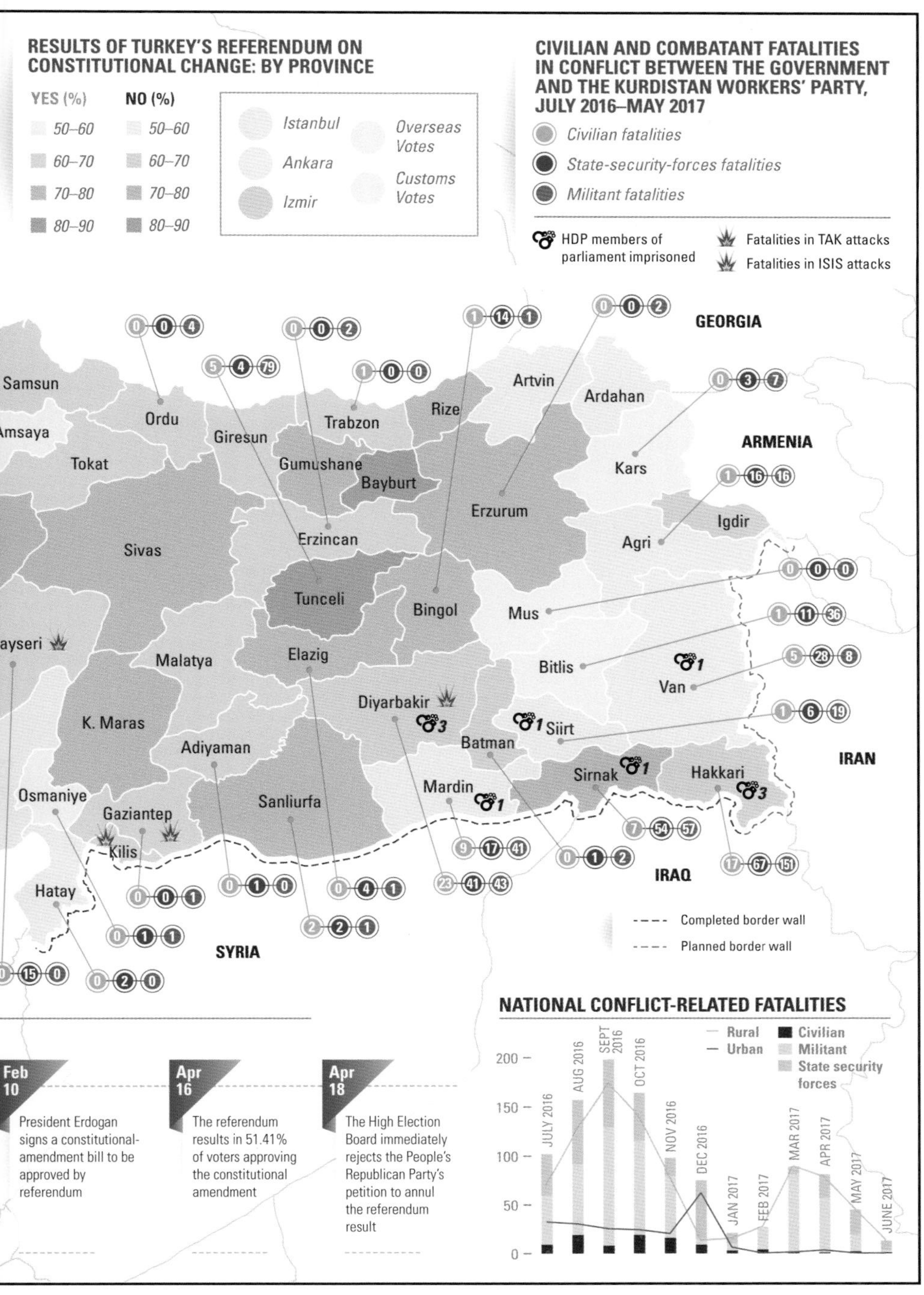
RESULTS OF TURKEY'S REFERENDUM ON CONSTITUTIONAL CHANGE: BY PROVINCE
YES (%)
NO (%)
50–60
60–70
70–80
80–90
50–60
60–70
70–80
80–90
Istanbul
Ankara
Izmir
Overseas Votes
Customs Votes
CIVILIAN AND COMBATANT FATALITIES IN CONFLICT BETWEEN THE GOVERNMENT AND THE KURDISTAN WORKERS' PARTY, JULY 2016–MAY 2017
Civilian fatalities
State-security-forces fatalities
Militant fatalities
HDP members of parliament imprisoned
Fatalities in TAK attacks
Fatalities in ISIS attacks
GEORGIA
ARMENIA
IRAN
IRAQ
SYRIA
Samsun
Amsaya
Ordu
Giresun
Trabzon
Rize
Artvin
Ardahan
Kars
Tokat
Gumushane
Bayburt
Erzurum
Igdir
Agri
Sivas
Erzincan
Tunceli
Bingol
Mus
Kayseri
Malatya
Elazig
Bitlis
Van
Diyarbakir
Siirt
Batman
K. Maras
Adiyaman
Sirnak
Hakkari
Mardin
Osmaniye
Gaziantep
Sanliurfa
Kilis
Hatay
0 0 4
0 0 2
5 4 79
1 0 0
1 14 1
0 0 2
0 3 7
1 16 16
0 0 0
1 11 36
5 28 8
1 6 19
7 54 57
9 17 41
0 1 2
17 67 151
23 41 43
0 4 1
0 1 0
0 0 1
2 2 1
0 1 1
0 15 0
0 2 0
1
1
3
1
3
1
Completed border wall
Planned border wall
NATIONAL CONFLICT-RELATED FATALITIES
Rural
Urban
Civilian
Militant
State security forces
200
150
100
50
0
JULY 2016
AUG 2016
SEPT 2016
OCT 2016
NOV 2016
DEC 2016
JAN 2017
FEB 2017
MAR 2017
APR 2017
MAY 2017
JUNE 2017
Feb 10
President Erdogan signs a constitutional-amendment bill to be approved by referendum
Apr 16
The referendum results in 51.41% of voters approving the constitutional amendment
Apr 18
The High Election Board immediately rejects the People's Republican Party's petition to annul the referendum result

Chapter 7

Middle East and North Africa

The Middle East and North Africa remained in disorder during the year to mid-2017. Intense competition between, and hedging by, the region's powers made for a troubled strategic landscape with sustained conflict exacting a rising humanitarian cost. Wars raged in Libya, Syria, Yemen and Iraq. The rapid erosion of the Islamic State, also known as ISIS or ISIL, accelerated territorial and political opportunism wherever the group was driven back; Turkey's instability fostered violence domestically and abroad; Russia made inroads across the region; and the election of Donald Trump as president of the United States created considerable uncertainty.

In this volatile environment, relations between major powers were tense. The rivalry between Saudi Arabia and Iran continued to be acute and corrosive, shaping conflicts and regional politics. Other frayed relationships also contributed to the chaos. Saudi Arabia and the United Arab Emirates allied against Qatar in an unprecedented manner, exacerbating rifts among Gulf Cooperation Council (GCC) states and their allies in the wider region. Turkey and Iran were distrustful of each other's aims in Iraq and Syria. Riyadh expressed discontent with Cairo's unwillingness to cooperate on crucial regional matters despite receiving Saudi political and financial support. Israel looked for opportunities to build ties with Arab states given their converging views on Iran.

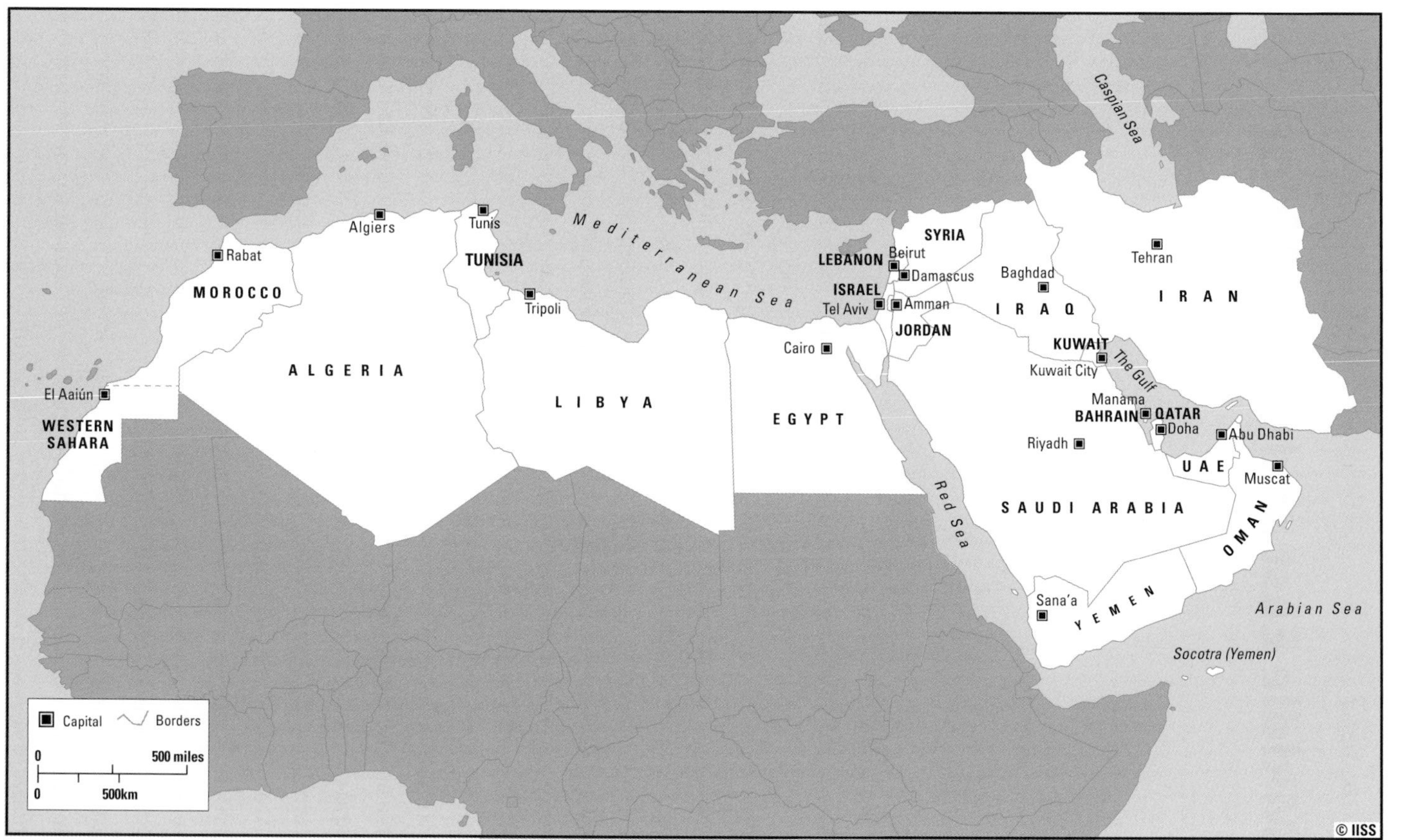

Caspian Sea
Tehran
IRAN
IRAQ
Baghdad
KUWAIT
Kuwait City
The Gulf
BAHRAIN
Manama
QATAR
Doha
Abu Dhabi
UAE
Muscat
OMAN
SAUDI ARABIA
Riyadh
YEMEN
Sana'a
Socotra (Yemen)
Arabian Sea
SYRIA
Damascus
Beirut
LEBANON
ISRAEL
Tel Aviv
Amman
JORDAN
Red Sea
EGYPT
Cairo
Mediterranean Sea
LIBYA
Tripoli
TUNISIA
Tunis
ALGERIA
Algiers
MOROCCO
Rabat
WESTERN SAHARA
El Aaiún
Capital
Borders
0
500 miles
0
500km
© IISS

Together, these dynamics thwarted meagre efforts at conflict mediation and detente, completely sidelining issues of governance and reform. The Obama administration had no success with diplomacy during its last months; the Trump administration simply discarded such efforts. The hope that the US and Russia would engage in talks that aimed at de-escalation in Syria and lowered regional tension proved unfounded. The United Nations' efforts at mediation in Yemen failed to persuade the warring sides to suspend the war. Competition for legitimacy and resources continued to fuel the fighting in Libya. Although the campaign against ISIS produced significant territorial advances, the considerably weakened group remained lethal.

Regional power dynamics

Throughout 2016, the Obama administration resisted calls to escalate US military involvement in Syria as Russian- and Iranian-facilitated regime advances threatened the rebellion and its stronghold in Aleppo. Then-secretary of state John Kerry stubbornly engaged in diplomacy with his Russian counterpart, Sergei Lavrov, to secure a ceasefire, dangling the promise of joint counter-terrorism operations in exchange for de-escalation by the Russian military and other pro-regime forces. By the time of Trump's inauguration, these efforts had proved inconclusive.

During his presidential campaign, Trump harshly criticised US policy on Syria, calling for an end to American support for the country's rebels and an exclusive focus on fighting ISIS in coordination with Russia. Initially, the lack of US diplomats at peace talks in Geneva and Astana generated concern among the Syrian opposition that Washington would disengage.

However, in April, the Assad regime conducted a chemical attack against the rebel-held town of Khan Sheikhoun. Within days, the White House had ordered a missile strike on the air base from which the attack was launched. Diplomatic escalation followed, albeit with conflicting messaging from Trump officials. While Nikki Haley, US ambassador to the UN, pushed for the ouster of President Bashar al-

Assad and introduced draft resolutions to sanction his regime, other Trump officials articulated more limited goals focusing on deterring further use of chemical weapons.

Within weeks, it became clear that Washington had not significantly altered its Syria strategy. Although US attempts to sanction the regime ended Moscow's hopes of cooperation with Washington on Syria, the White House did not increase its support for the Syrian rebels. Instead, it concentrated on defeating ISIS and dislodging the group from Raqqa. After conducting a policy review, the Trump administration largely held to the strategy of its predecessor by maintaining and, from May, upgrading military support for Syrian Kurdish and allied Arab militias operating within the Syrian Democratic Forces (SDF). Turkey lobbied heavily against US cooperation with Kurdish forces but had no success in the effort, partly because it was unable to propose a realistic alternative strategy or muster a credible anti-regime force. Washington tried to mitigate Turkish concerns about the long-term empowerment of the Kurds by offering guarantees, including those on the governance of SDF-held areas.

However, US priorities in Syria increasingly clashed with President Assad's desire to restore his rule nationwide and, more importantly, with Iran's ambitions to create a land bridge from its own borders, through Iraq, to Syria and Lebanon, and to extend its presence in southern Syria, along the Jordanian and Israeli borders. Seeming to presage a greater struggle, in May and June the US conducted strikes against regime forces and Shia militias advancing towards a base hosting US and UK special forces, as well as Syrian rebels, fighting ISIS in the southeastern town of Tanf. The potential for confrontation between US forces and Iran-aligned militias in Syria grew considerably.

Washington's new approach to the Middle East came to the fore with Trump's trip to Saudi Arabia in May 2017, his first official foreign visit as president. The theatrics and tone of the event demonstrated substantive US–Saudi alignment. A US$110-billion arms deal – years in the making – was announced during the trip. Trump pleased the Gulf Arab autocracies by downplaying traditional US advocacy of political reform and human rights, while the Saudis unveiled new initiatives to combat extremism. The president's denouncement of Iran for allegedly fuelling 'the fires of sectarian conflict and terror' exacerbated fears that he had adopted Saudi Arabia's sectarian view of regional politics. Coinciding with the Riyadh summit, the re-election of Hassan Rouhani as Iranian president failed to moderate either US or Gulf Arab hostility towards Tehran. Nonetheless, Trump's seemingly binary view of the Middle East was soon complicated by a re-emerging challenge. Just weeks after the visit, Riyadh and Abu Dhabi took unprecedented steps to isolate and punish Doha – partly for its support for radical Islamist movements and its amicable relationship with Iran, but more importantly for opposing their attempts to lead the region. The resulting crisis threatened to confound Gulf Arab security planning, as well as US policy.

Having exceeded expectations in its Syrian campaign, Russia increased the costs of counter-escalation by Turkey, Saudi Arabia and Qatar while outmanoeuvring the Obama administration during intensive diplomatic talks in the latter half of 2016. Partly due to then-president Barack Obama's reluctance to threaten or employ force, Washington's peace efforts crumbled in September as Russian or Syrian warplanes bombed a UN humanitarian convoy bound for Aleppo. This failure damaged the image of the US among its allies in the region and the Syrian rebels. The fall of Aleppo three months later crowned Russia as the dominant external power in Syria.

By late 2016, Moscow had created a diplomatic track on Syria in Astana that included Iran and Turkey but initially excluded the US, and that operated in parallel with UN-led negotiations. In an apparent attempt to achieve a nationwide ceasefire on terms favourable to Assad, Russia brokered talks between the regime and select rebel groups, attempting to guarantee the process alongside a more compliant Turkey and an ambivalent Iran.

The Gulf Arab states were excluded from the negotiations, forcing Saudi Arabia and Qatar to recalibrate their ambitions: having lost the capacity to provide significant operational assistance and endured the setbacks of a costly conflict, they seemed to recognise that their initial objectives had become unrealistic. As a consequence, Ankara became Moscow's key interlocutor just as Turkish forces intensified their fight against ISIS – largely to check Kurdish ambitions – and US–Turkey relations further deteriorated.

When excluded from the early rounds of the Astana negotiations, Washington devoted little policy or bureaucratic attention to diplomacy on Syria – a trend underlined by its decision not to appoint a new special envoy for the purpose. Although the US dispatched relatively high-level representatives to later Astana meetings, it was noticeably less involved than it had been in earlier stages of the UN-led peace process, generating concern among other Western countries and the Syrian rebels.

The Astana track failed to deliver the promised countrywide ceasefire and to alleviate the humanitarian situation in Syria. Regime forces and Iranian-backed militias displayed no inclination to suspend the fighting. Instead, the regime used the ceasefire to reallocate military resources, capturing strategically important territory across Syria. Relatively moderate rebel groups were weakened by the ceasefire, leaving space for jihadist and other extremist organisations to grow more powerful. Having largely neutralised the mainstream rebellion, Russian and other pro-regime forces finally invested significantly in the fight against ISIS – notably in the northeast, the east and Palmyra, seeking to break the group's siege of Deir ez-Zor.

Thus, throughout the year to mid-2017, Russia played an increasingly active role in Middle Eastern politics. The perception that the country had outwitted the US in several regions of the world drove Middle Eastern leaders to move closer to Moscow. Capitalising on its successful intervention in Syria and apparent US disengagement, Russia positioned itself as a decisive military player and an alternative pole for countries seeking to balance their relationship with Washington. For several Middle Eastern nations, Trump's ostensible affinity for Russia seemed to significantly reduce the risks of such hedging.

At the same time as it pursued goals inimical to the interests of the GCC in Syria, Russia maintained strong ties with the UAE based on their converging views on Egypt, Islamism and other issues, as well as the good personal relationship between Russian President Vladimir Putin and UAE leader-in-waiting Sheikh Mohammed bin Zayed Al Nahyan. Moscow improved its links with Middle Eastern states in the hope of gaining strategic and economic benefits. Estranged from the US under Obama, Egypt emerged as a Russian partner of choice, with President Abdel Fattah Al-Sisi meeting Putin to discuss defence agreements and other forms of cooperation. Libyan military strongman Khalifa Haftar used his links with Cairo and Abu Dhabi to build a relationship with Moscow – in the hope of receiving Russian military assistance and political cover in his struggle against the UN-recognised government in Tripoli.

Initially centred on securing Assad's survival, the Russia–Iran partnership also expanded. Whatever their differences, each country saw cooperation with the other as a force multiplier and a check on US policy. For the first time, Iran allowed Russia to use one of its air bases – that in Hamadan – to conduct operations in northern Syria. (In a sign of lingering distrust, Tehran temporarily suspended this arrangement after Russia's public discussion of it generated discontent in Iran.)

Eager to modernise its military, Tehran initiated negotiations to increase its procurements of Russian weapons. Moscow began the delivery of the S-300 missile-defence system to Tehran, and the sides began talks on a US$10bn arms package that included armoured vehicles, artillery, helicopters and fighter jets. Working to revive the Iranian economy after the repeal of nuclear-related sanctions, the Rouhani administration also sought Russian investment in energy ventures.

This rapprochement caused concern in Israel and Gulf Arab states, which feared that it would increase Iran's reach while providing weaponry to the country and its Shia allies in the region. Russia's role in the Syrian conflict created operational challenges for Israel, but sustained communication between the countries allowed the latter to continue its air campaign against Iranian and Hizbullah targets in Syria. Israel demanded that Russia refrain from selling weaponry to Iran and its allies, seemingly to no effect. Saudi Arabia remained distrustful of Russia due to its support for Iran and Assad. Senior Saudi officials, including Crown Prince Mohammed bin Salman Al Saud, lobbied Moscow to downgrade its ties with Tehran. However, Riyadh had little influence on Moscow: the latter's cooperation on energy production was necessary to stabilise oil prices, while its ties to Iran and Yemen's Houthi movement made it both an important diplomatic actor and a potential threat.

Iran, Saudi Arabia and Turkey

Iran and Saudi Arabia maintained the most potent geopolitical rivalry in the Middle East. The countries moved even further apart in the year to mid-2017, seeking to solidify their respective alliances and adjust their positions in response to fluctuating US policy. Riyadh resented Obama's approach to the Middle East, accusing him of tolerating Iranian expansionism to protect the nuclear deal. With the Trump administration indicating its willingness to increase pressure on Iran, Saudi Arabia saw an opportunity to shape US policy to its benefit. However, it was unclear how Washington and Riyadh could cooperate against Iran outside existing frameworks.

Tehran extended its influence and military reach in Syria, Iraq and Lebanon, despite Riyadh's efforts at containment through its allies and proxies. The Saudis orchestrated condemnation of Iran in various forums, including the Arab League, the GCC and the Organisation of Islamic Cooperation. They also sought to enrol their allies in institutions that could mobilise political and military power in the service of Saudi interests, not least the Islamic Military Alliance to Fight Terrorism, which was announced in 2015 and unveiled in the year to mid-2017. The coalition excluded Shia-majority countries such as Iran and Iraq, limiting its membership to Sunni-majority states. Crown Prince Salman travelled extensively to generate support for the alliance, with varying levels of success. Many Asian, Arab and African countries joined the coalition as a symbolic gesture, but were reluctant to politically or militarily commit to the venture due to their fear of entanglement in Saudi policy.

In his harshest criticism of Iran to date, Salman promised in May 2017 that his country 'will not wait until the battle is in Saudi Arabia, but we will work so the battle is there in Iran'. Such combative rhetoric mirrored that of Iranian officials. Major-General Mohammad Ali Jafari, commander of Iran's Islamic Revolutionary Guard Corps (IRGC), accused Saudi Arabia of 'trying to create division and insecurity in Shi'ite countries, but, by God's grace, has failed to do so thus far'. The IRGC and other hardline Iranian institutions accused Saudi Arabia of facilitating the attack on the Iranian parliament in June 2017, the first large-scale ISIS assault in Iran. Similarly, the Iranian foreign minister claimed that his country had intelligence that Saudi Arabia was 'actively' supporting terrorist groups near Iran's eastern and western borders (without producing evidence). This climate of hostility pervaded Middle Eastern politics and generated anxiety among states wary of further conflict.

The rivalry played out on several battlefields. Saudi Arabia initiated a long-awaited rapprochement with Haider al-Abadi, the Iraqi prime minister, even while maintaining its harsh criticism of Shia movements seen as obedient to Iran. However, Tehran continued to be significantly more powerful in Iraq. In Lebanon, Michel Aoun and Saad Hariri, the Iranian-supported presidential candidate and Saudi-backed prime-ministerial candidate respectively, reached a power-sharing agreement that favoured Aoun. The outcome reflected the ascendancy of Hizbullah, which achieved military victories in Syria as it amassed political power in Lebanon.

Bahrain stepped up its repression of the Shia-dominated opposition by banning major parties and jailing leaders – a sign that government hardliners were confident in Saudi support and US acquiescence. Radicalisation among young Bahraini Shi'ites increased as Iranian and Iraqi preachers appealed to their discontent. The increasing complexity of improvised explosive devices used in Bahrain and pervasive Iranian media coverage of the country lent credence to the notion that Tehran was attempting to influence a divided Bahraini society.

On 26 August 2016, six days after an ISIS suicide bombing killed 56 people at a wedding in the southeastern city of Gaziantep, Turkey launched a ground offensive into ISIS-held territory in Syria, code-named *Operation Euphrates Shield*. Publicly, Turkish officials maintained that the goal of the operation was to push ISIS back from the border. But, as its name implied, the effort was also designed to prevent the Syrian Kurdish Democratic Union Party (PYD), a close affiliate of the Kurdistan Workers' Party (PKK), from launching its own offensive against ISIS. Ankara feared that if the PYD were to drive ISIS out of the territory it held to the west of the Euphrates River, the Kurdish group would gain control of a long strip of territory along the Syria–Turkey border.

Around 3,000 Turkish troops and 5,000 members of Syrian rebel militias backed by Ankara gradually advanced southwards. On 23 February 2017, they expelled ISIS from the town of Bab, 30 kilometres south of the Turkish border. However, Ankara's plan to then move east to the PYD-controlled town of Manbij was blocked by Washington, which had established a close partnership with the PYD's military wing, the Kurdish People's Protection Units (YPG), and deployed special-forces personnel alongside YPG units in the town. Moscow then brokered an agreement between Damascus and the PYD that resulted in the insertion of Syrian-regime forces between the PYD in Manbij and the forces deployed by Ankara.

By June 2017, the result was a stalemate. Although *Operation Euphrates Shield* succeeded in driving ISIS back from the Turkish border, and created a de facto Turkish protectorate wedged between two PYD-controlled territories in northern Syria, the Turkish troops were boxed in, with Ankara unable to advance for fear of a military confrontation with the Syrian regime, Russia and the US.

Iran and the Syrian regime feared that *Operation Euphrates Shield* would inhibit their military operations. By prioritising the containment of Kurdish ambitions in Syria, Ankara diverted Syrian rebels away from the fight against the regime. The fall of rebel-held eastern Aleppo in December 2016 was a significant setback for Turkey. It was made worse by Iranian-backed militias' decisive role in seizing the city and subsequent expansion across northern Syria.

In the face of these setbacks, the Turkish government engaged in increasingly strident and sectarian rhetoric. President Recep Tayyip Erdogan and other Turkish leaders warned against Persian 'expansionism' and Iranian 'sectarian policies', expressing concern about the emergence of two 'Shia states' on their southern border. The approach drew criticism from Tehran: although the Iranian government adopted an accommodating tone, hardline Iranian leaders derided, and vowed to counter, Erdogan's alleged imperial ambitions. Turkey's apparent alignment with Saudi Arabia on Yemen and other matters also caused concern in Iran, as did Erdogan's attempts to influence the Trump administration. Turkish businessmen linked to Erdogan had hired Michael Flynn, a proponent of a hardline approach to Iran, as a lobbyist. But Trump's decision to fire Flynn as his national security adviser after just 24 days in post, combined with Erdogan's failure to sway US officials on Kurdish policy and the operation to retake Raqqa, illustrated the limits of Turkey's power in Washington. Indeed, Iran watched with satisfaction as Turkey's relations with the US and many other Western states deteriorated, apparently forcing Ankara to seek detente on its eastern border and with Asian powers sympathetic to Iran.

Iran's swift, unconditional expression of support for Erdogan after the July 2016 coup attempt in Turkey helped keep the countries' rivalry in check. They also found common ground in their opposition to re-energised Kurdish separatist groups, which provided a basis for cooperation between their security services. However, the complexities of the Iraqi and Syrian battlefields created discord between Ankara and Tehran. Iran maintained good relations with the Patriotic Union of Kurdistan and the PKK in Iraq, seeking to help the latter group establish control of the strategically important Sinjar region. In contrast, the PKK's activities compelled Turkey to conduct airstrikes in the region. Simultaneously, both Ankara and Tehran opposed Kurdish bids for independence in Syria and Iraq.

Syria's civil war

In Syria, the Assad regime and its allies had gained the upper hand militarily and politically. The rebels' significant territorial losses had not led to total defeat but blocked any path to victory. The capture of rebel-held eastern Aleppo dealt a debilitating blow to the non-jihadist rebellion and the political opposition. Driven from its largest urban base, the fragmented rebellion lost standing and influence at home and abroad. Some rebel groups, including Islamist forces in Idlib and those east of Damascus, once again descended into infighting.

Following their conquest of Aleppo, pro-regime forces conducted high-tempo joint operations to recover strategically important territory along the western routes linking Aleppo to Damascus. Rebel weakness and the Astana de-escalation process also freed Assad's troops to conduct operations in Idlib and Hama provinces. Attempts by Iranian forces and their militia allies to control areas around the Iraqi border and to establish a presence next to Jordan and Israel were unacceptable for both countries, as well as the US – which sought to shore up rebels fighting ISIS and even conducted strikes against regime forces. This escalation threatened to turn eastern Syria into an arena of direct confrontation between Washington and Tehran. Uncertainty about the extent to which the US would commit to this fight, and what strategy it would adopt, loomed over the calculations of all powers involved in the Syrian conflict.

Some forces, primarily those of the regime, engaged in ethnic cleansing. There were increasing transfers of fighters and civilians from besieged and defeated areas across the country to Idlib, turning the jihadist-dominated region into a prime recipient of internally displaced persons, as well as a focal point of the violence. Illustrating the complexity of the conflict, an agreement mediated by Iran and Qatar allowed for the sieges of Shia towns in Idlib and Sunni villages in the south to be lifted simultaneously, and civilians subsequently transferred to other areas. The UN expressed its reservations about the deal as it contravened international humanitarian law.

The weakened mainstream was increasingly vulnerable to jihadist predation and enticement, as al-Qaeda affiliate Jabhat al-Nusra became a pivotal player in the conflict. Operating primarily from the province of Idlib, the group rebranded itself as Jabhat Fateh al-Sham and announced a formal break with al-Qaeda in July 2016. While the split had organisational effects, the new entity retained its jihadist ideology. The move was partly meant to attract other groups. Following the fall of Aleppo, Jabhat Fateh al-Sham once again rebranded itself as Tahrir al-Sham, an umbrella group that absorbed smaller extremist units such as Harakat Nour al-Din al-Zenki.

Groups opposed to Jabhat al-Nusra gathered under Ahrar al-Sham, a powerful Salafist organisation. The two alliances clashed regularly but, facing militarily superior regime forces, US and Russian airstrikes, and a loss of foreign support, they sought to limit their conflict with each other. Nonetheless, the rivalry between them detracted from rebel unity and combat effectiveness.

The battered central government had varying levels of control within the areas held by pro-regime forces. The magnitude of the devastation, a scarcity of resources, the development of local militias and a growing dependency on Iran and Russia all weakened Assad's authority. Nonetheless, he remained the indispensable orchestrator of regime politics and sought to appeal to sympathetic external audiences. Although the regime had little hope of being accepted by the international community, the faltering rebellion and the rise of Sunni extremists demoralised Assad's detractors at home and abroad, leading to tacit acceptance of his role. By mid-2017, Syria had effectively been partitioned into Turkish, Russian, Iranian and US zones of influence.

This development was a consequence of the contest to capture ISIS-held territory. The SDF – dominated by the YPG, the Syrian wing of the PKK – proved militarily competent and politically savvy. Having secured Western support and recognition for its fight against ISIS, the YPG sought to consolidate its authority over Rojava, a set of non-contiguous territories in northern Syria, and to develop a civilian administration there. Despite stabilising living and security conditions in Rojava, the YPG faced criticism for its alleged autocratic tendencies and discrimination against dissidents and Sunni Arab groups.

Stridently opposed to Kurdish aspirations for autonomy, Turkey supported competing anti-ISIS Syrian forces that sought to conquer territory west of the Euphrates River. Ankara's distrust of the Kurds converged with Russian concern about developing US–Kurdish ties. Importantly, Assad and Iran were also concerned about Washington's support for the SDF, as well as US attempts to establish a military presence in northern and eastern Syria. Such tensions made for a volatile battlefield, with occasional clashes between the various forces threatening to escalate into a greater confrontation. Moscow appeared unable or unwilling to compel pro-Assad and Iranian-backed forces to abide by its de-confliction arrangements with Washington.

Decline of the ISIS 'caliphate'

The nascent 'caliphate' ISIS proclaimed in June 2014 faced serious challenges as it entered its fourth year. The group had dramatically shrunk since its peak in 2015, losing some of its key leaders. By the end of 2016, it had also lost more than one-quarter of the territory it once held in Iraq and Syria, and all the territory it once held in Libya.

These territorial losses resulted from a combination of factors dating back to late 2014, especially *Operation Inherent Resolve*, the aerial campaign against the group launched by a US-led coalition in August that year. Other important factors included ad hoc, short-lived coordination between enemies of ISIS such as Shia, Sunni and Kurdish militias.

The coalition effectively degraded the group's ability to expand the territories it captured during its first year as a self-styled global state, while engaging in train, equip, advise and assist missions that enhanced the capabilities of the Iraqi security forces and Kurdish Peshmerga groups battling ISIS on various fronts. With the support of the aerial campaign, the Iraqi Army played a key role in retaking Ramadi and Fallujah, while Peshmerga fighters captured Sinjar. In October 2016, the coalition supported the Iraqi security forces, Peshmerga fighters, Sunni tribes and militias, and Shia groups in a combined effort to retake Mosul, the de facto ISIS capital in Iraq. The following January, the Iraqi government declared that it had driven ISIS out of the eastern side of the city; by June, the Iraqi security forces had recaptured 95% of Mosul and were advancing on the remaining ISIS-held areas of the Old City.

The activities of the controversial Hashd al-Shaabi, or Popular Mobilisation Units (PMU), also contributed to ISIS territorial losses. Responsible for documented atrocities against Arab Sunnis in Iraq, the predominantly Shia forces of the PMU were vital in expelling ISIS from Tikrit, Baiji and several areas of eastern Diyala province.

In August 2016, Turkey's *Operation Euphrates Shield* forced ISIS out of Jarablus, a key transit point for many foreign fighters crossing the Turkey–Syria border. This contributed to the reported fall in the number of foreign fighters crossing the border, from a peak of 2,000 per month to 50 per month. In February 2017, Turkey's offensive expelled ISIS from Bab, a city that connected ISIS-controlled areas of Aleppo with those it held in the provinces of Raqqa and Deir ez-Zor.

Although ISIS leader Abu Bakr al-Baghdadi remained at large, the group lost several senior figures who were critical to its military strategy and propaganda campaign. In July 2016, its de facto minister of war – Georgian-born Tarkhan Batirashvili, also known as Abu Omar al-Shishani – was killed in an airstrike while fighting Iraqi forces. One month later, long-time spokesman Taha Subhi Falaha, also known as Abu Muhammad al-Adnani, died in Aleppo. In September, a US airstrike in Raqqa killed the group's de facto minister of information, Wa'il Adil Hasan Salman al-Fayad, also known as Abu Muhammad al-Furqan. The following June, there were reports that Turki al-Binali, a Bahraini national who emerged as an influential ISIS cleric, had also died. Yet, although these losses had a noticeable effect on operations, the group continued to function coherently

In November 2016, as the battle for Mosul continued, Baghdadi released a statement highlighting what he saw as the increasingly important role of the *wilayat* (ISIS provinces) in relation to the group's territorial losses in Iraq and Syria. Although ISIS claimed to have established 39 *wilayat* across ten countries, the group no longer existed as a caliphate in a territorially coherent way. Not all of its territories in Iraq and Syria were contiguous, while its *wilayat* were geographically separated from the core and largely failed to provide governance to the populations it claimed to control (except for in small areas of Libya). As the political identities of the *wilayat* were only partially tied to those of ISIS territories in Iraq and Syria, they did not depend on the core for survival.

Responsible for a series of high-casualty attacks, the South Asian branch of ISIS, *wilayat* Khorasan, may have suffered major losses that degraded its capabilities. In April 2017, the US dropped a GBU-43 Massive Ordnance Air Blast, known colloquially as the 'mother of all bombs', on the group's stronghold in the Afghan province of Nangarhar. The same month, US and Afghan forces killed the leader of the *wilayat*, Sheikh Abdul Hasib.

A group referring to themselves as the 'soldiers of the Khilafah in Misr [Egypt]' carried out several operations in Egypt, some of which targeted Coptic Christians. In an interview with ISIS magazine *Al-Naba*, the group's leader made clear that it was distinct from the Sinai *wilayat*, but that they coordinated with each other as 'brethren'. This separate structure suggested that support for ISIS in Egypt was growing beyond the peninsula.

In May and June 2017, the security forces in the southern Philippine city of Marawi battled former members of the Abu Sayyaf Group who had sworn allegiance to Baghdadi. These militants included Indonesians and Malaysians, suggesting that ISIS was gaining momentum in, and appealing to foreign fighters across, Southeast Asia. In June the previous year, ISIS had released a video produced by what it referred to as 'the Philippines', which featured several Syria-based groups composed of fighters from that country, as well as Indonesia and Malaysia. They called on their supporters in Southeast Asia to join the caliphate in Syria or, failing that, the 'caliphate in the Philippines'. (From August 2016 onwards, the group's statements were produced under the name 'East Asia'.) In response to the violence in Marawi, Philippine President Rodrigo Duterte imposed martial law on the southern Philippines, while *Al-Naba* claimed that supporters of ISIS had 'taken control' of the city.

Nonetheless, the group's territorial losses in Iraq and Syria looked set to continue. Although this undermined its ideological narrative predicated on territorial strength, and despite the dramatic decrease in foreign fighters joining the group, ISIS continued to conduct or inspire attacks in the West, particularly Europe.

Iraq's disorder and divisions

The accelerating campaign against ISIS combined with political paralysis in Baghdad to empower the PMU, a fragmented sub-state structure comprising around 50 militias and at least 60,000 fighters. Although they were often described as strategic assets of Iran, the numerous constituent groups had varying ideological and political inclinations. Shia militias in the PMU were broadly divided into three categories, affiliated with either Ayatollah Ali al-Sistani; the Shia politician Moqtada al-Sadr; or Iran and, for tactical reasons, former prime minister Nuri al-Maliki. The third set appeared to be the most powerful, as it included larger militias such as Kata'ib Hizbullah and Asa'ib Ahl al-Haq. Against this background, the rise of the PMU did not entail a concentration of power within a single coherent entity, but rather the proliferation of heavily armed non-state actors vying for influence in Iraq. Although Christian, Sunni, Turkmen and other groups operated under the PMU umbrella, the more powerful Shia militias co-opted many of them, such as the Yazidi force in Sinjar.

Many of the more organisationally coherent, Iranian-backed PMU units have undermined the Iraqi government's objective of rebuilding its security apparatus and implementing a process of reconciliation with communities that had previously been dominated by ISIS. This caused tensions across the northwest of Iraq that exacerbated political competition in Baghdad and attracted criticism from Gulf Arab states, particularly Saudi Arabia.

Iranian-backed PMU groups sought to secure strategic victories and translate their military standing into political influence ahead of the 2018 national election. In an effort to increase their political legitimacy and influence, the PMU militias carefully cultivated their public image, celebrating their victories and sacrifices in an effort to embarrass and constrain the government. As a consequence, in post-Mosul Iraq they aimed to become political and social movements. Geographically, they focused on Tal Afar and Sinjar in an effort to establish a zone of influence, allowing them to join with allied militias operating in Syria and complicate US plans in northern Iraq and Syria. Members of the PMU were implicated in human-rights violations involving captured ISIS fighters, as well as civilians from Sunni communities across northern Iraq.

Sadr, founder of the Saraya al-Salam militia, embodied these trends. His complicated relationship with Iran and historical rivalry with Maliki set him apart from many other Iraqi Shia leaders. He defied Tehran by opposing PMU involvement in Mosul, criticising Iraqi Shia groups' intervention in Syria and calling for Assad to step down. Sadr demonstrated his widespread appeal from 2015 and especially in 2017 by mobilising thousands of Iraqis to demand extensive political reform. This campaign for reform put intense pressure on Prime Minister Abadi, who was unable to deliver on its demands. Abadi also sought to counter the influence of the PMU by sidelining its component militias on the battlefield and empowering the Iraqi security forces, especially the Golden Division of the Counter Terrorism Service. More generally, he sought to rebuild the prestige of the Iraqi military, which had lost the public's faith by collapsing before the ISIS advance on Mosul in 2014.

Abadi's efforts had ambiguous results: several edicts and laws, designed to bring the PMU under government control, actually gave the organisation recognition and access to state resources. Order 91, issued by the prime minister's office in July 2016, described the PMU as an independent military formation that was part of the Iraqi armed forces. A law passed by parliament in November established the PMU as a separate military corps.

After the government prevented the PMU from participating in the fight for Mosul, Iranian-backed Shia militias chose to conquer ISIS territory south and west of the city, an area in which the town of Tal

Afar was the main strategic prize. By June 2017, they had made significant advances, reaching the Iraqi–Syrian border and linking up with advancing forces loyal to Assad and Iran in Syria. By seizing control of contiguous areas on the two battlefields, anti-US forces had gained an advantage in any future confrontation, as they would be able to move fighters and weaponry through their territory relatively quickly and cheaply.

Political wrangling in Baghdad and a loss of faith in Iraqi institutions also encouraged the military forces loyal to the Kurdish Regional Government to assert their control over Kirkuk and other disputed territory. Masoud Barzani, president of the Kurdish Regional Government (KRG), announced that it would hold a referendum on independence in September 2017. Leaders in Baghdad reacted angrily to the news. However, given the unstable nature of its politics and the perilous state of its economy, the KRG remained heavily dependent on Baghdad for financial support. Thus, Barzani's announcement of a referendum was most likely a bargaining ploy rather than the start of a quick march to independence. Meanwhile, Abadi was keen to use the recapture of Mosul to discredit his detractors, publicly criticising his predecessor for having overseen the collapse of the Iraqi Army before the ISIS advance in 2014, and for having allowed some Shia militias to persecute Sunni communities. It seemed likely that these political and sectarian tensions would be accentuated in the 2018 national election campaign.

Turkey's descent into authoritarianism

At first sight, the year to mid-2017 was one in which Turkish President Erdogan strengthened his grip on domestic power. After surviving a bloody, if shambolic, coup attempt during 15–16 July 2016, Erdogan declared a state of emergency that he used to implement massive purges of perceived opponents and to tighten his control over Turkey's already largely cowed and submissive media. In a constitutional referendum held on 16 April 2017, Turks voted by 51.4% to 48.6% to replace the country's parliamentary system with one in which all political power would be concentrated in the presidency. Scheduled to come into effect in November 2019, the new system will remove virtually all constitutional checks and balances.

However, Erdogan's growing authoritarianism was also a sign of weakness, a tacit acknowledgement that – unlike during his early years in office – he no longer believed that he could remain in power by democratic means. By June 2017, 12 elected members of the Turkish parliament – all of them members of the pro-Kurdish Peoples' Democratic Party – had been imprisoned, and there were pending charges against another 34. More than 150 journalists had been jailed and thousands more dismissed from their jobs due to pressure from the government. The crackdown also extended to the general public, with more than 4,000 people facing charges – mostly under laws that forbid 'insulting the president' – for posts on social media or alleged overheard comments.

By June 2017, the state of emergency had been used to close 131 media outlets and 1,552 non-governmental organisations, as well as to dismiss 102,000 civil servants and suspend 30,000 others. The dismissals included more than 5,000 academics at the country's universities. Moreover, the government removed – and, in most cases, imprisoned – elected officials in 79 of the 106 eastern municipalities won by pro-Kurdish parties in the March 2014 local elections. It replaced them with political appointees loyal to Erdogan's Justice and Development Party (AKP).

Even the constitutional referendum was marred by unprecedented restrictions on 'No' campaigners and, on the day of the vote, numerous allegations of fraud and voting irregularities. Many of these allegations appeared to be well founded, as they were backed up by photographs and videos posted on social media. The Supreme Electoral Board – which is responsible for overseeing all voting procedures in Turkey and is dominated by AKP appointees – refused to investigate any of the allegations. Most extraordinarily, on the night of the referendum, after the counting had begun, the board abruptly announced that it had acceded to a request from the AKP to suspend the legal requirement that all valid ballot papers carry an official stamp – thereby removing the main safeguard against the practice of stuffing ballot boxes.

As concern about the rule of law in Turkey intensified, there was a steep rise in reports of the torture and wider maltreatment of people who had been taken into custody, particularly those who had been detained in relation to the July 2016 coup attempt.

On the evening of 15 July 2016, units of the Turkish Land Forces took control of a handful of locations in Istanbul, including the city's main international airport and the two bridges over the Bosphorus, while helicopters and F-16 warplanes struck several targets in Ankara, among them the headquarters of the National Intelligence Organization, the police Special Operations Forces, the parliament building and Erdogan's palace – although, at the time, he was on holiday in the Mediterranean resort of Marmaris. At midnight, a squad-sized unit of putschists stormed the offices of the state-owned TRT television channel and forced a presenter to read out a statement, live on air, that the military had seized power to reverse Erdogan's accelerating Islamisation of the Turkish state.

Yet, by the time of this broadcast, it was already clear that the putsch was doomed. Virtually all of the 510,000 members of Turkey's military and its 250,000 police officers had remained loyal to the regime. These forces had surrounded the putschists in most locations. Nonetheless, at around 12.45am on 16 July, Erdogan appeared on national television to call for his supporters to take to the streets to resist the coup attempt. An estimated 200 civilians lost their lives in the subsequent clashes. By 10am, the coup was effectively over: the authorities had detained the 3,000 troops who had actively participated in it, most of them conscripts and cadets who had been told by their commanders that they were participating in a military exercise.

On the evening of 15 July, as soon as news of the attempted putsch broke, the Turkish government immediately blamed the followers of Erdogan's former ally, the 75-year-old Islamic preacher Fethullah Gülen, who has been living in self-imposed exile in the United States since 1999. However, it soon became apparent that, although some of Gülen's followers may have been involved, the putschists also included Turkish ultranationalists and hardline secularists. Indeed, by

June 2017, many of the details of the putsch remained unclear, including the identity of the ringleaders, how the putschists expected to seize power with such limited resources and how they planned to govern the country if the coup succeeded.

Turkey's aggressive stance on the PYD led to further deterioration in its relations with the US, which had already been strained by Washington's refusal to extradite Gülen without convincing evidence that he was behind the July 2016 coup. To Ankara's fury, Washington announced on 8 May 2017 that it would begin direct supplies of weapons and equipment to the YPG.

By June 2017, US–Turkish relations appeared to be on the verge of a major crisis. Ankara's relations with its other traditional allies were equally parlous. Members of the European Union, particularly Germany, were reluctant to jeopardise the March 2016 agreement with Ankara that had resulted in a steep decline in the number of Syrian refugees entering Europe. Nonetheless, there was a growing sense that something had to be done about Turkey's descent into authoritarianism and the rapid erosion of not only human rights but also the rule of law in the country.

Although the full transition to the new political system was due to take place following the presidential election scheduled for November 2019, there was a widespread expectation that Erdogan would try to bring the election forward – likely to sometime in 2018. But there appeared to be little prospect that the new system would be adequate for addressing the instability in Turkey, much less resolving the country's many other problems. Indeed, Erdogan's purges had caused social turmoil and stripped the state apparatus of much-needed expertise. There were particularly acute concerns about Turkey's economic prospects, amid fears that a downturn would severely exacerbate the dangerously high tensions in Turkish society.

Rouhani's re-election and Iran's regional relations

The Obama administration spent its last six months in office trying to strengthen the Iran nuclear deal. Reports from the International Atomic

Energy Agency (IAEA) confirmed that Tehran was implementing the Joint Comprehensive Plan of Action (JCPOA). Yet support for the deal from major international powers contrasted with growing Arab distrust of Iran, stinging criticism of the agreement from Republicans in Washington and virulent attacks from Trump, who disparaged its terms.

Iran engaged in a lively domestic debate in the lead-up to the May 2017 presidential elections. The battle over the legacy of President Rouhani and the merits of maintaining a relationship with the US, especially after the election of Trump, framed the process. On 19 May, Rouhani – whose mentor and protector Akbar Hashemi Rafsanjani had recently died – achieved a surprise first-round victory in the elections on a high turnout, gaining 57% of the vote against 38% for his more conservative opponent, Ebrahim Raisi. Contrary to expectations, the arms of the state associated with the Supreme Leader, Sayyid Ali Khamenei, did not intervene to alter the results as they had in 2009.

Rouhani had fought a short but energetic campaign in which he mobilised large crowds across the country, flaunted the 2015 nuclear deal as a success vindicating his approach to international affairs and promised to focus on improving daily life and the economy. Raisi – a former hardline judge and reportedly a leading candidate to succeed Khamenei – became the conservative choice after the withdrawal of his competitors. Raisi mounted relentless attacks on Rouhani's strategy of regional and international engagement.

The election results prompted spontaneous celebrations in large cities, where support for Rouhani was strongest. He also scored well in regions with sizeable Kurdish and Sunni populations, as well as among young people and other social groups – and even in Mashhad, Raisi's hometown. His success was broadly interpreted as a mandate for normalising Iran's relations with other countries and for reviving the domestic reforms of Mohammad Khatami, president during 1997–2005.

Nonetheless, the election seemed to be first of all a vote against Raisi and the potential return to self-imposed isolation. A majority of

Iranians also rejected the conservatives' inflationist, redistributive economic policies. Raisi campaigned on a contradiction: while adopting a discourse of social justice in which he was the defender of the poor, he also headed the religious foundation Astan-e-Quds, one of the largest conglomerates in Iran. This marriage of crony capitalism and leftist discourse failed to gain public support. Raisi's defeat also appeared to be the result of revolutionary fatigue among most Iranians, who dismissed his advocacy of the 'revolutionary preference'.

Raisi had proposed redistributing oil income through direct handouts and other state benefits, a strategy that failed to strengthen the economy under the Ahmadinejad administration and that seemed even more problematic at a time of low oil prices. Although almost one million Iranians had slipped into poverty during Rouhani's first term, many feared that the economy would fare even worse under a radical, isolationist president. The middle class appeared to prefer a centrist president whose foreign policy prioritised socio-economic development over confrontation.

During the start of his second term, Rouhani strengthened his position by managing public discontent, an ability that proved his value to Khamenei. His popularity among both the public and parts of the economic elite provided another layer of protection against criticism from hardliners. Rouhani's performance was likely to be critical to the future of Iran; if sufficiently successful, he might have considerable influence on the process of selecting Khamenei's successor.

However, Rouhani faced a complex task and considerable challenges. To advance the civil liberties that many Iranians yearned for and to neutralise his conservative critics, he had to improve economic conditions for the population. This task depended on regional and international economic integration, which in turn rested on the implementation of the nuclear deal and continued sanctions relief. Unelected clerical and security leaders have the ability to hinder the implementation of this agenda, particularly on civil rights. Moreover, the IRGC sought to protect its business interests and advance an economic agenda that prioritised relations with Russia and China. Rouhani's efforts to obtain further sanctions relief also had to overcome a Trump administration and US Congress that sought to impose sanctions on Iran's missile programme and politico-military activities across the Middle East, areas largely controlled by hardline Iranian leaders.

Even as Iran maintained its military involvement in Syria, Iraq and – to a considerably lesser extent – Yemen, Rouhani made overtures of detente towards GCC states. He visited Kuwait and Oman in the hope that they would persuade other GCC states to improve their relations with Iran. Yet Rouhani's attempts at de-escalation were undercut by the IRGC's deepening role in Syria, where it contributed to the capture of Aleppo and large-scale displacement, and its backing of Shia militias in Iraq. Rouhani reportedly opposed the force's more limited role in Yemen. The visible presence of Qassem Suleimani, head of the IRGC's Quds Force, on the Syrian and Iraqi battlefields reinforced the notion that Rouhani was either too weak or too obedient to oppose Iranian hardliners on regional policy.

The president and his foreign minister made a great effort to protect the JCPOA, obtaining European and other international support for the deal despite criticism from the incoming Trump administration. In the last months of the Obama administration, Tehran and the Financial Action Task Force reached an agreement to slowly integrate Iran's banking sector into the international financial system, thereby encouraging trade and investment. Under the deal, Iran was required to reform the structure of its banking system in line with international standards and to end its financial support for proxy groups in the Middle East that Washington designated as terrorist groups. The agreement also demanded that the country address international concerns about its role in money laundering.

European support for the JCPOA, as well as the IAEA reports noting Iran's compliance with its terms, alleviated some pressure. Tehran finalised high-profile deals with Boeing and Airbus to modernise its commercial aircraft fleet. However, by mid-2017, it had yet to strike any new, large-scale oil deals. Many international energy companies showed an interest in Iranian projects, with French firm Total signing a US$4.7bn agreement covering parts of the South Pars gas field. But the prospect of new sanctions, combined with the difficulty of doing business in Iran, slowed negotiations on major commercial ventures. There was a possibility that additional US sanctions would bolster Iran's hardliners, undermining the JCPOA and deterring foreign investment.

Much hinged on relations with the US. The Trump administration seemed torn between a dramatic pressuring of Iran – as demanded by Saudi Arabia, many in Congress and powerful members of the administration – and a less confrontational approach. There was a considerable risk of escalation in Syria, Iraq and elsewhere. Split between two camps that dreaded and courted such escalation respectively, Iran faced many domestic and foreign challenges to Rouhani's narrative of a peaceful economic rise.

Saudi Arabia's new leadership and the Qatar crisis

Saudi Crown Prince Salman decisively strengthened his hold on power in the year to mid-2017. Having acquired key responsibilities in national security and economic development, he had become a pivotal figure in Riyadh's major decisions. Many of his close advisers received appointments to senior positions: his brother Khaled as ambassador to the US; his military assistants as senior leaders in the intelligence services and the armed forces; and allied royals as governors of important provinces.

Internally, Salman cultivated an image as a moderniser attuned to the aspirations of young Saudis, keen to replicate the economic success of the UAE. Projecting dynamism and marketing his reform plan as 'Vision 2030', Salman appealed to domestic and foreign audiences seeking to accelerate the pace of reforms and open up the Saudi economy. A flagship element of the plan was an initial public offering for 5% of state oil firm Saudi Aramco. Yet Riyadh faced a budgetary challenge: low oil prices combined with high defence spending to force cuts in public contracts, subsidies, salaries and benefits. The measures were lifted within a year due to the discontent they generated among important constituencies, including public-sector employees and influential trading families.

Salman also nurtured and deployed Saudi nationalism in the service of a hawkish foreign policy. Some at home and many abroad worried that his interventionist ventures, particularly in Yemen, would be extremely costly and lead to blowback. The rapid depletion of Saudi foreign-exchange reserves, military setbacks and the difficulty of maintaining consensus among nominal allies seemed to vindicate such concern.

Salman spearheaded Saudi engagement with the Trump administration, conducting high-profile meetings with the US president and orchestrating his May 2017 trip to Saudi Arabia. He also developed strong ties with UAE leader-in-waiting Mohammed bin Zayed. The alliance between the political and economic powerhouses of the Arabian Peninsula appeared to be designed to compel regional actors to align with their interests, while also serving as the backbone of an anti-Iran and anti-Islamist strategy. However, setbacks in Yemen and a rupture in relations with Qatar indicated the limits of such an alliance and its regional ambitions.

On 21 June, Salman replaced Mohammed bin Nayef as crown prince, a predicted yet momentous move that significantly altered Saudi politics and internal family dynamics. Indeed, it broke with a long tradition of maintaining a balance between the branches of the royal family and avoiding a concentration of power.

Two weeks earlier, Salman had reportedly backed an unprecedented move in intra-GCC relations. Following years of tension, Saudi Arabia and the UAE moved to confront and isolate Qatar. The proximate cause of the showdown was a statement attributed to Qatari leader Emir Tamim bin Hamad Al Thani, which according to Doha had been planted by hackers. The Saudi, Emirati and Bahraini governments cut all political, diplomatic and economic ties to Qatar, accusing Doha of fuelling dissent within their countries and endangering regional stability by supporting terrorist organisations and other Islamist groups, as well as by maintaining cordial relations with Iran. Among the severe measures they announced were bans on Qatari nationals and the closure of their airspace, waters and land borders to Qatar. The maximalist, public nature of Saudi Arabia's and the UAE's denunciations and demands suggested that this would be a protracted confrontation fuelled by a desire to subdue Qatar and assert their dominance of Gulf Arab politics.

The crisis threatened to upend Middle Eastern politics. It shattered claims of a broad Sunni Arab front against Iran; threatened already fragile efforts at Gulf political, security and economic integration; and deepened the divide between governments that supported the Muslim Brotherhood and those that viewed the group as a terrorist organisation. Jordan and other beneficiaries of Saudi and Emirati largesse sided with Riyadh and Abu Dhabi; Ankara affirmed its support for Qatar and sped up the deployment of Turkish soldiers to the country. Hamas, a frequent recipient of Qatari support, initiated a rapprochement with Iran, several years after parting ways with the Iranians because of their role in the Syrian conflict.

Heavily dependent on imports of food, goods and construction material, as well as access to foreign workers, Qatar reached out to Turkey and Iran. By the end of June 2017, there was a real possibility that the Saudi–Emirati move would stall and then possibly backfire, but Qatar had already incurred considerable economic costs and damage to its brand.

The crisis complicated Washington's policy in the region. Eager to maintain relations with its main Arab allies while operating from the Udeid air base in Qatar, the US resorted to mediating between its partners in the battle against ISIS amid accelerating operations to defeat the group and rising tension with Iran. Washington's approach appeared contradictory. Trump initially sided with Saudi Arabia and the UAE, publicly chiding Qatar for supporting extremism. The State Department and the Pentagon sought to resolve the crisis diplomatically while continuing to pursue weapons deals with Doha.

The Qatar crisis brought Saudi Arabia and Egypt back into alignment after a period of uneasy relations. Indeed, ties had soured over bilateral and regional matters in the year to mid-2017, but were ultimately sustained by overriding strategic interdependence. Ironically, it was an Egyptian attempt to pander to Riyadh that ignited discontent on both sides. Widespread popular opposition, criticism from regime supporters in parliament and legal challenges compelled President Sisi to temporarily halt his plan to transfer the Red Sea islands of Tiran and Sanafir to Saudi Arabia. Riyadh expressed its discontent with the delay through state media. For the Saudi government, Egypt's hesitation and the obstacles to the transfer raised by the Egyptian courts fuelled a sense of humiliation and injury inflicted by an ally that it had supported at great political and financial cost.

Bilateral relations came under further strain due to Cairo's conflicting positions on regional issues, particularly the Syrian conflict. In October 2016, Riyadh described Cairo's vote in favour of a Russian-backed Security Council resolution that benefited President Assad as 'painful'. Shortly thereafter, Sisi publicly declared his support for the Syrian president, describing Egypt's aim to back 'national armies to impose control over the territory, deal with extremists and impose the necessary stability in Libya, Syria and Iraq'. At the height of this tension, Saudi Aramco announced that it would suspend oil shipments to Egypt, despite a US$23bn deal for monthly deliveries of 700,000 tonnes of petroleum. Riyadh had already been disappointed by Egypt's merely symbolic contribution to the Saudi-led coalition in Yemen, which involved only naval deployments in the Bab al-Mandeb Strait.

The countries' diverging regional outlooks and objectives illustrated the limits of Riyadh's investment of around US$25bn in the Sisi government over four years to steer Egyptian foreign policy. Saudi Arabia sought a reliable partner in its rivalry with Iran and seemingly moderated its views of the Muslim Brotherhood. Egypt prioritised the reinstatement of a military-led state after the Arab Spring. For Cairo, Iran was not the main threat, while the Assad regime was preferable to the Islamist and jihadist groups that dominated the Syrian opposition.

Yet Cairo's retrenchment with Tehran was often overstated. Sisi sought to secure foreign support to strengthen his regime and pursue domestic objectives. This was evident in his attempts to diversify Egypt's alliances given its uneven relations with the Obama administration. Sisi's potentially risky strategy required him to balance key allies while maintaining a level of domestic credibility, an especially difficult challenge in light of his hyper-nationalist discourse and the severe deterioration of the Egyptian economy.

Facing their own economic challenges, many in Saudi Arabia viewed the effort to bankroll Sisi as having produced poor returns. But they could not accept the risk of spillover that would come with allowing the Egyptian regime to collapse. Acknowledging their mutual reliance in a volatile region, Egypt and Saudi Arabia moved towards rapprochement in March 2017, motivated in part by the sense that the Trump administration would back a Saudi–Egyptian alliance that respected US interests. This amounted to a mutual understanding rather than reconciliation. Their fundamental disagreements remained unresolved, with both parties seeking to minimise the damage.

In fact, tension between Riyadh and Cairo was neither new nor unexpected. Saudi Arabia's ascendance in the Middle East challenged – and, arguably, marginalised – Cairo's traditional role as a regional leader, a shift that Riyadh created with massive financial resources and a willingness to employ force. Egypt struggled to adapt to its diminished position.

War in Libya and Yemen

The conflict in Yemen entered its third year with no serious prospects for peace and neither side able to make a military breakthrough. Front-lines were largely static even as sieges in Ta'izz, and fighting in Ma'rib, Ibb and other provinces, caused massive damage and a humanitarian crisis. Superior Saudi and Emirati firepower did not translate into decisive victories against, or split, the alliance between the Houthi movement and the forces of former president Ali Abdullah Saleh. Although there were signs of increasing Iranian assistance to the Houthis, Tehran continued to see Yemen as an arena in which to pin down and harass Saudi Arabia at low cost. With the UN diplomatic mediation mission in Yemen faltering, the Saudi–Emirati side appeared to have no viable exit strategy. Saudi Arabia was targeted in raids across its border with Yemen and in ballistic-missile strikes, a humiliation that hardened Riyadh's view of the war.

Saudi Arabia and the UAE hoped that a large operation to capture Hodeida – a major port city on the Red Sea and the economic lifeline of Houthi-controlled areas – would change the dynamics of the conflict. Yet the UN and others criticised the move for endangering food supply as famine spread throughout the country. Indeed, the humanitarian toll of the war and numerous attacks violating the Law of Armed Conflict generated increasing media coverage and international condemnation, forcing Riyadh and Abu Dhabi to publicly defend their intervention. The collapse of Yemen's health sector and food supply led to large-scale outbreaks of cholera.

There were tactical differences between Saudi Arabia and the UAE. Riyadh, at least rhetorically, maintained the capture of Sana'a and the restoration of the Hadi government as its main objectives. In contrast, and reflecting the difficulty of the fight, the UAE shifted its focus to southern Yemen. Abu Dhabi sought to stabilise areas in the south, particularly those along the coast, and to combat al-Qaeda in the Arabian Peninsula – which lost the city of Mukalla to joint US–UAE operations conducted alongside local groups. However, discontent with the internationally recognised but largely dysfunctional Hadi government encouraged groups in the south to pursue their own separatist agendas. This led to battles between nominally allied forces in Aden and other areas, in which the UAE supported anti-Hadi forces.

Libya remained divided between multiple forces vying for control of what was left of its political institutions, territory and resources. The international community, especially the EU, grew increasingly concerned that deteriorating conditions in the country would foster terrorism and force a growing number of refugees to flee to Europe across the Mediterranean Sea.

The main contest in Libya pitted the UN-backed, Tripoli-based Government of National Accord (GNA), headed by Fayez al-Sarraj, against the Libyan National Army (LNA), led by Khalifa Haftar. The latter derived its legitimacy from the Tobruk-based House of Representatives, receiving support from Egypt and the UAE. The war in Libya also involved a variety of local, Islamist and jihadist militant groups, including Misratan militias, a Benghazi-based Islamist group, al-Qaeda and ISIS.

Sarraj and Haftar both faced internal challenges to their authority. In late 2016, Sarraj foiled a coup mounted by his predecessor, Khalifa al-Ghawil. Sarraj's and Haftar's factions competed partly by seizing territory from other groups, thereby expanding their areas of control and claims to legitimacy. Haftar's forces were stronger – not least due to their air capabilities and superior organisation – but were nonetheless unable to decisively defeat the GNA.

Sarraj and Haftar held direct talks in Abu Dhabi in May 2017, their second meeting since December 2015, when the former assumed his position. Yet the peace proposal put forth by the UAE as a basis for an agreement faced significant hurdles, particularly as it lacked the support of various actors on the ground. This problem came to the fore in May, when the GNA foreign minister suggested that Haftar lead a unified national army, causing outrage among Tripoli- and Misrata-based militias. They doubted that they would have a place in a force commanded by an avowed anti-Islamist such as Haftar, and remained wary of the UAE. On 18 May, GNA-aligned militias carried out an attack that killed 41 members of the LNA.

Against this background, the GNA's authority continued to wane within the areas it claimed to control. Not only was the GNA seen as dependent on militias that had their own, often competing agendas, but it had a poor governance record. Lacking an official budget, the GNA was only able to provide basic services intermittently, while inflation continued to spiral. Its faltering authority on the ground cast doubt on the worth of controversial agreements signed by Sarraj and the EU in February 2017 to stem the flow of African migrants travelling to Europe through Libya. As a result, the international community began to accept Haftar as a key actor in Libya's future.

Despite expressing support for the UN peace process, Egypt and the UAE were involved in military operations in Libya. In May and June, Egypt conducted airstrikes on the Derna-based Mujahideen Shura Council in retaliation for the killing of 28 Coptic Christians south of Cairo, an attack that ISIS claimed to have carried out. The countries also complicated mediation efforts by hosting parallel peace talks. Using counter-terrorism as a pretext, Egypt and the UAE worked alongside foreign powers to support – and allegedly arm (in defiance of UN sanctions) – Haftar, allowing him to act independently of the GNA.

Cairo viewed Haftar as a strategic asset able to secure Libya's eastern border and prevent the conflict there from spreading to Egypt. Egyptian officials believed that only a strong army led by Haftar could bring an end to the chaos. Furthermore, a secure, oil-exporting Libya would bring economic benefits to Egypt by hosting Egyptian labourers. Turkey, Qatar and Sudan backed Islamist militia groups in Libya, some of them loyal to the GNA. These groups included the Benghazi Defence Brigades, an organisation that was allegedly linked to al-Qaeda in the Islamic Maghreb, and that engaged in ferocious battles with Haftar's forces in the eastern 'oil crescent' the following March.

Following its successful intervention in Syria, Russia saw faltering Western efforts in Libya as providing another opportunity to pursue its interests, partly by countering NATO's influence there. The resulting confrontation affected diplomacy at the UN. At Israel's urging, the US blocked Salam Fayyad's appointment as UN special representative to Libya, prompting Russia to veto that of Richard Wilcox, a candidate put forward by the US. The decision was widely interpreted as Moscow's attempt to display its interest in, and influence on, Libyan affairs. With Martin Kobler remaining in position as special representative, this lack of consensus further marginalised the UN in Libya.

Russia also used the Libyan conflict to expand its regional alliances. Its convergence with Egypt led to cooperation between the countries. In March, Russian special forces deployed to an air base near Salloum, close to the Egyptian border with Libya, while Russian aircraft reportedly flew operations in Libya out of Marsa Matrouh.

In January, Russia invited Haftar aboard the *Admiral Kuznetsov*, an aircraft carrier that had supported operations in Syria. He also visited Moscow in an attempt to garner Russian material and political support. However, by mid-2017 he had not received a shipment of Russian weapons worth US$2bn, under a deal announced six months earlier.

Although Washington saw the fight against ISIS in Libya as a lower priority than that in Syria and Iraq, the US military conducted operations against the group there alongside European forces, particularly French troops. In early December 2016, following months of airstrikes and heavy fighting on the ground, local allied forces expelled ISIS from Sirte. However, the group retained a presence in the oil crescent between Sirte, Ras Lanuf and Benghazi, generating concern that access to smuggling networks and flows of foreign fighters – especially those crossing Libya's southern and western borders – would allow it to re-emerge.

The operation against ISIS in Libya also created a power vacuum in some areas. The LNA clashed with groups such as the Benghazi Defence Brigades for control of territory formerly held by ISIS, not least in the oil crescent. Largely focused on fighting Haftar, the Benghazi Defence Brigades dealt him a significant blow by capturing LNA-controlled oil ports in March.

In this context, the future of al-Qaeda affiliates in Libya remained unclear. Ansar al-Sharia, one such affiliate, announced its dissolution on 27 May. The declaration came after some of its members defected to ISIS in Sirte and many others, including most of its leaders, died in battle. *Operation Dignity*, an anti-Islamist military offensive launched by Haftar in Benghazi in 2014, had taken a heavy toll on the group.

Israel's regional outreach

The Obama administration's efforts to revive the Israeli–Palestinian peace process met with little success. Israeli settlement expansion continued to be the largest obstacle to talks and a two-state solution. In December 2016, the UN Security Council adopted Resolution 2334 condemning Israel's settlements in 'Palestinian territories occupied since 1967'. Washington's decision to abstain on the vote for the resolution

– rather than use its veto – was the culmination of years of bitter, antagonistic relations between the Obama administration and Israeli Prime Minister Benjamin Netanyahu. After experiencing a long period of diplomatic tension, mostly rooted in the 2015 Iranian nuclear deal and the international rehabilitation of Tehran, the outgoing US administration eventually decided to express its public disapproval of Israel's policy. However, the abstention came too late to make a difference, as did a speech by Kerry outlining his view of a final settlement. However, the US–Israeli defence relationship remained strong: a few months before the showdown, Obama approved a record package of US$38bn in US military aid to Israel.

The November 2016 election of President Trump, who repeatedly expressed his full support for Israel, marked a clear break with the Obama administration. Predictably, Netanyahu and other Israeli hardliners greeted Trump's anti-Iran and pro-Israel inclinations with enthusiasm. Rhetorically, especially while campaigning for office, Trump embraced views on Israel that ran counter to established US policy. After vowing to relocate the American Embassy in Israel from Tel Aviv to Jerusalem, he asserted on 16 February 2017 that a two-state solution may not be the only way to resolve the Israeli–Palestinian conflict. By breaking with the international consensus at a time when Israel faced growing criticism, he confirmed the opening of a new era of cooperation between the US and Israel. Netanyahu calculated that Trump could help persuade Egypt and Saudi Arabia to normalise their relations with Israel without a peace settlement, and could shape Palestinian politics to isolate Hamas and compel the Palestinian Authority to revise its demands.

More settlement buildings were constructed in the West Bank and East Jerusalem in the first half of 2017 than in all of 2016, a year in which settlement construction had risen by 40% compared with 2015. During his visit to Jerusalem in May 2017, Trump recalled his commitment to broker what he called 'the ultimate deal' in the peace process. Nonetheless, his actual engagement with the process remained highly uncertain: Trump's team, comprising his son-in-law Jared Kushner and special envoy Jason Greenblatt, had yet to provide details on how they would restart negotiations.

The instability of the region also had a significant impact on relations between Israel and Gulf Arab states, whose interests partially converged due to the fallout from the 2011 Arab Spring and the polarising effect of Saudi–Iranian rivalry. A committed opponent of Iran, Israel worked to court Gulf Arab states by capitalising on their shared strategic interests. Yet Arab public opinion meant that their ties remained discreet and limited: Israeli security and high-tech companies won contracts in several Gulf Arab states, while an Israeli representative of the International Renewable Energy Agency was welcomed in Abu Dhabi. There were also reports of secret meetings to discuss Iranian activities in the region, as well as limited intelligence sharing.

Nonetheless, relations between Israel and the Gulf Arab states were constrained by the ongoing Israeli–Palestinian conflict, a critical issue for the populations of GCC countries. Therefore, this convergence was tentative, and seemingly aimed at testing how the region would respond to a deal with Israel.

The UAE backed Mohammed Dahlan, a Gaza strongman and former leader of Fatah, as an alternative to the chairman of the Palestinian Authority. In Riyadh, members of the establishment publicly called for a more conciliatory approach towards Israel (albeit without the government's imprimatur). The *Wall Street Journal* reported in May 2017 that the UAE and Saudi Arabia had created an unprecedented proposal to partially normalise relations with Israel, on the condition that the Netanyahu government froze settlement construction in the occupied territories and eased trade restrictions in Gaza. These posited Israeli concessions were far less stringent than those in the 2002 Arab Peace Initiative, which demanded the establishment of an independent Palestinian state. Although there was no official response to the alleged plan, reports of such an agreement seemed to signal a period of re-evaluation in the Gulf region. In June, Israeli Defense Minister Avigdor Lieberman seized on the Qatar crisis as an opportunity to enhance counter-terrorism cooperation between Israel and what he called 'moderate Arab states'. By mid-2017, it was still unclear whether they would enter into a formal arrangement.

Zemlya Frantsa Iosifa
Severnaya Zemlya
Arctic Ocean
Novaya Zemlya
Novosibirskiye Ostrova
RUSSIAN FEDERATION
Moscow
Kaliningrad (Russia)
Minsk
BELARUS
Kiev
UKRAINE
MOLDOVA
Chisinau
Astana
KAZAKHSTAN
Bering Sea
GEORGIA
Tbilisi
Yerevan
ARMENIA
AZERBAIJAN
Baku
TURKMENISTAN
Ashgabat
UZBEKISTAN
Tashkent
Bishkek
KYRGYZSTAN
TAJIKISTAN
Dushanbe
Pacific Ocean
Capital
Borders
2000 miles
3000km
©IISS

Chapter 8

Russia and Eurasia

Throughout the year to mid-2017, Eurasian politics continued to be dominated by Russia's stand-off with the United States and Europe, and Russia's involvement in the conflicts in Ukraine and the Middle East. Russia and the West viewed each other as a defence priority, if not an outright threat. In an updated foreign-policy concept released in November 2016, Moscow accused the Euro-Atlantic community of promoting instability and regional conflict, warning that it would take action if Western countries sought to interfere in the internal affairs of other states outside the framework of international law.

The election of Donald Trump as US president in November 2016 raised the possibility of a fundamental shift in the relationship between Moscow and Washington – one with major implications for European security and the conflicts in Ukraine and the Middle East. Trump's agenda appeared to imply a desire for greater cooperation with Russia in combating international terrorist groups – particularly the Islamic State, also known as ISIS or ISIL – in the region. He had shown little interest in the war in Ukraine, prompting speculation that the United States might lift the sanctions imposed on Russia for its annexation of Crimea and wider role in the conflict.

Yet by mid-2017, Trump had failed to articulate a clear vision for the future of the US–Russia relationship. The resulting uncertainty was compounded by allegations that Russia interfered in the US presidential elections, and that members of Trump's campaign team had colluded with Russian officials. As a consequence, there remained a risk that the relationship would deteriorate further. The US military conducted a missile strike on a Syrian air base in April and downed a Syrian aircraft in June, casting doubt on prospects for US–Russia counter-terrorism cooperation and reviving Moscow's fear that Washington would continue to push for the removal of Syrian President Bashar al-Assad, a Russian ally. Trump's presidency did nothing to allay Russian concerns about the missile-defence programme and evolving conventional capabilities of the US. Ongoing militarisation by both sides imperilled arms-control treaties: in March 2017, US officials for the first time publicly accused Russia of violating the 1987 Intermediate-Range Nuclear Forces (INF) Treaty. Trump made no move to ease Ukraine-related sanctions on Russia; in June 2017, the US Senate put forward additional sanctions in response to Russian interference in the elections, as well as to codify the existing regime.

While the relationship with Moscow became a source of controversy in the US, Russia's foreign policy appeared to have entered a holding pattern after the shock of its direct intervention in the Syrian conflict in September 2015. This reflected uncertainty about future relations with the US, the desire to create room for easing tension with Washington and a partial shift in focus towards domestic issues in the run-up to the Russian presidential elections, scheduled for early 2018. In contrast to those of previous years, President Vladimir Putin's December 2016 state of the nation speech primarily dealt with domestic and social issues.

Although Russia's military intervention in Syria tipped the conflict decisively in the regime's favour, it remained unlikely that Assad would restore his control of the entire country. Following the capture of eastern Aleppo from the rebels in December, regime forces held almost all major population centres in Syria. Russia subsequently stepped up its efforts to reach a political settlement by launching peace negotiations in Astana, Kazakhstan's capital, in parallel with the process in Geneva.

Moscow seemed to have achieved its goals of shoring up the Assad regime and safeguarding Russian military assets in Syria. However, having established itself, alongside Iran, as one of the pre-eminent external actors in the conflict, Russia became responsible for orchestrating peace talks that were far from achieving a lasting settlement. Russia's intervention in Syria also failed to recast its relations with the West, with the brutal aerial campaign to recapture Aleppo eliciting strong criticism from the European Union.

While Russia increased its diplomatic activity in Syria in the year to mid-2017, it expended little effort to move the conflict in Ukraine towards a resolution. Relations between the EU and Moscow were still shaped by the Ukraine conflict and broader concerns about Russian expansionism. The EU retained the unity to keep in place its sanctions on Russia's defence, energy and financial sectors. As in the previous year, the Ukraine conflict persisted at a relatively low intensity, with neither the government nor rebel forces making territorial gains. As the Ukrainian and Russian governments had little reason to make concessions that would alter the status quo, negotiations within the 'Normandy format' of France, Germany, Russia and Ukraine made no substantive progress. By mid-2017, it appeared that the conflict in eastern Ukraine would continue to simmer for the foreseeable future.

In Uzbekistan, the most populous state in Central Asia, the death of President Islam Karimov in September 2016 led to an apparently peaceful transition of power to Shavkat Mirziyoyev, until then the prime minister. The transition seemed to create the opportunity for a limited thaw in the country's relations with Kyrgyzstan and Tajikistan.

The economies of the post-Soviet region struggled to deal with the impact of low oil prices and the recession in Russia, which led to financial turbulence and currency depreciation across much of Eurasia. Although Russia emerged from recession in the first quarter of 2017, the region's growth prospects to 2020 fell short of pre-2014 levels.

Persistent tension between Russia and the West

Russia's relations with the West remained stuck in a pattern of confrontation and mutual distrust, despite Trump's pledges to seek improved relations with Moscow. Dialogue between Western leaders and the

Kremlin on the conflicts in Syria and Ukraine retained their narrow focus, reflecting their fundamentally opposed positions on the Assad regime and the future structure of Europe's security architecture.

Russia's November 2016 foreign-policy concept, the first to be published since the start of the war in eastern Ukraine and its military intervention in Syria, held to many of Moscow's long-standing concerns. These included rising transnational terrorism, NATO expansion and the increasingly multipolar nature of the international system – which had eroded the power of the West and enhanced the importance of new regional blocs, such as the Russian-led Eurasian Economic Union. The authors of the concept argued that the international system was growing increasingly disorderly, not least due to the Euro-Atlantic community's promotion of regime change. While expressing a willingness to cooperate with the West on an equal basis, they also explicitly warned that Western interventionism would meet with a robust response:

> Russia does not recognise the US policy of extraterritorial jurisdiction beyond the boundaries of international law and finds unacceptable attempts to exercise military, political, economic or any other pressure, while reserving the right to react very strongly to unfriendly actions, including the bolstering of national defence and taking retaliatory or asymmetrical measures.

NATO devoted much of its July 2016 summit in Warsaw to responding to the perceived security threat posed by Russia. Members of the Alliance accused Russia of having breached the commitments underpinning the 1997 NATO–Russia Founding Act and challenging the fundamental principles of the global and Euro-Atlantic security architecture. Building on the Readiness Action Plan they had agreed on in Wales two years earlier, NATO members agreed to establish the Alliance's forward presence in Eastern Europe by deploying four multinational battalion-sized battle groups to Estonia, Latvia, Lithuania and Poland on a rotational basis. They also announced land-operations training within a multinational framework brigade in Romania, and measures to increase the NATO naval presence in the Black Sea. The Alliance and the EU pledged to deepen their security cooperation with a view to countering 'hybrid threats' emanating from Russia. The move likely reaffirmed Moscow's view of the Union as a proxy for NATO and the US; this was the lens through which it viewed EU integration with Ukraine and other post-Soviet states.

Although Russian officials promised a 'military-technological response' to the forward deployments, their public reaction to the summit was relatively muted. This reflected both the small size of the deployments and the fact that the substantive decisions on them had been publicly known for some time. As a result, Russia had already formulated a military response, creating three new divisions in its Western Military District. While NATO was preoccupied with the threat posed to its members in the Baltic and Nordic regions, Moscow's primary focus remained the conflict in Ukraine and the potential for further Western integration with post-Soviet countries. On these issues, the conclusions of the NATO summit were more reassuring for Russia. The potential accession of Georgia to NATO received only a passing reference at the conference, and its final communiqué made no mention of the agreement to eventually admit Ukraine as a member of the Alliance, reached at the 2008 summit in Budapest.

With NATO and Moscow blaming each other for the breakdown of the European security order, they appeared set to maintain an adversarial relationship. By the end of Barack Obama's tenure as US president, there had been a near-total breakdown in communication between the White House and the Kremlin. Following the collapse of a ceasefire in Syria in September 2016, then US secretary of state John Kerry said that discussing the conflict there with his Russian counterpart could feel like living in a 'parallel universe'. The sides grew even more distant in December, when Obama expelled 35 Russian diplomats from the US and seized two diplomatic compounds in response to Russia's alleged interference in the presidential elections, including its cyber operations against the Democratic National Committee.

Trump's victory in the elections raised the prospect of a fundamental shift in US foreign policy, with potentially far-reaching implications for bilateral ties. In his election campaign, Trump repeatedly made the case for improved relations with Russia and spoke of his admiration for Putin. He appeared to show understanding for Russia's position on Ukraine, even suggesting that he could recognise Crimea as part of Russian territory and lift US sanctions linked to the Ukraine conflict. Casting doubt on US security guarantees to Europe under Article 5 of the NATO treaty, Trump stated that the Alliance was an 'obsolete' organisation that imposed excessive costs on Washington (although he later reversed this position). He also appeared interested in the possibility of greater cooperation with Moscow in a counter-terrorism alliance – of the kind Putin had called for in his September 2016 speech to the United Nations, shortly before Russia directly intervened in the Syrian conflict.

Trump's foreign-policy agenda appeared to be a repudiation of the liberal international order, and therefore aligned with several of Russia's long-standing positions. The Trump administration showed little interest in democracy promotion or involving itself in the internal affairs of other states. Indeed, US Secretary of State Rex Tillerson's visit to Moscow in April did not include meetings with civil-society and human-rights activists, which had been customary under previous administrations. For Moscow, the 'unipolar' system that formed after the fall of the Soviet Union is fundamentally opposed to Russian interests. Speaking at the Munich Security Conference in February 2017, Russian Foreign Minister Sergei Lavrov observed that

> the historic era that could be called the post-Cold War order has come to an end. Its main result, as we see it, was the complete failure of the Cold War institutions to adapt to new realities … This global model was preprogrammed for crisis right from the time when this vision of economic and political globalisation was conceived primarily as an instrument for ensuring the growth of an elite club of countries and its domination over everyone else. It is clear that such a system could not last forever.

Yet there was no certainty that Trump's 'America First' policy would lead to a sustainable improvement in bilateral relations. Although Trump expressed a wish to free the US from international commitments, he was no conventional isolationist. He continued to make the case for a confrontational foreign policy, remained committed to high levels of defence spending and, as illustrated by a missile strike on a Syrian government air base in April 2017, appeared ready to employ force rapidly and unexpectedly in a manner that could easily work against Russian interests.

Moreover, by mid-2017, there was no indication that the contours of a putative 'grand deal' between the US and Russia would be quickly formulated. Trump's foreign-policy team included several more conventionally minded cabinet secretaries, such as James Mattis at the Pentagon and Tillerson at the State Department. In February, H.R. McMaster was appointed national security adviser, replacing Michael Flynn, who had been one of the strongest advocates of increased cooperation with Russia. Once in office, the Trump team appeared to step back from several of its more radical foreign-policy positions. At the February 2017 Munich Security Conference, Pence pledged 'unwavering' support for the transatlantic alliance and told delegates that the US 'will continue to hold Russia accountable, even as we search for new common ground'. In May, Tillerson expressed doubt about the prospects for improved relations, stating that he hoped Washington and Moscow 'can begin to build a way in which we can learn how to work with one another', before adding: 'I don't know whether we can or not.'

Trump's pro-Russian statements caused consternation in parts of the US political and security establishment. This dismay grew into a political storm after US intelligence agencies reported that the Kremlin had interfered in the presidential elections, conducting cyber attacks on the Democratic National Committee. In March 2017, James Comey, then head of the FBI, revealed that he had opened a counter-intelligence investigation into links between Trump's team and Russian officials. By June 2017, Trump was at the centre of overlapping judicial and congressional investigations into allegations of Russian interference in the presidential elections; collusion between members of his campaign and the Kremlin; and subsequent obstruction of the investigations. With his links to Russia under intense scrutiny, Trump had little room for manoeuvre.

News of Trump's victory was greeted with applause in the Russian parliament and prompted Russian state media outlets to soften their anti-US rhetoric. But there was no indication that Moscow was willing to make concessions on any points of principle to improve relations. Even before the domestic political backlash against Trump's pro-Russia line, Russian officials were likely to have taken a conservative view of Trump's ability to change the hostile tenor of US policy towards Russia. The November 2016 Russian foreign-policy concept framed Western foreign policy as fundamentally opposed to Russian interests, casting the West as entirely responsible for reframing relations between the sides.

Meanwhile, the US and Russia continued to see each other as posing a major military challenge. Trump gave no indication that he would address long-standing Russian concerns about Washington's ballistic-missile-defence (BMD) programme in Europe or its new generation of conventional weapons – both of which Russian officials believe could undermine its nuclear deterrent. Speaking at the end of March 2017 in Geneva, Lieutenant-General Viktor Poznikhir, deputy head of the Russian General Staff's Main Operation Directorate, reiterated Russian concerns about the BMD programme. He argued that existing BMD facilities could be adapted to fire cruise missiles at Russia, and that the US intended to deploy more than 1,000 ballistic-missile interceptors by 2022. At the June 2017 St. Petersburg International Economic Forum, Putin issued another warning that the US was undermining the global strategic balance, and that Russia would be obliged to respond. His tone and language were almost unchanged from May 2016, when he discussed the deployment of an interceptor and radar site in Deveselu, in Romania, as part of a global approach that had created a US–Russia arms race.

Growing Russian concern about the evolution of US conventional and nuclear capabilities threatened key arms-control agreements, such as the 2010 New START. Trump's contradictory statements on nuclear disarmament and the value of existing arms-control treaties only exacerbated this concern. In March 2017, General Paul Selva, vice-chairman of the Joint Chiefs of Staff, told the US House Armed Services Committee that Russia's deployment of the 'SSC-8' (the designation given to a land-attack cruise missile that he claimed violated the spirit and intent of the INF Treaty) was designed 'to pose a threat to NATO and to facilities within the NATO area of responsibility'. The US had been hinting for some time that the development of the missile violated the INF Treaty, but this was the first public statement of this view by a named official. In November 2016, the US sought to address compliance concerns about the development of the missiles with Russian officials at a meeting of the Special Verification Commission, but did not appear to make progress in the effort.

Thus, by mid-2017, there was little prospect of a significant reduction in tension between Russia and the West. Buffeted by frequent leaks and allegations relating to ties with the Kremlin, the Trump administration was at risk of developing an incoherent Russia policy. From Moscow's perspective, Trump's election was a symptom of an inevitable and welcome US retreat from global leadership; but the subsequent controversy over his ties to Russia also underlined the anti-Russian consensus within the US political establishment. Trump's approach to global affairs appeared to presage a period of greater turbulence and unpredictability that could easily work against Russian interests. Neither side had put forward realistic proposals to address the structural problems in their relationship, despite the need for such measures in arms control and the security architecture of the post-Soviet region. The new Cold War dynamic looked set to remain in place. With Congress pushing to expand US sanctions on Russia, Putin extended countermeasures banning imports of Western food until the end of 2018.

Low-level conflict in eastern Ukraine

The conflict in eastern Ukraine continued to dominate relations between Russia and the EU, to the exclusion of almost all other issues. The dynamics of the war were virtually unchanged, as were the terms of EU–Russia interactions, in the year to mid-2017. Although EU member states often disagreed on Russia policy and the efficacy of sanctions – as illustrated by Hungary's decision to host Putin for an official visit in February 2017 – these disputes had little effect on EU policy. Critics of the sanctions policy failed to offer a viable alternative approach, and the most influential EU members showed no interest in broadening their engagement with Russia. If anything, shocks such as the United Kingdom's vote to leave the EU and the election of Trump only strengthened EU unity. Official attitudes towards Russia in France, Germany and the UK hardened further over the year in response to the Russian military's brutal bombing campaign in Syria. Increasingly, EU sectoral sanctions, Russian counter-sanctions and mutual antagonism came to be viewed as normal. The European Council renewed rolling sanctions on Russia in July 2016 and January 2017, apparently with minimal internal debate.

The Special Monitoring Mission (SMM) of the Organization for Security and Co-operation in Europe (OSCE) registered almost daily violations of the ceasefire agreement. However, the intensity of the conflict was still significantly lower than it had been before the signing of the second ceasefire agreement in Minsk in February 2015. By mid-June 2017, the SMM had confirmed 45 civilian casualties since the start of the year. In the preceding year, the Line of Contact between Ukrainian forces and Russian-backed separatists had barely moved, while ceasefire violations were generally concentrated in a few areas. The humanitarian situation remained serious, with issues relating to the payment of utility bills leading to shortages of water and electricity, particularly in areas of the Luhansk region outside government control.

The level of violence fluctuated, with particularly intense fighting recorded in August and November 2016. Russia may have timed the latter flare-up to coincide with the US elections, as an early test of the incoming administration. In August, the conflict intensified across the Line of Contact after Moscow accused Ukrainian forces of killing two Russian servicemen in Crimea. Claiming that Ukraine had 'resorted to the practice of terror', Putin responded by pulling out of a planned meeting on the conflict with the leaders of France, Germany and Ukraine on the margins of the G20 summit in China. The circumstances surrounding the alleged attack – which the Ukrainian government denied had taken place – were never made clear and Russia quietly allowed the matter to slide.

The sides announced several attempts to renew the ceasefire, but each effort led to only a temporary lull in the fighting. This failure underlined the lack of progress on implementing the Minsk II agreement, even in basic de-escalation measures such as the withdrawal of heavy weaponry from the front-line.

Neither Ukraine nor Russia appeared interested in moving beyond the status quo. The decentralisation and constitutional reforms mandated by the Minsk II agreement, designed to grant a special status to the separatist-controlled regions of Donetsk and Luhansk, were highly controversial in Ukraine. Given its declining popularity among the electorate, the Ukrainian government seemed unlikely to risk further destabilising the political situation by attempting to push through the measures. In September, President Petro Poroshenko said that he expected parliament to vote on constitutional amendments that granted autonomy to parts of eastern Ukraine 'in the nearest possible future'. Alexander Zakharchenko, leader of the self-declared Donetsk 'People's Republic' (DNR), responded by announcing a unilateral ceasefire. However, the ceasefire quickly collapsed and by mid-2017 the vote on the constitutional amendments had not taken place.

The Ukrainian government's approach to the conflict in the east was constrained by its unpopularity and its desire to avoid being outflanked by Ukrainian-nationalist forces. In January, demobilised soldiers and veterans of Ukrainian volunteer battalions imposed a makeshift blockade on the edge of separatist-controlled territories, to prevent them from trading with the rest of Ukraine. This followed several moves to isolate these regions by the government, which had placed financial and trade restrictions on the DNR and the Luhansk 'People's Republic' (LNR), suspended social transfers to citizens in the regions and disrupted the provision of basic utilities there. Nonetheless, the government initially criticised the embargo, warning that it could lead to significant economic losses and limit access to heating. On 15 March, after efforts to remove the blockade provoked public protests, the National Security and Defence Council adopted the measure as government policy, announcing it would halt all freight traffic across the front-line in the Donbas region. According to an initial estimate by the National Bank of Ukraine, the move would reduce the country's GDP growth by 1.3 percentage points in 2017.

The prospect of eventually reintegrating the separatist-controlled regions was further undercut by Russia's decision in February 2017 to temporarily recognise identity documents issued by the DNR and LNR authorities, enabling residents of the areas to travel, work and study in Russia. Moscow claimed to have made the decision on humanitarian grounds, in response to the Ukrainian economic blockade. German Chancellor Angela Merkel said that the move 'directly contradicts everything that was agreed in Minsk', while Poroshenko described it as 'another proof of Russian occupation as well as Russian violation of international law'. Yet Moscow could argue with some justification that the Ukrainian government's policy of isolating the DNR and the LNR economically further reduced the likelihood that the territories would eventually be reconciled and reintegrated with Ukraine.

In further encroaching on Ukrainian sovereignty, Russia held out the implicit threat that it could recognise the independence of the DNR and LNR – as it had the breakaway territories of Abkhazia and South Ossetia, *de jure* part of Georgia, in 2008. But Moscow was unlikely to take this step: its overriding aim in the Ukrainian conflict is to prevent the consolidation of a pro-Western government in Ukraine that could facilitate the country's accession to the EU or NATO. To achieve this, Russia needs to ensure that the contested territories remain part of

Ukraine. Russia's strategy in the conflict had been broadly unchanged since the signing of the Minsk II agreement in February 2015, although several alternate courses of action remain open to it. Since all Ukrainian governments will remain formally committed to EU and NATO integration for the foreseeable future, Russia's strategy focused in the first instance on disruption. This could be achieved either by embedding its proxies in a de-centralised Ukrainian state through the Minsk process, or by maintaining a low-level conflict that depletes the Ukrainian government's resources, resolve and political capital. Russia's continued military build-up on Ukraine's border in 2016 suggested that the Kremlin was considering another option: escalating the conflict.

While still heavily reliant on external support from the EU and the IMF, by mid-2017 Ukraine's finances and economy were starting to look less precarious, with the latter organisation projecting that the country would meet its short-term fiscal and monetary targets. Ukraine continued to reorient its trading relationships away from Russia and towards the EU. Russia accounted for 11.6% of Ukrainian trade by value in 2016, compared with 20.7% in 2014. The EU accounted for 40.6% of Ukrainian trade by value in 2016, five percentage points more than in 2014. A rise in domestic gas prices put Naftohaz, Ukraine's state gas company, on a more sustainable financial footing, depriving Russia of a traditional instrument of influence on the Ukrainian elite. Naftohaz avoided potential costs of more than US$30 billion in May, when an arbitration court ruled in its favour in a case brought by Russian energy firm Gazprom over a 'take or pay' claim for undelivered gas.

Nonetheless, Moscow had cause to hope that Ukraine's dysfunctional, unstable politics would gradually shift the domestic balance of power to its benefit, and that the EU would lose the will to maintain its Ukraine-related sanctions on Russia. Ukrainian efforts to tackle corruption continued to have little success in the year to mid-2017, prompting several reform-minded figures to quit the government in protest. In May 2017, Valeria Gontareva resigned as head of the National Bank of Ukraine, having encountered strong resistance to her efforts to clean up the banking sector. The fusion of business and politics continued to block implementation of reforms, leading the IMF to hold back disbursement of credit under the Extended Fund Facility on several occasions. In May 2017, the EU granted Ukrainian citizens visa-free travel in its member states. But with the EU highly unlikely to offer a path to membership to act as a policy anchor, there was a risk that the Union's relationship with Ukraine would be allowed to drift. Moreover, the Ukrainian political elite had limited will and capacity to complete the slow, complex process of implementing Ukraine's EU Association Agreement.

Russia's strengthened position in the Middle East

Despite Putin's announcement of a drawdown in March 2016, the Russian military was deeply involved in the Syrian conflict throughout the year to mid-2017. In summer 2016, Moscow increased Russian air-power in Syria by deploying additional Su-25 SM and Su-24 M aircraft. Russia also tripled its ground component in Syria – largely comprising special-forces personnel – to around 3,000 troops in the second half of 2016. Moscow continued to use the Syrian conflict to test its long-range precision-strike capacity, launching cruise missiles at targets around the city of Aleppo from ships based in the Eastern Mediterranean. In a further demonstration of its desire to be a major power in the Middle East, Russia deployed the *Admiral Kuznetsov*, its only aircraft carrier, to the Eastern Mediterranean in October 2016 (although the vessel was withdrawn in early 2017 after losing two aircraft to accidents).

Russia's intervention in the Syrian conflict placed only a small burden on the national budget. This was primarily because of its heavy reliance on non-precision munitions, whose use resulted in large-scale civilian casualties and destruction of property. The Russian military lost an estimated 50–100 personnel in the conflict (excluding the victims of the crash of a Syria-bound Tu-154 airliner off the coast of Russia in December 2016).

Russian officials expressed few concerns about the progress of the campaign or the risk of entrapment in an open-ended conflict. They regularly stressed the valuable military experience gained from the intervention, as well as its potential benefits for the Russian defence industry. There were suggestions that the Russian military used the conflict in Syria as a testing ground for its expeditionary capabilities, regularly rotating its deployments of personnel to provide them with experience of active service. According to an estimate by one Russian military think tank, by early 2017 more than half of Russia's military pilots had been deployed to Syria, while the country's artillery specialists had also reportedly been deployed there on a rotational basis. Thus, the Obama administration's warnings that Syria would become a 'quagmire' for the Russian military appeared to have been ill-founded.

Russia's bombing campaign allowed the Assad regime to decisively strengthen its position. By the end of December 2016, pro-regime forces had retaken the eastern side of Aleppo, Syria's second city, and thus controlled all the major population centres in the country. The high civilian death toll of the bombardment of Aleppo provoked further Western criticism of Russia's military campaign. In October, Putin cancelled a planned visit to France after François Hollande, then the president, accused Russia of war crimes. This tension dispelled any hope that the conflict in Syria would allow Moscow to reframe its relations with the West away from a policy of containment of Russia. But despite expressing outrage at the humanitarian cost of the war, Western powers failed to take any significant action to protect civilians in Syria.

Nonetheless, the Syrian government's advances in 2016 also underlined the limits of Russia's military operation. Severely degraded after six years of conflict, regime forces struggled to maintain control of captured areas. As they moved to encircle Aleppo in September, they lost territory to rebel advances in the province of Hama. In December, ISIS briefly recaptured the city of Palmyra, the scene of a triumphant Russian concert the previous May. While continuing to conduct a heavy bombing campaign, Russia increased its diplomatic efforts with the intention of at least bringing the conflict into a more manageable equilibrium. From Moscow's perspective, vague and inconsistent Western policy on Syria allowed Russia to shape the course of the conflict through force and thereby dictate the terms of a future political settlement.

Russia still hoped to push the US into increased military cooperation and engagement with a negotiation process that would preserve a pro-Russian regime in Damascus. Although Moscow presented its military intervention in Syria as a counter-terrorism campaign, the Russian air campaign focused on relatively moderate anti-regime forces. In January 2017, outgoing US defence secretary Ashton Carter commented that Russia's intervention had done 'virtually zero' to degrade the capacity of ISIS. At the same time, Russia increased its engagement with the Syrian opposition, indicating that it could countenance a political settlement that did not involve Assad retaining power indefinitely.

However, there were considerable obstacles to both improved cooperation with the US and a political settlement along the lines sought by Russia. The US and the Syrian rebels shared a deep distrust of Russia's and the regime's intentions. Furthermore, Moscow seemed to lack either the leverage or the inclination to prevent regime forces from targeting US-backed opposition groups. The growing entanglement of jihadist groups and more moderate rebel forces also presented a challenge, as Russian-brokered ceasefire agreements only covered the latter. Assad appeared to have been emboldened by his military advances: in mid-September, hours before a proposed ceasefire was due to come into force, he reiterated his intention to re-establish control over all of Syria. Unlike Iran – the regime's other major ally – Russia viewed this proposition as unrealistic. The September ceasefire agreement unravelled almost immediately, following the destruction of a UN aid convoy bound for eastern Aleppo in what US officials identified as a Russian or Syrian airstrike. The incident effectively ended any prospect of dialogue between the US and Russia on Syria until January, when the Trump administration took office. As a result, the US had no role in another ceasefire Russia and Turkey brokered with rebel groups in December.

Russia's interests in the conflict partially differed from those of Iran, which was more committed to maintaining and expanding areas of Syria under Assad's control. While Iran regarded its Syrian campaign as part of a broader struggle against Gulf Arab countries, Russia was eager to maintain constructive relationships with Saudi Arabia and other Sunni-majority states.

For Moscow, the election of Trump may have had the potential to partially align Washington's policy on the Syrian conflict with its own. The Trump administration focused on the campaign against ISIS, while leaving the future of the Assad regime in question. 'It's important that we keep our priorities straight, and we believe that the first priority is the defeat of ISIS', Tillerson said in April, adding: 'once the ISIS threat has been reduced or eliminated, I think we can turn our attention directly to stabilising the situation in Syria'. However, his comments came shortly after the April 2017 US missile strike, which targeted a Syrian air base identified as the launch pad for a chemical-weapons attack on the rebel-held town of Khan Sheikhoun. Describing the missile strike as an act of aggression, Putin announced that he would suspend an agreement to deconflict US and Russian air operations in Syria. In June, the US military shot down a regime warplane, prompting Russia to declare that it would view US jets in western Syria as 'air targets'.

Moscow pushed ahead with peace talks in the first half of 2017, holding several rounds of negotiations with Iran, Turkey and representatives of the Syrian opposition in Astana, the capital of Kazakhstan. Although there was little prospect of an overarching political settlement, the powers built on a December 2016 ceasefire by agreeing to create four 'de-escalation zones' that recognised some key areas controlled by the rebels. After members of the opposition abandoned the talks, it was unclear whether Russia and other external powers would be willing or able to secure the safe zones – particularly given that some anti-government groups not covered by the agreement were active in these areas. Moreover, prominent rebel organisations connected to al-Qaeda were absent from the negotiations and the parties had not addressed the issue of Assad's future. Nonetheless, Russia could plausibly argue that the Astana negotiations yielded better results than most observers had anticipated at the outset of the process.

By mid-2017, Russia's military intervention had met several important objectives. Moscow had further strengthened its position as one of the two dominant external actors in Syria. Although there was little prospect that the Assad regime would re-establish control over all of Syria, Russia's bombing campaign had seen off the threat of regime change, secured Russian military assets in the country and ensured that any future political transition would be conducted on Moscow's terms. Despite its support for the Assad regime and close cooperation with Iran, Russia also managed to maintain a positive working relationship with traditional US allies in the region, including Israel, Egypt and Gulf Arab states. Russia's inclusion in the OPEC oil-supply deal allowed for close diplomatic engagement with Saudi Arabia (concluded in December 2016 and extended the following May, the agreement aimed to halt the fall in oil prices).

Moscow's expanding dialogue with the parties to the Libyan conflict hinted at its ambitions to influence events in other parts of the Middle East. Khalifa Haftar, head of the Libyan National Army, visited Moscow in November, and in January reportedly held talks with defence officials aboard the *Admiral Kuznetsov* off the coast of Libya. According to US military officials, Russia deployed special forces to eastern Libya in support of Haftar. The Russian government denied this claim.

The year to mid-2017 also saw increased Russian engagement in Afghanistan, amid continued claims in the US and Afghan media, denied by the Kremlin, that Russia was providing active support to the Taliban. In December 2016, Russia hosted a trilateral consultation in Moscow with officials from China and Pakistan, to the consternation of the Afghan government, which was not represented. However, Moscow maintained contact with the US-backed government in Kabul, and then Afghan foreign minister Salahuddin Rabbani met his Russian counterpart in Moscow in February. In April, Russian newspaper *Izvestia* reported that Afghan officials had discussed the possibility of receiving military aid from Moscow with the Russian foreign ministry. The same month, Lavrov met former Afghan president Hamid Karzai in Moscow.

Russia's increased diplomatic engagement with these conflicts was driven by several factors. In part, it was a response to genuine concerns in Moscow regarding terrorism and international stability caused by unresolved conflicts on the Eurasian periphery. For example, in May 2017 Russia led military exercises in Tajikistan that simulated an invasion of armed groups from across the border with Afghanistan. As in Syria, questions of international prestige also played a role: Moscow continued to assert its status as a great power with an indispensable role to play in all major global issues.

Economic stagnation in Eurasia

The fallout from low commodity prices and the contraction in Russia's economy continued to affect Eurasia in the year to mid-2017. Russia's economy performed better than expected, with GDP falling by just 0.2% in 2016 and the country emerging from recession in the first quarter of 2017. But most economists shared the Russian central bank's view that without systemic reforms, long-term growth was unlikely to exceed 1.5–2% per year. Thus, Russia's economy was forecast to account for a declining share of global GDP. In time-honoured tradition, the Kremlin commissioned two groups of experts – one of them led by former finance minister Alexei Kudrin – to formulate a plan of action. But with parliamentary elections in September 2016 and the presidential elections scheduled for March 2018, the Russian elite was focused on maintaining stability and creating the conditions to ensure a high turnout and a vote in favour of the incumbent.

With the Russian government assuming that oil prices would remain low to 2019 and beyond, the ministry of finance remained committed to a stringent programme of fiscal consolidation designed to maintain macroeconomic stability. This included a reduction in defence spending in 2017, a measure that called into question the government's goal of modernising 70% of Russian military hardware by 2020. However, defence spending would have passed its peak at this stage even under the government's pre-crisis plans; moreover, 'modernisation' was an elastic term that did not necessarily imply the introduction of advanced technology. There were few indications that the economic outlook would prompt the Russian elite to seek an accommodation with the West to boost investment.

The weak outlook for Russia's economy was mirrored across the Eurasian region, owing either to lower revenues for hydrocarbon exports or a fall in remittances from Russia in migration-dependent countries such as Moldova, Belarus, Tajikistan, Uzbekistan and Kyrgyzstan. Media reports suggested that much of Central Asia was experiencing increasingly severe economic problems – although official figures often failed to reflect this trend. In Turkmenistan, which relies almost exclusively on gas exports for foreign currency, the unemployment rate was around 65–70%, according to a central-bank estimate quoted by Radio Free Europe. In June 2017, Turkmenistan's government ended the free provision of water, gas and electricity. Having essentially destroyed the foundations of a paternalist state, the regime had few means to maintain control other than repression and enforced isolation. Tajikistan, the poorest post-Soviet state, began talks on financial assistance with the IMF and the European Bank for Reconstruction and Development. Due to the country's poor record on cooperation with international financial institutions, the organisations were likely to approach the discussions with caution. There was a possibility that Tajikistan would instead seek concessional funding from Russia, which could demand the country's accession to the Eurasian Economic Union in return. Indeed, at a conference on inter-regional cooperation held in Dushanbe in December 2016, Alexander Tsybulskiy, a Russian deputy minister of economic development, noted the benefits of joining the union for Tajikistan.

Given the weak economic outlook in Eurasia, China's Belt and Road Initiative continued to gain significance as the most likely external driver of growth in the region. However, China's expanding role in Central Asia continued to generate controversy. Kazakhstan's government revised planned land reforms in February 2017, following a public backlash caused by the widespread belief that they would allow Chinese investors to gain control of agricultural areas. Chinese firms announced few new investment projects in Central Asia or Russia in the year to mid-2017. In March, there were reports that the construction of a fourth Turkmenistan–China gas pipeline – planned to run through Tajikistan and Kyrgyzstan – had been indefinitely postponed.

The economic slowdown had not yet led to increased political instability in Central Asia. The political transition in Uzbekistan in 2016 also challenged assumptions about the sustainability of personalised authoritarian regimes in the post-Soviet region. There were no outward signs of conflict among Uzbekistan's elite following the death of President Karimov, who had ruled the country for 27 years. While public confirmation of Karimov's death appeared to have been delayed by several days, political leaders quickly united around Mirziyoyev, allowing him to be appointed as acting president in contravention of the constitution. A highly managed election in November secured Mirziyoyev's position.

There were signs that the transition would lead to a thaw in Uzbekistan's relations with neighbouring Tajikistan and Kyrgyzstan, which had long been dominated by territorial disputes, ethnic tension and conflicts over resources. After coming to power, Mirziyoyev quickly established warmer relations with his counterparts in Tajikistan and Kyrgyzstan. In November, Uzbekistan and Kyrgyzstan announced an agreement on 49 non-demarcated sections of their border. The following April, direct flights between Uzbekistan and Tajikistan resumed for the first time in two decades. In June, the countries held bilateral talks on improving their economic ties and ending the visa regime. But it was unclear whether Uzbekistan's government would take further steps to end the country's relative economic and political isolation, given that the security services appeared to resist plans to lift short-term visa requirements for tourists from a range of countries in the Organisation for Economic Co-operation and Development.

Kazakhstan's president, 77-year-old Nursultan Nazarbayev, was the last Central Asian leader to have remained in power since before the fall of the Soviet Union. Although he had not appointed a successor, there were strong indications that the state had begun planning for an eventual transfer of power. Constitutional reforms adopted in March 2017 were intended to devolve powers from the presidency to parliament, thereby improving parliamentary oversight of government and legislation. These measures were unlikely to have a practical impact during Nazarbayev's presidency. However, they seemed to pave the way for a more collective system of rule, in recognition of the fact that Kazakhstan's second president would struggle to achieve the authority and legitimacy of his predecessor.

There was little certainty about when and how a presidential transition in Kazakhstan would be coordinated. Given Kazakhstan's large ethnic-Russian community and key role in the Eurasian Economic Union, it seemed likely that Russia would play a role in the transition process, if only as external guarantor of the chosen candidate. Limited Western economic and security engagement with Kazakhstan reduced the risk that the political transition would trigger an international crisis.

Chapter 9

Europe

Populism, the threat of EU disintegration and the impact of the Trump administration on the transatlantic relationship dominated European politics in the year to mid-2017. The challenges posed by large-scale migration, financial fragility and terrorism also continued to draw significant attention from policymakers. Against this backdrop, Europe's political leaders worked to craft a compelling vision for the future. Within the European Union, they sought to explain the continuing relevance of the European project. In the United Kingdom, they worked to forge a new identity alongside Europe as the country moved to depart the Union. By mid-2017, neither of these grand visions had been fully articulated – although both showed signs of development. Yet it remained unclear whether the people of Europe would wait patiently for the completion of the respective narratives, and whether the continent's elites retained the credibility to chart a course the public would accept. At stake was Europe's ambition to re-emerge as a source of peace and stability amid regions beset by conflict and civil unrest. There was a danger that Europe would continue to be introspective despite the instability on its borders, and that outside actors such as Russia – or even Turkey – would foment discontent on the continent.

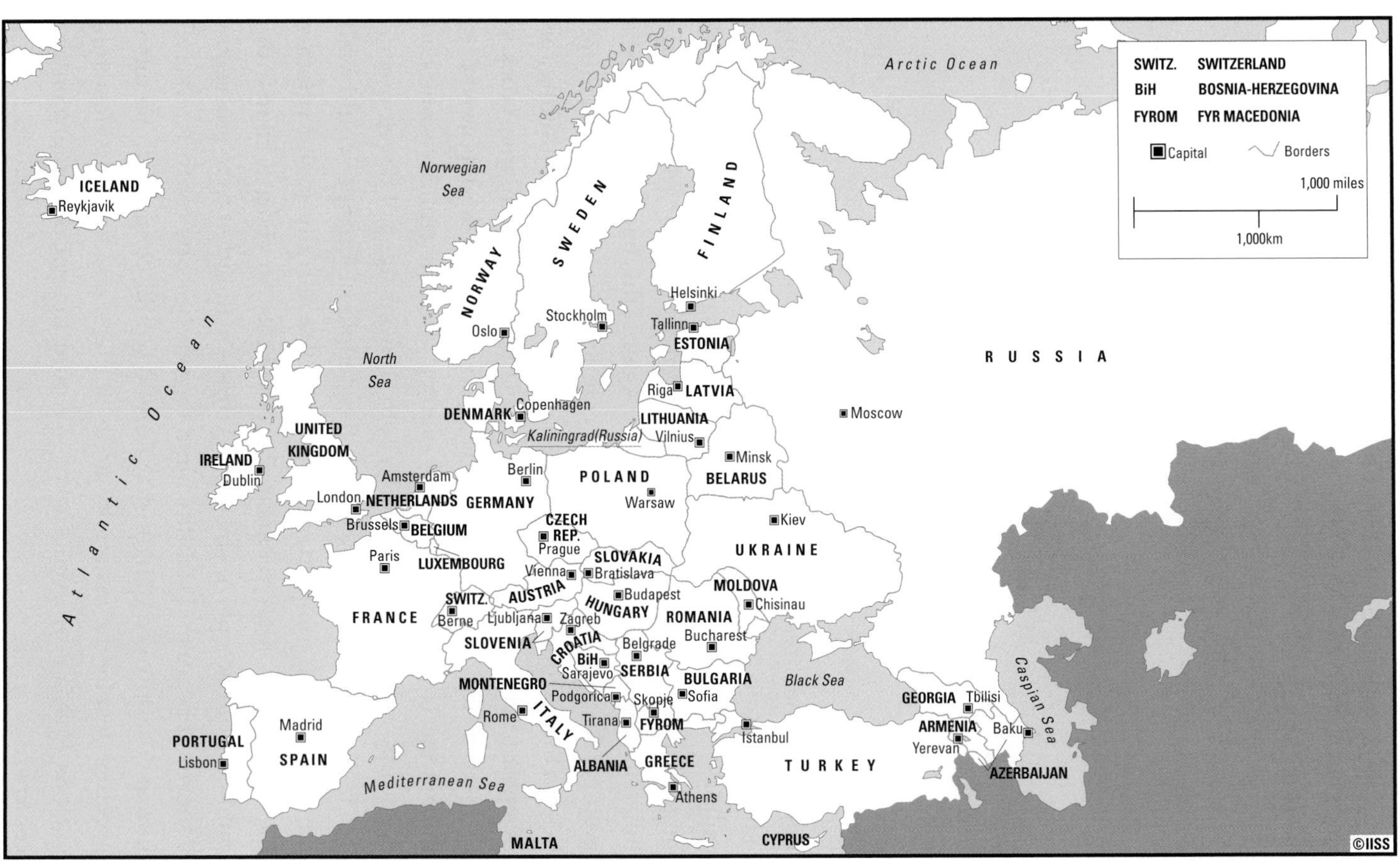
SWITZ. SWITZERLAND
BiH BOSNIA-HERZEGOVINA
FYROM FYR MACEDONIA
Capital
Borders
1,000 miles
1,000km
Arctic Ocean
Norwegian Sea
North Sea
Atlantic Ocean
Mediterranean Sea
Black Sea
Caspian Sea
ICELAND
Reykjavik
NORWAY
Oslo
SWEDEN
Stockholm
FINLAND
Helsinki
Tallinn
ESTONIA
Riga
LATVIA
LITHUANIA
Vilnius
Kaliningrad(Russia)
RUSSIA
Moscow
Minsk
BELARUS
DENMARK
Copenhagen
UNITED KINGDOM
IRELAND
Dublin
London
Amsterdam
NETHERLANDS
Brussels
BELGIUM
GERMANY
Berlin
POLAND
Warsaw
CZECH REP.
Prague
Kiev
UKRAINE
Paris
LUXEMBOURG
SLOVAKIA
Vienna
Bratislava
AUSTRIA
Budapest
MOLDOVA
Chisinau
SWITZ.
Berne
FRANCE
Ljubljana
Zagreb
HUNGARY
ROMANIA
SLOVENIA
CROATIA
Belgrade
Bucharest
BiH
Sarajevo
SERBIA
MONTENEGRO
BULGARIA
Podgorica
Skopje
Sofia
Rome
ITALY
Tirana
FYROM
Istanbul
ALBANIA
GREECE
Athens
Madrid
PORTUGAL
Lisbon
SPAIN
TURKEY
GEORGIA
Tbilisi
ARMENIA
Yerevan
Baku
AZERBAIJAN
MALTA
CYPRUS
©IISS

Populism and electoral volatility

The implications of the UK's vote to leave the EU were slow to surface. The event was most often described as an effect of populism, or a popular revolt against ruling elites if not the entire political class. The majority of the urban electorate voted in favour of continued membership, as did much of the business community, particularly the financial sector. In England and parts of Wales, most voters living outside major cities voted to leave. This held true even in places that gained significant benefits from EU funding or agricultural subsidies, or from access to European markets. As the economic rationale for the Leave vote was controversial, the outcome of the referendum appeared to turn more on emotion than any strict measure of costs and benefits.

The British referendum was only the first in a series of political contests in which populism predominated. Italy followed next with a referendum on a raft of constitutional amendments designed to make government more decisive by strengthening the executive – and thus more able to undertake much-needed economic and social reforms. Prime Minister Matteo Renzi led the campaign, promising early on to resign if the amendments were rejected. This personalisation of the contest was unnecessary – and proved to be fatal. The reforms had been sketched out long before Renzi's February 2014 appointment as prime minister, and were then agreed on through multiple votes in both chambers of parliament. Nonetheless, Renzi felt confident in his personal popularity and sought to cement his reputation as a transformative force in Italian politics.

As the referendum campaign unfolded, the polls moved decisively against the reforms. This trend resulted partly from opposition to Renzi as the old guard mobilised against him, but even more from broader distrust of all political elites among younger voters. Populism played a role on both sides of the debate. Although Italians were dissatisfied with the way in which politics functioned, they did not agree on an alternative. Stasis became the default option. On 4 December, the constitutional reforms were rejected by a margin of 18 percentage points. Renzi resigned as prime minister and the Italian political class found itself at a constitutional impasse: parliament's mandate had only one year to run and there was no clear majority in favour of reforming the country's political institutions.

On the same day as the Italian referendum, Austria reran the second round of its presidential elections. The latter contest once again illustrated European voters' discontent with traditional elites. Originally held in April and May 2016, the presidential elections had seen candidates from the Green Party and the Freedom Party, on the left and far right respectively, eclipse their centrist rivals. The Green Party candidate went on to win a narrow victory in the second round, only to have the courts overturn the result the following July. Many European leaders worried that the Freedom Party would capture the presidency in the repeat second-round vote, but in the event the Green Party candidate triumphed by an even larger margin. Nonetheless, their subsequent expressions of relief at the result appeared to ignore the underlying levels of electoral volatility in Austria, as evidenced by the large number of voters willing to switch parties from one contest to another.

This electoral volatility was also evident in March 2017, when the Dutch went to the polls. Many foreign observers were concerned that the far-right Party for Freedom would emerge as the largest political grouping in the Netherlands parliament. As the Dutch electoral system is constructed around proportional representation and has only one district, the difference between first and second place can be determined by coalition bargaining. Therefore, cooperation between moderate parties can be crucial to the formation of a government that limits the power of the far right. Although the Party for Freedom underperformed expectations in the election, moderate Dutch politicians still struggled to form a workable coalition. By mid-2017, the coalition talks were continuing and it was unclear whether they would result in a minority government or another election. The problem appeared to be not so much unbridled emotion as a deeper disaffection with the workings of democracy. Dutch voters had grown weary of consensus and of politicians campaigning on a set of promises only to compromise on these commitments when forming a coalition government. They wanted a clear choice and disliked the traditional alternatives on offer.

This critique of democracy was also evident in France, which held its presidential elections in April and May, followed by two rounds of legislative elections in June. There, National Front candidate Marine Le Pen threatened to lead a far-right populist revolt, consistently maintaining a lead in the polls. Few believed Le Pen would win in the second round of the contest or that her party would gain a majority in the legislative elections. There was widespread concern that she would gain more votes than any of her rivals in the first round, a result that would be symbolically important and would have implications for the 2022 elections.

The contest unexpectedly saw the emergence of two more populist insurgencies, led by far-left candidate Jean-Luc Mélenchon and the centrist Emmanuel Macron respectively. Together, these forces marginalised the ruling Socialist Party just as the campaign of the centre-right candidate imploded in scandal. This left the field open for Macron to achieve the largest vote share in the first round, and to overwhelmingly defeat Le Pen in the second. Macron then consolidated his position by converting the movement that brought him to power, En Marche!, into a broader vehicle to contest the legislative elections, La République en Marche. He won an outright majority in the legislature by appealing to the centre of the French political spectrum. The combination of a strong presidential mandate and a working majority in the National Assembly created opportunities for meaningful reform of French labour markets, social services and the public sector. Nonetheless, the volatility of the French electorate – which denied both major parties a place in the presidential run-off – and the low turnout in the second round of the legislative contest suggested that there was still potential for populist mobilisation against the ruling class. Neither Mélenchon nor Le Pen retreated from the political stage and both were preparing to oppose the Macron administration.

Meanwhile, the UK provided yet another example of electoral volatility. On 18 April, less than a month after formally triggering the two-year countdown to the country's departure from the EU, British Prime Minister Theresa May called for a snap election, ostensibly to reinforce her mandate to negotiate a new relationship with the Union. Talks with the EU were scheduled to begin on 19 June. At the time she called the election, May's Conservative Party was around 20 percentage points ahead of Jeremy Corbyn's Labour Party in most opinion polls. After Parliament agreed to the elections, voters went to the polls on 8 June. Seemingly due to a series of political missteps by May and her government, a collapse in support for non-traditional political movements such as the UK Independence Party and increased turnout among the British electorate (rising from 66.1% in 2015 to 68.7% in 2017), the prime minister strengthened support for her Conservative Party by more than five percentage points yet still lost her overall majority in Parliament. Labour closed the gap with the Conservatives to slightly more than two percentage points, gaining 30 parliamentary seats and prompting their rivals to strike a confidence and supply deal with the Northern Irish Democratic Unionist Party to remain in government.

Threats to EU unity

The combination of Macron's strength and May's weakness created divergent perceptions of the European project among electorates. Macron ran on an explicitly pro-European platform. He promised to reinvigorate the Franco-German relationship, reform the EU and strengthen Europe's place in the world. After he won both the presidency and a legislative majority, many of his colleagues in other countries began to feel a sense of optimism, as did political leaders in EU institutions. In contrast, May became embroiled in a fierce debate over economic policy and social services with Corbyn, whose domestic platform was far more prominent than his ambivalence towards Europe.

By losing her majority, May threw the UK's departure from the EU into doubt. Although most observers believed that the country would complete the process, few still expressed concern that its example would spark an exodus by other member states. Indeed, polls by the Pew Foundation indicated that support for the European project had strengthened outside the UK. As a consequence, the EU no longer appeared to be threatened with disintegration.

The growing popularity of German Chancellor Angela Merkel only confirmed that perception. She encountered a series of tests in summer 2016. The EU and Turkey maintained their deal to stop refugees and other migrants from the Middle East and North Africa travelling through the Western Balkans to Europe. But the number of immigrants already in Germany as a result of Merkel's August 2015 decision to suspend the Dublin Regulation – under which refugees are stopped at the first safe country they reach – continued to chip away at confidence in the chancellor's leadership, even within her own party. The persistent strength of the right-wing Alternative for Germany also posed problems for Merkel, as did continuing pressure from the IMF to grant debt forgiveness to Greece as part of the country's third bailout package. The situation came to a head in early 2017, when Martin Schulz left the European Parliament to lead the largest rival of Merkel's Christian Democratic Union (CDU), the Social Democratic Party (SPD). The SPD's poll ratings rose sharply following the move, presenting a credible challenge to the chancellor.

Then Merkel's fortunes suddenly changed for the better. The popular leader of Alternative for Germany became embroiled in scandal, the IMF softened its stance on Greece and support for Schulz dissipated almost as quickly as it had arisen. By the end of the year, Alternative for Germany appeared likely to miss the threshold for representation in the German parliament, the IMF accepted Berlin's terms on the third bailout package and the SPD suffered a crippling defeat in Schulz's home state of North-Rhine Westphalia. As a consequence, the press began to speculate that Merkel would forge a strong partnership with Macron even before the September 2017 German elections, and that the two leaders would reshape the European project together.

Yet not all European countries were enamoured of the prospect of a rejuvenated Europe. Part of this scepticism stemmed from differing political priorities. For example, the governments of Hungary and Poland sought less to reinvigorate European institutions than to secure control of domestic politics – even at the expense of democratic checks and balances. Hungarian Prime Minister Viktor Orbán's regime had been engaged in this process since 2010, often with the tacit acceptance of the European People's Party, a transcontinental grouping of which Merkel's CDU is a member. Poland's Law and Justice party ruled during 2005–07 and returned to power in 2015. At the European level, it is connected to the Alliance of Conservatives and Reformists in Europe, of which the British Conservative Party is the largest member. Law and Justice party leader Jaroslaw Kaczynski embarked on an effort to rapidly consolidate his power without political cover from other parts of Europe, often coming into conflict with EU institutions and the governments of other member states as a result. On 27 July 2016, the European Commission issued a 'Rule of Law Recommendation' on a dispute between the Law and Justice party government and the Polish Constitutional Tribunal, giving the government three months to comply with EU recommendations. This elicited little response, perhaps because such a recommendation has no immediate enforcement or sanction. Instead, the disagreement dragged on throughout the year, with the European Commission reiterating its warnings and extending its deadlines for compliance only to see the Polish government engage in repeated rounds of brinkmanship. By May 2017, the European Commission's frustration with what it perceived to be threats to fundamental values extended to Hungary as well. When the issue was put to a vote in the European Parliament, it split the European People's Party. By mid-2017, neither the Polish nor the Hungarian government had conceded. Thus, while membership of the EU continued to be popular in both countries, support for strengthened European institutions was limited.

Such ambivalence could be seen beyond Central and Eastern Europe. Italy was, if anything, even more conflicted in its attitude towards the European project. Indeed, in the Pew survey that showed a strengthening of support for integration across the EU, Italy went against the trend. The Italians' grievances – as revealed through a series of polls commissioned during their referendum campaign – reflected the ongoing migration and financial challenges the EU faced. The problem was that although these challenges were labelled as 'European', Italians experienced the consequences of migration and financial fragility far more keenly than most EU countries, perceiving Italy's interests to be at odds with those of wider Europe on the issues.

There was a sharp contrast between migration movements across the Eastern Mediterranean into the Western Balkans and those across the Central Mediterranean into Italy. The agreement with Turkey effectively closed down the eastern route, leaving thousands of migrants stranded in Greece while preventing new arrivals. However, to the south of Italy, there was no government capable of stemming the flow of migrants; negotiations with different political groups in Libya succeeded on paper but failed to have an effect on the ground. As a result, a record 180,000 migrants crossed the Mediterranean into Italy in 2016, and it was estimated that another 200,000 would arrive in 2017. The Italian government attempted to deal with the pressure by relocating migrants across the country. It also called upon European partners to lend a hand. Although these domestic efforts were broadly successful – particularly under the government that was formed after the constitutional referendum – those abroad largely failed. By 21 June 2017, only around 7,000 migrants had been relocated to other parts of Europe from Italy, despite a commitment to relocate approximately 35,000.

Meanwhile, Italy's financial problems could be seen in the fate of Monte dei Paschi di Siena, the world's oldest bank, as well as a clutch of smaller institutions based in central Italy and Veneto. Italian banks were slow to feel the effects of the 2007–08 economic and financial crisis, and successive Italian governments even slower to respond. In the meantime, the EU had changed the rules for bailing out financial institutions to ensure that investors rather than taxpayers carried much of the burden. This burden-sharing arrangement is politically toxic for

Italy due to the geographical concentration of the country's banks – in terms of both funding and lending. Therefore, by trying to wind up four small banks based in central Italy in December 2015, the Renzi government inadvertently caused large numbers of families in affected regions to suddenly lose all their savings. The resulting scandal played into the negative sentiment that surrounded the referendum campaign, contributing to the failure of the constitutional-reform efforts backed by Renzi.

When Monte dei Paschi di Siena's future became uncertain, Italy's financial problems increased by several orders of magnitude, threatening financial stability in the euro area. Unlike the four smaller banks, Monte dei Paschi di Siena is systemically important for Italy and hence Europe. It is also the main financial institution in Tuscany, a political stronghold for both Renzi and his Democratic Party. Worse still, more than 40,000 households stood to lose their investments under the new European bailout. Finding a way to rescue Monte dei Paschi di Siena without imposing unacceptable losses on retail investors involved a series of high-profile negotiations in which the Italian government publicly positioned itself against the European institutions. As the negotiations dragged on, efforts to save two smaller banks in Veneto also failed to gain traction because of perceived European constraints. A solution emerged in outline in spring 2017 and began to crystallise in June. However, by that time, an increasing number of Italians perceived the European project as constraining their country rather than supporting it.

The lesson of these experiences is that a combination of factors relating to growing disaffection with democracy, instability on Europe's periphery and the legacy of the economic and financial crisis has created divisions among member states that run between West and East, North and South. A strengthened Franco-German partnership may be able to forge a strong response to this tension, but will need to establish its credibility with both domestic constituencies and across national governments. This is a difficult challenge in the best of circumstances. It is even more taxing with the global environment under stress in ways that emphasise European divisions more than they underscore common interests or values.

New transatlantic relationship

What was true for Europe was also true for the transatlantic relationship. The election of Donald Trump as the 45th president of the United States highlighted the significance of common values in underpinning the transatlantic relationship and the success of the European project. Trump's victory also raised the prospect that the US would downgrade its security commitment to Europe. Moreover, it suggested that influential figures in the White House might seek to undermine European integration in favour of bilateral relationships beneficial to the US. This raised the spectre of a new, transactional transatlantic relationship.

Merkel was the first leader to publicly acknowledge the values theme. In her congratulatory letter to Trump, she stressed that 'Germany and America are bound by common values … it is based on these values that I wish to offer close cooperation'. The theme remained close to the surface throughout their interactions. Merkel underscored the importance of common values when she met Trump in March 2017, and she reiterated it when they gathered for the NATO summit and the subsequent meeting of the G7 in May. However, by the end of those meetings, Merkel had concluded that Europe would have to stand on its own. At a campaign rally in Munich on 28 May, she stated that 'the times in which we could completely depend on others are, to a certain extent, over ... We Europeans truly have to take our fate into our own hands.' In reaction to the Trump administration's decision to withdraw from the COP-21 climate accord, Macron took that argument one step further. Speaking directly to the American people on 2 June 2017, he said that he would continue to push for protection of the environment as a value shared across the globe, underscoring that the Trump administration's view of the issue was an outlier in global opinion.

Prime Minister May tried a different tack. She quickly embraced the new Trump presidency and sought to position herself within the so-called 'special relationship' between the UK and the US. She was the first European leader to visit Trump, and she used that opportunity to invite him to the UK for a state visit. The invitation was immediately controversial. Opposition groups within the UK declared their outrage, promising to stage large-scale protests during his visit. This reaction returned the focus to differences in values across the Atlantic; it also revealed cleavages between May's foreign-policy aspirations and her connection to the British people. After May lost her majority in the election the following June, she and Trump agreed to postpone the state visit.

Trustworthiness also became an issue in the transatlantic relationship, as Merkel's assessment of the NATO summit suggested. The debate focused on American commitments to collective defence under Article 5 of the North Atlantic Treaty. In many ways, this disagreement was an effect of Trump's unconventional presidential campaign. In the context of an argument about burden sharing within the Alliance in April 2016, Trump made it sound as though he might favour US withdrawal from NATO, calling the organisation 'obsolete'. The suggestion captured headlines. So did his intimation that Washington might not defend NATO allies perceived as having failed to live up to their financial obligations. Moreover, Trump initially maintained his position on NATO after becoming president. Critics such as former defence secretary Robert Gates pivoted from accusing him of being 'wilfully ignorant' prior to the election to saying that 'there is some value in a disruptive approach' after joining Trump's transition team. It was not until April 2017 that Trump appeared to moderate his position, stating during a press conference with NATO Secretary-General Jens Stoltenberg that the Alliance was 'no longer obsolete'.

At the NATO summit the following month, Trump broke with protocol to again stress the importance of burden sharing and he failed to reiterate the US commitment to collective defence. After the event, Trump's advisers argued that such commitment went without saying. However, the fact that Trump was willing to take such a disruptive line as candidate – and his seemingly impromptu removal of a commitment to Article 5 included in the written version of the speech – contributed to a strong impression among European leaders that he could not be trusted. This was another reason why Merkel contended that Europeans had to take their fate in their own hands.

Trump's posturing was disconcerting for European allies, but it also played into a narrative about the need for greater European security cooperation pushed strongly by France and Germany in the aftermath of the British referendum. The narrative took root in the EU global strategy released soon after the vote. The strategy was conceived and drafted before Britain voted to leave the EU and only subsequently rebranded as 'a springboard to relaunch the process of European integration'. Nonetheless, the idea of re-energising European security cooperation was attractive to a German government that had grown tired of leading controversial discussion of macroeconomic-policy coordination and a French government exhausted by failed attempts at domestic economic reform. Therefore, when the Slovak presidency of the European Council convened a special summit in Bratislava in September 2016 to craft a new vision for Europe's future, the gathered heads of state and government insisted that 'we need the EU not only to guarantee peace and democracy but also the security of our people.' And while the Bratislava Declaration refers to the importance of creating economic and social opportunities for young Europeans, it does so in the context of concern about conflict-related migration, terrorism and external threats.

This mixture of social issues, migration, terrorism and external challenges was intentional. It was a coherent response to a tragic turn in the pattern, frequency and nature of terrorist attacks against European targets. On 14 July, Mohamed Lahouaiej-Bouhlel, a Tunisian living in France, drove a truck into a crowded beach-front promenade in Nice, killing 86 people and wounding many others. This use of a civilian vehicle in an act of extraordinary violence created a heightened sense of insecurity – particularly for Europeans used to gathering in large urban pedestrian areas. Moreover, the attack was followed the same month by a botched suicide bombing in the German city of Ansbach, and the brutal slaying of a priest in the French city of Rouen. The perpetrators of these assaults included foreign residents, recent migrants and European citizens whose parents had migrated to Europe. Hence, tackling the sources of this threat required a comprehensive mixture of initiatives.

This pattern of terrorist activity continued throughout the year to mid-2017, despite attempts to bolster intelligence-sharing and related security measures. The vehicular attacks were particularly dramatic. Terrorists drove into crowds at a Christmas market in Berlin in December, on a street in Stockholm in April and on two of London's bridges in March and June. Terrorists also indiscriminately targeted civilians with axes, knives and suicide bombs. The Manchester attack in May reflected the scale of the challenge. The perpetrator was born in England to Libyan parents. He had little or no outside support. And while he was known to British police as a potential threat because of his links to the Islamic State, also known as ISIS or ISIL, they had no reason to believe he was planning an attack.

British efforts to respond to the Manchester bombing revealed the changed nature of the transatlantic relationship. The British authorities shared intelligence on the matter with the US and France. Soon thereafter, some of these details – including images from the scene – were leaked to the *New York Times*. The British government appeared to immediately presume that the Trump White House was the source of the leak. Home Secretary Amber Rudd decried the lack of confidentiality, while the British police announced that they would temporarily suspend intelligence-sharing on the attack with the US. Although violent extremism was a common threat for Americans and Europeans, effective transatlantic cooperation in tackling the problem could no longer be taken for granted.

Complex negotiations and regional insecurity

Europeans were forced to devise an effective response to domestic and foreign threats while at the same time relaunching their integration project. There was no obvious solution to this combination of challenges. As a consequence, when it published the White Paper on the Future of Europe in March, the European Commission offered a menu of five possible scenarios ranging from 'carrying on' (read: muddling through) to 'doing much more together'. The most realistic options implied a flexible arrangement that either allowed willing countries to cooperate on a range of projects, or focused member states' attention on a smaller number of tasks in which they were likely to have the most impact. Subsequent reflection papers detailed the implications of these approaches for social policy, globalisation, the monetary union and security.

The process of agreeing to this agenda required immensely complex negotiations. The search for a consensus was further complicated by the need to forge and maintain a common negotiating position on the UK's exit from the Union, and relations with Russia and Turkey. The UK is key to European finance, Russia is critical to energy security and Turkey is important to migration. By the end of June 2017, each of these issues remained open-ended. The European Central Bank made important moves to relocate euro-denominated transactions inside the euro area, and yet the fate of the City of London as a global financial capital was undecided. The European Council retained its sanctions on Russia, and yet individual member states, including Germany, pushed back against efforts by the US Congress to extend those sanctions to transactions related to infrastructure connecting Russia to Europe. Even as the European Commission sustained the migration agreement with Turkey, there was rising tension between European capitals and Ankara during and after the April 2017 Turkish constitutional referendum, which formalised and expanded the power of President Recep Tayyip Erdogan.

Not all of Europe's neighbours were eager for European integration to succeed. Vladimir Putin's Russia actively sought to disrupt the European project, Erdogan's Turkey was at best indifferent to it and May's Britain (though still within the EU) hoped to get the best deal it could in forging a new relationship. Thus, relations with these countries were likely to shape the fortunes of the Union in the coming year.

Instability in the Western Balkans

The Western Balkans region has suffered from domestic crises, political fragmentation, regional tension and endemic corruption since the end of the Cold War. External powers have acted to stabilise the region, but their aggregated influence became less effective and benign in the year to mid-2017. At the same time, pressure from transnational threats, including Islamist militancy, has increased. The combined impact of the refugee crisis – involving the large-scale movement of people fleeing conflicts in North Africa, the Middle East and Afghanistan to a Europe reluctant to receive them – and the EU's inward turn following the UK's June 2016 vote to leave the Union, changed the strategic dynamic for the worse. As a consequence, the Western Balkans is in its most vulnerable position in a decade.

Although the region has distinct hubs of crisis, all of them are linked. Disputed borders, economic failure, corruption and constitutional and ethnic divisions have made Bosnia-Herzegovina dysfunctional, turned Macedonia into a tinderbox and left Kosovo and Serbia on course for a conflict only prevented by the NATO presence in Kosovo. In the year to mid-2017, both Macedonia and Bosnia-Herzegovina came closer to armed conflict. Whereas international engagement has routinely dampened the risks of war, a change in the constellation of external actors in 2016 exacerbated instability and insecurity.

Western commitments in the Balkans were calibrated in light of priorities in other regions. By contrast, Russia has been less resource-constrained and has demonstrated a significant appetite for risk. Moscow has been prepared to trial, most notably in Montenegro, techniques of covert intervention honed in Ukraine. Although it failed in Montenegro and had only mixed success elsewhere in the Western Balkans, the Kremlin showed little sign that its commitment to defending and extending its influence by supporting allies and undermining adversaries was set to diminish.

At the same time, radical Islamism and organised crime in the region were undercutting still immature political structures and feeding off social or economic marginalisation. The presence across the Western

Balkans of radicalised Muslims – some with experience as foreign fighters, others the product of local circumstances and actors – constituted a long-term threat to stability and integration. Kosovo had the highest number of foreign fighters per capita of any European country; their presence inspired many others to at least entrench their Muslim identity. Separately, the power of (principally Albanian) organised-crime networks proved increasingly difficult for either Balkan or Western European countries to contain.

The most troubling dimension of these developments was the growing interdependence, or at least coincidence of interest, of forces that undermined stability. For example, organised criminal groups were a ready and reliable supplier of weaponry and fake identities for terrorists, as well as a potential resource for Russian covert operations (especially those in the cyber domain). Although there is no shared interest between Russian ambitions and those of Islamists, they may have increasingly needed each other as adversaries. Both were feeding sectarian identity and politics. Since 2012, Russia had shown in the Balkans and elsewhere a steady interest in harnessing the unifying force of Orthodox Christianity. This created an increasingly tense relationship with radicalised and extremist Muslim actors, as well as with religious conservatives who had ties to Turkey and the Middle East.

As a consequence, the resilience of institutions was being tested. In Macedonia and Montenegro, they were surviving. Similarly, there were limits to how far criminal organisations and terrorist groups would seek to undermine states. Their interests were potentially better served by a weak but functioning government than by none. The same could be said of Russia, but the voracious appetite for risk displayed in Montenegro gave little comfort that Moscow would practise restraint. In this context, its activities in Republika Srpska (RS), the Serb entity in Bosnia-Herzegovina, potentially served as a test case.

Political transition in Macedonia

Macedonia was scheduled to hold elections in June 2016, but a gathering political crisis delayed the vote. The crisis began in January 2015 when the government, led by the Internal Macedonian Revolutionary Organization–Democratic Party for Macedonian National Unity (VMRO–DPMNE), accused the leader of the opposition Social Democrats, Zoran Zaev, of plotting a coup. Zaev responded with allegations that the government had wiretapped thousands of citizens, sparking large-scale anti- and pro-government demonstrations. Protests erupted once more in April 2016, when the country's president, Gjorge Ivanov, stopped the investigation into VMRO–DPMNE leader Nikola Gruevski, who had been the country's prime minister since 2006, and pardoned officials involved in the case. Finally held in December 2016, the parliamentary elections changed the established political order. The VMRO–DPMNE won only 51 of the 120 parliamentary seats, while Zaev's Social Democrats won 49 seats, having received the support of swathes of ethnic-Albanian voters who had previously voted for ethnic-Albanian parties but responded positively to Zaev's pledge to tackle high-level corruption and reinvigorate the country's faltering efforts to join the EU and NATO. After the two established ethnic-Albanian parties – both of which had served in Gruevski-led coalition governments since 2006 – lost half of their support, it became impossible for the VMRO–DPMNE to form a new majority coalition of the kind that was widely perceived to be self-serving and corrupt.

Ivanov, who had won the presidency in 2014 as the VMRO–DPMNE candidate, refused for six months to allow Zaev to form a coalition government, leaving Macedonia rudderless. The president claimed that Zaev sought to turn the country into a binational state and was working with an external power to undermine its sovereignty. The questionable basis for this claim was that in January 2016 the country's ethnic-Albanian parties had, with the involvement of the government of Albania, agreed on a platform to make Albanian a second official language. This measure went further than the 2001 Ohrid Agreement, which ended the armed conflict between the government and militant group the National Liberation Army, and made Albanian an official language in Albanian-majority areas. The platform also included a call for renegotiations on national symbols such as the flag to make them more representative of ethnic Albanians, as well as reform of the security sector and support for an EU-sponsored special prosecutor to investigate political corruption and wire-tapping allegations that implicated Gruevski. While elements of the platform (and Albania's involvement) could be seen as provocative and were guaranteed to foster ethnic-Macedonian nationalism, many observers suspected that Ivanov was seeking to protect Gruevski and others.

In April 2017, as the impasse continued, pro-VMRO–DPMNE nationalists broke into parliament and assaulted at least 12 parliamentarians in response to protests that demanded Zaev be allowed to form a ruling coalition. The government defended the assaults as political rather than criminal. This stance pushed the country closer to the brink of violent unrest and, potentially, armed conflict.

NATO has a strong presence in the Western Balkans, but its members failed to pursue a unified approach there. Bulgaria tended to support a more ethnic-Slav, Macedonian-nationalist perspective, as represented by the government of VMRO–DPMNE. Greece had long been at loggerheads with Skopje because it objected to the name 'Macedonia' and thus blocked progress on NATO and EU membership. The VMRO–DPMNE refused to compromise. Albania had long supported Macedonia's ethnic-Albanian population, which is closely linked to the ethnic-Albanian majority in neighbouring Kosovo, an entity with disputed status that hosts a NATO-led peace-support operation. Albania's prime minister and foreign minister acted with little restraint in signing the platform, as the move undermined moderate efforts to build a coalition and sharpened ethnic divisions, increasing the likelihood of ethno-political violence. Any outbreak of violence in Macedonia would affect Kosovo, as both were part of the former Yugoslavia and have maintained strong ties (Kosovo provided armed support to the insurgency during Macedonia's 2001 conflict).

By mid-2017, the prospect of violence had receded: Zaev had become prime minister and formed a government that quickly acted to defuse tension and improve the country's international relations. In this, the government embraced ethnic-Albanian political parties and took steps to temper ethnic tension. It also indicated a willingness to alter the country's legal name, to settle the dispute with Greece. Athens responded positively. Options for the new name included Vardar Macedonia (after the main river running through the country) or North Macedonia. Another possibility was interim name the Former Yugoslav Republic of Macedonia. After UN Special Representative Matthew Nimetz visited Skopje and Athens in July 2017, it seemed that quick advances might be possible after a quarter-century of deadlock and intransigence. Swift progress on NATO membership would perhaps give Zaev's coalition sufficient impetus to succeed with its anti-corruption agenda. However, as the regional and domestic political environment remained fragile, it was still possible that Macedonia would slide closer to armed conflict.

Crisis in Bosnia-Herzegovina

Bosnia-Herzegovina, a weak state comprising the RS and the Muslim-Croat Federation, also slipped deeper into crisis in the year to mid-2017. The country faced conditions similar to those shortly before the 1992–95 war broke out; the difference two decades later was the international presence there. However, this presence has weakened over ten years – declining sharply since 2015, as the EU became distracted by its internal dynamics – and may be unable to prevent violence if it diminishes further. The country completed its EU Questionnaire (a preliminary step on the path to membership), adopted an EU Stabilisation and Association Agreement and conducted a defence review in the year. However, some political leaders behaved in a manner that seemed calculated to destabilise Bosnia-Herzegovina and to exacerbate the crisis.

The most provocative moves were made by the RS president, Milorad Dodik, who announced that he would hold a referendum on independence from Bosnia-Herzegovina by the end of 2018. Such a plebiscite would run counter to the constitution and risk igniting armed hostilities once again. Although Western actors, international organisations and Bosnian Muslims broadly condemned Dodik's proposal, only Serbia and Russia had the ability to force him to back down – and neither did so. He had violated the constitution once before, holding a referendum to establish a Bosnian Serb national day on 9 January, a date with historical and cultural significance. By organising celebrations of the national day and announcing the independence referendum, Dodik demonstrated his disregard for the rest of the country, international opinion and the rule of law. He also struck a blow against the unity of the Armed Forces of Bosnia and Herzegovina by involving the (Bosnian Serb) 3rd Infantry Regiment in the celebrations.

Dodik also announced plans to – with support from Bosnian Croats seeking to secede from the federation – hold a referendum intended to force the removal of the three international members from the nine-member Constitutional Court of Bosnia and Herzegovina. He could use the attempt to mobilise further nationalist support and build his case for independence. Other politicians also contributed to the growing sense of dismay and decay. In a report to the UN Security Council, Valentin Inzko, international high representative for Bosnia-Herzegovina, noted the dangers of the country's formal request to the International Court of Justice (ICJ) in February 2017, which sought to revise the court's 2007 judgment in the Bosnia–Serbia genocide case. That case had found that, while Bosnian Serbs were directly responsible for genocide, Serbia was not – although Belgrade had failed to prevent the July 1995 act of genocide in and around Srebrenica or punish its perpetrators. This request to revise the 2007 judgment was essentially an initiative by Bakir Izetbegovic, the Bosnian Muslim member of the tripartite presidency of Bosnia-Herzegovina. He alleged that there were grounds to do this because of new material from the trial of General Ratko Mladic at the International Criminal Tribunal for the former Yugoslavia (ICTY) – although the new material pointed more in the opposite direction, to Mladic's personal role in particular. Unsurprisingly, Bosnian Serbs rejected the move as unconstitutional and boycotted parliament, while also threatening to block government and presidential decisions. At its core, the ICJ request could be regarded as would-be retribution aimed at Dodik. But it also underlined the degree to which emotions about the genocide continued to run high in Bosnian Muslim communities, in which a growing number of young people – many of them with no direct personal experience of the 1992–95 war – were becoming radicalised.

Due to conclude by November 2017, the Mladic case was set to define the reputation and legacy of the ICTY. It offered the international community a chance to remedy the failure to convict those responsible for the 1992–93 acts of genocide that prompted the creation of the court (the lack of convictions fuelled resentment among Muslims) and to confirm Mladic's responsibility for the act of genocide in and around Srebrenica. Such an outcome would dismay Bosnian Serbs but would have a positive psychological effect on Bosnian Muslims, providing official recognition of what victims (and observers) have long regarded as genocide. It would temper the enduring sense of injustice among Bosnian Muslims, which has prevented reconciliation and state-building, while also contributing to radicalisation and preserving the potential for a resumption of violence.

Izetbegovic's request to the ICJ deepened political divisions in the country and made it difficult for institutions to function effectively, due to the lack of a common perspective shared by the three principal ethnic communities. Detailed social research showed that Bosnia-Herzegovina had experienced an exceptional decline in social trust during 1998–2007 and a lack of affective attachment to the country, compounded by low regard for citizenship. All of this was underpinned by separate curricula in schools for Croats, Bosnian Muslims and Serbs. Inzko had a sensible vision for breaking down barriers between communities through a mass-exchange scheme, but he was unlikely to be able to implement it in the face of opposition within the country and a lack of support internationally. The strength of ethnic intolerance, citizenship preferences and nationalism – exacerbated by other factors – presented a major threat to the viability of the state.

Economic troubles added to the malaise in Bosnia-Herzegovina. The debt crisis suffered by Croatia's largest company, Agrokor, left supermarket shelves in Bosnia-Herzegovina half empty and threatened the jobs of its many employees. International financing, which had for years kept the dysfunctional state afloat, was likewise in jeopardy. The proximate cause of this was the failure to secure a new excise-duty law in April 2017, a condition for an IMF Extended Fund Facility agreed on in September 2016. The fund did not disburse the second tranche of payments, amid arguments that Bosnia-Herzegovina would have to start afresh with the IMF. That failure had further consequences because World Bank funding is conditional on a working IMF programme. European Bank of Reconstruction and Development infrastructure projects were also cast into doubt. Overall, the EU judged that Bosnia-Herzegovina would lose €2 billion (US$2.3bn) in international support and investment. Perhaps most critical of all, without the Extended Fund Facility money, the state and its entities, particularly the RS, faced a liquidity crisis and possible bankruptcy. Such economic degeneration could only be expected to increase nationalist divisions, political instability and the likelihood of violence.

Growing major-power competition

International engagement across the region – especially in Bosnia-Herzegovina, Kosovo and Macedonia – has been critical to mitigating the combination of nationalist tension, economic failure, corruption and mass migration that could lead to armed violence. However, the composition and effects of international engagement are changing. Competition between Western countries, Russia and a range of Islamic countries has diluted the stabilising impact of this engagement in the Western Balkans.

The key to a prosperous and peaceful future for the region is eventual EU membership. The most critical case in this respect is Bosnia-Herzegovina. There are many people in the country and outside it who wish to see the international presence withdrawn and the constitution rewritten. These calls are fundamentally misguided, as Bosnia-Herzegovina's most significant problem is not the constitution but the lack of consensus in the country. At present, the RS government is oriented more towards Serbia than Bosnia-Herzegovina and works to disrupt the latter. The most viable way to change this dynamic is to create a realistic prospect of EU membership for Serbia. This would compel the RS to behave in ways that would not impede Serbia's progress. Meanwhile, to secure EU membership, Serbia would close its border and act in other ways calculated to give the RS a stark choice: stay locked into a dysfunctional Bosnia-Herzegovina without support from Belgrade, or cooperate with Sarajevo to turn Bosnia-Herzegovina into a more politically and economically effective entity. Such an entity might eventually achieve EU membership, thereby securing an open border with Serbia.

Serbia appeared to be on a fast track to an accession agreement until 2015, but the subsequent migration crisis and the UK's vote to leave the Union inhibited the process. London had been one of the most ardent supporters of EU enlargement as part of a strategy to enhance regional stability. In the wake of the UK referendum, support for enlargement weakened and the prospective EU27 prioritised efforts to preserve unity and address internal problems. At that point, the migration crisis had already reduced the pace and likelihood of Serbia's accession. Indeed, most EU member states responded to the influx of migrants from the south by putting pressure on the vulnerable states of the Western Balkans to stem the flow. Their actions turned the Western Balkans into a frontier region to impede the transit of migrants, in a manner that echoed the Austro-Hungarian Empire's use of the Western Balkans as a barrier to the Ottoman advance on Central Europe – albeit that the Austro-Hungarian leadership sought to halt a military operation, not merely human migration.

However, there was another long-standing impediment to Western Balkan states' chances of EU accession: corruption. Albania, Bosnia-Herzegovina, Macedonia and Kosovo all ranked poorly in the Corruption Perceptions Index. Brussels adopted a strong anti-corruption stance in its dealings with Western Balkans countries that aspired to EU membership. Yet corruption threatened more than just these aspirations. It undermined economic performance, restricted development and prosperity, and fuelled instability and insecurity.

This could be seen in Croatia as much as in the non-EU states in the region, especially in the troubles of Agrokor. The company employed more than 40,000 people and its annual revenue of €6.5bn (US$7.6bn) was equal to 15% of GDP. It had expanded through debt financing but proved unable to control costs; when it failed to secure a refinancing deal in January 2017, the firm suffered damaging debt-rating downgrades and its suppliers halted deliveries. The prospective collapse of Agrokor threatened Croatia's social stability and economic health. With debts of €5.7bn (US$6.4bn), the company was too large for the state to bail out and to do so would have invited controversy. In April 2017, a series of irregularities in the firm's dealings led the prime minister, Andrej Plenkovic, to dismiss Zdravko Maric, a former Agrokor senior executive, as finance minister. These irregularities included Maric's alleged failure to declare a conflict of interest, actions to aid the troubled company, non-disclosure of his knowledge of its problems and use of personal loans. However, Croatian parliamentary rules – and voting – meant that Maric survived, albeit damaged and under threat as more alleged evidence of his concealment of Agrokor's difficulties emerged in July. Thus, the Croatian government had few options but to encourage investment in the firm or to seek arrangements with its creditors, most of whom were Russian.

Agrokor's debts to Russia's Sberbank and VTB formed part of a broader pattern of increased Russian presence in the Western Balkans, associated with a mixture of destabilisation, security infiltration and economic and political domination. Agrokor, as with much of the regional economy, had become dependent on Russia through state weakness and corruption. Russian loans at rates unrealistically favourable to the borrowers, linked to energy sales by Gazprom, left companies such as Agrokor and countries such as Croatia indebted to the Russian state and its proxies. As a consequence, these entities became dependent on Moscow in ways that raised security concerns and threatened greater instability.

Serbia's position was more perilous than that of Croatia, as it was outside the EU and had lost a credible prospect of membership in the short term. The country's president, Aleksandar Vucic, who was re-elected in 2017, continued to engage in a fine balancing act between the West and Russia. Despite his nationalist past, Vucic was oriented towards the EU and recognised that the best future for Serbia and the region lay in accession to the Union. However, his position was constrained by Russian penetration of Serbian political life, as prospects of EU membership were put on hold after 2015. It was likely that he did not trust and could not rely on the chiefs of his security and intelligence services, while a cadre of Western-trained and -oriented military officers had been largely pushed aside. Meanwhile, Russia's relative economic strength left Serbia with little room for manoeuvre. In December 2016, Vucic was obliged to accept Russian military aircraft and other materiel that Serbia did not need for operational purposes: six MiG-29 fighter aircraft, 30 T-72 tanks (similar to the M-84 model once produced in the region and familiar to the Serbian military) and 30 combat reconnaissance vehicles. Although welcomed by many in the Serbian security sector, these gifts would be costly. Vucic estimated that modernisation of the aircraft would cost Serbia an unaffordable €180m–230m (US$210m–268m), plus maintenance costs, while imposing a military and security dependency on Moscow at odds with the country's neutrality.

Moscow's increased influence on Serbia was apparent at the UN General Assembly. In 2015 Serbia had sought to mediate in the Ukraine conflict and pressed for enhanced conflict monitoring by the Organization for Security and Co-operation in Europe. Yet, in December 2016, Serbia voted with Russia and 24 other states against a General Assembly resolution tabled by Ukraine that called for an international monitoring force in Crimea. Serbia's 'no' vote reflected increased Russian leverage over the country.

Russian influence was apparent across the Western Balkans, with Moscow issuing proposals designed to deepen states' dependence on Russia and leave them unable to diversify trade and other economic activity. Dodik, the RS president, visited Moscow more often than he did Sarajevo. After one such trip to the Russian capital, in March 2017, he made his only visit to Sarajevo since being interviewed by prosecutors in late 2016, to meet the EU foreign secretary, Federica Mogherini. There, he announced that the RS would not hold an independence referendum for the time being, while insisting that it would do so eventually. It appeared that he did this at the behest of Russia, which had calculated that its interests were best served by holding the referendum in reserve and appearing to support EU efforts in Bosnia-Herzegovina.

In Macedonia, Russia suffered a setback with the formation of Zaev's government. During a visit to Moscow in May 2017, the president, Ivanov, was told by Putin that the Russian government was closely monitoring Macedonia. Putin also signalled support for Ivanov and the nationalist agenda. Zaev made clear that the possibility of rapprochement with Greece and swift progress towards NATO membership were priorities for his administration in light of Russian interference in Macedonia. Yet while Moscow had been rebuffed, it retained levers of influence in the country that meant the risk of armed hostility there could not be dismissed.

Russia's ambitions were more firmly checked in Montenegro, which joined the Alliance in June 2017. However, the outcome might have been very different had Russian security operatives succeeded in their coup attempt on the day of the country's October 2016 election. The plot was to begin with demonstrators attacking the parliament building, after which agents provocateurs disguised as policemen would fire into the crowd. The resulting disarray would be used to assassinate the prime minister, Milo Djukanovic. The plotters were Serbian nationals who took orders from Russian military-intelligence officers via parts of the Serbian security apparatus. Although Moscow reportedly apologised to Belgrade and insisted the two officers were rogue operators, this explanation was implausible. NATO states rallied to aid Montenegro and thereafter Moscow's influence in the country declined. Russia then placed economic sanctions on Montenegrin goods; Russians accounted for 19.2% of tourists in Montenegro in March 2016, but just 7.3% one year later.

NATO, the US and terrorism

While the EU is important to the states of the Western Balkans, NATO remains critical because of its military remit, narrow focus and the involvement of the US. The Alliance forms the core of the Kosovo Force (KFOR), which conducts peace-support operations and provides territorial defence. The NATO-led presence in Kosovo is central to supporting stability in the wider region. A reluctance to cross NATO or the US has placed a limit on the extent to which Kosovo's ethnic-Albanian-dominated authorities will support the Albanian minority in Macedonia. Furthermore, KFOR's presence reduces the risk of a return to hostilities between Kosovo and Serbia – which remains a possibility because Serbia (backed by Russia) claims sovereignty over Kosovo, while the Kosovo authorities (backed by the US) assert their independence. The delicate nature of the stand-off was underlined in early 2017, when the prime minister of Kosovo, Hashim Thaci, suggested that the existing Kosovo Security Force – effectively a civilian carabinieri intended to support the civilian authorities – should grow from 3,000 to 5,000 personnel and become a fully fledged army. All members of NATO and the EU swiftly rejected the proposal. It became clear that such an initiative would not make Kosovo more secure but instead increase the chance that the far larger and more capable Serbian army would take action to protect Kosovo Serbs. Seemingly, Thaci's proposal had been inspired by a remark made by US National Security Advisor H.R. McMaster in Senate hearings to the effect that the US could reduce its presence in Kosovo if the territory were to have its own army. It is likely that McMaster was merely stating a basic military calculation. And the US responded decisively to Thaci's proposal. However, there was concern in the Western Balkans that a larger crisis might draw the attention of the new US president, Donald Trump, and potentially trigger a reappraisal of the US commitment to the region.

The aspect of the Western Balkans' security complex most likely to attract top-level attention in Washington was a key concern of the Trump administration: rising Islamist extremism and potential terrorism. The issue was of particular concern in Kosovo, where in January 2017 seven people were convicted of 19 terrorism-linked offences. One was found guilty of having recruited members of ISIS in Kosovo; the other six were found guilty of joining a terrorist organisation, after travelling to Syria to fight alongside ISIS.

Western security services and observers assessed that hundreds of Muslims from Bosnia-Herzegovina, Serbia, Kosovo, Macedonia and Albania had travelled to Syria, while others remained in the Western Balkans but were ready to launch terrorist attacks against local state institutions and other targets. The authorities foiled plots to attack people celebrating New Year in Sarajevo in December 2015, and to attack the Israeli football team in Albania in November 2016. The region was also used as a base for attacks in Western Europe: residents of Kosovo and Serbia were arrested for terrorism offences in Belgium and Germany. The Western Balkans featured many of the conditions associated with a present and growing terrorist threat: poverty; high unemployment; a widespread sense of injustice; declining secularism and rising religious conservatism in parts of society; and proselytising by actors from Kuwait, Qatar, Saudi Arabia and Iran, as well as Turkey. The prospective demise of the ISIS 'caliphate' in Iraq and Syria suggested that the threat of Islamist terrorism would grow in the Western Balkans as natives who had fought in the Middle East returned home to a poor, unstable and divided region. Such terrorism could, in turn, provoke retaliatory nationalist or ethnic violence. Although some prominent figures such as Dodik exaggerated the dangers posed by Islamist terrorism, the issue continued to be of genuine concern. It was evident that NATO, with the US in the lead, would be an integral part of the policy response to the threat in and from the Western Balkans.

©IISS
Atlantic Ocean
Pacific Ocean
MEXICO
Mexico City
THE BAHAMAS
Havana
CUBA
DOMINICAN REPUBLIC
BELIZE
JAMAICA
HAITI
Santo Domingo
Belmopan
Kingston
Port-au-Prince
GUATEMALA
Tegucigalpa
Guatemala City
HONDURAS
EL SALVADOR
San Salvador
NICARAGUA
COSTA RICA
Managua
Panama City
San José
PANAMA
TRINIDAD & TOBAGO
Caracas
Georgetown
VENEZUELA
Paramaribo
Cayenne
GUYANA
SURINAME
FRENCH GUYANA
Bogotá
COLOMBIA
Quito
ECUADOR
PERU
Lima
BRAZIL
Brasília
La Paz
BOLIVIA
PARAGUAY
Asunción
CHILE
URUGUAY
Santiago
Buenos Aires
Montevideo
ARGENTINA
Falkland Islands (UK)
South Georgia (UK)
Capital
Borders
0
1,000 miles
0
1,000km

Chapter 10

Latin America

On the night of 2 October 2016, Colombian President Juan Manuel Santos and his administration received the shock results of a national referendum on a peace accord with FARC. Having begun in secret in Havana years earlier, the process that led to the plebiscite was designed to end Colombia's 52-year conflict with the rebel group. Santos had thrown his entire political weight behind the accord, and with its signing won praise around the world. He was already the clear favourite to win the Nobel Peace Prize. In the weeks before the vote, most polls indicated that the 'Yes' campaign would win by a small but comfortable margin. But instead the 'No' campaign – capitalising on widespread mistrust of FARC and discontent with Santos – won by less than half a percentage point. Although the government quickly renegotiated controversial parts of the deal and went through congress to approve it (while Santos still received the Nobel Prize), the result caused considerable damage to the peace process and Colombia's already fractured politics.

This sense of disappointment – with politics and politicians, unachieved promises and obstacles to progress – was common in Latin America, and indeed the rest of the world, in the year to mid-2017. The election of Donald Trump as president of the United States dealt a major blow to the strategies and ambitions of many countries in the region, not least Mexico.

Meanwhile, longer-term challenges remained unresolved. Latin American countries accounted for nine of the ten highest homicide rates in the world. In 2016 Venezuela, El Salvador, Honduras and Jamaica all registered murder rates of more than 50 per 100,000 people, according to either their public-security authorities or civil-society organisations. Drug trafficking and other forms of organised crime continued to threaten the rule of law and public security in almost every country in the region. The political and economic crisis in Venezuela, in which protesters clashed with an increasingly authoritarian government, grew more severe and lacked any clear path to resolution. Brazil's president, Dilma Rousseff, was impeached amid a severe economic crisis and one of the largest corruption scandals in modern history. In most other Latin America countries, cases of graft – both related and unrelated to Brazil – further undermined trust in the government. The region's economies showed no sign of returning to the prosperity of the 2003–13 commodity boom.

As in Colombia's peace process, some of these disappointments were offset by what many saw as positive trends. Proliferating corruption scandals were often the product of improved transparency and respect for the rule of law. With rare exceptions – Venezuela, Nicaragua, Cuba – Latin America remained unquestionably democratic. Most of the region's economies weathered the economic downturn far better than in past decades. And even the inauguration of the Trump administration had some benefits for the region, hastening its decades-long effort to engage with the world independently of the US.

Nonetheless, in the eyes of Latin American citizens, many of these shifts in fortune were unacceptable. They retained high expectations for improvements in government transparency and ethics, public services, anti-crime efforts, social equity and economic growth, as well as respect and dignity on the world stage. Yet there appeared to be little prospect that these expectations would be met in the short term.

Turmoil of the Trump era

Trump's ascent to the presidency was likely the most significant strategic development for Latin America in the year. Although the event initially had only a limited tangible impact, its symbolic and political implications quickly became clear. In some respects, the Trump era immediately challenged long-held assumptions about regional alignments, diplomatic interests and countries' strategic orientations.

On the campaign trail and in his first months in office, Trump was particularly critical of the North American Free Trade Agreement (NAFTA), calling it 'the worst trade deal ever approved by this country' and pledging to unilaterally withdraw from the arrangement unless certain conditions were met. He came close to starting the withdrawal process on 26 April 2017, but personal phone calls from the leaders of Canada and Mexico – and pleas from several of his close advisers – convinced him to wait.

Depending on its terms, any cancellation or renegotiation of NAFTA, the world's second-largest trading bloc, would likely affect Mexico more than any other country. The US accounted for 73% of Mexico's exports and 51% of its imports in 2016. Much of northern Mexico's industrial base is built on cross-border manufacturing processes and integrated value chains enabled by NAFTA.

Nonetheless, Mexico had several negotiating tools that it could use against Trump. Firstly, were NAFTA to be cancelled, bilateral trade would fall back to the World Trade Organisation's 'most favoured nation' status, under which Mexico is legally permitted to impose substantially higher tariffs than the US. Such a development would have major effects: both countries' economies would suffer, while some US industrial and agricultural exports to Mexico would be hit particularly hard. Secondly, Mexican cooperation on immigration is critical to Trump's broader agenda. Seven out of every ten migrants from Central America bound for the US are apprehended at Mexico's border with Guatemala. In theory, Mexico could cease these detentions. Finally, cooperation with Mexico on border security and efforts to fight drug trafficking, terrorism and illicit financial flows is vital to US national security.

Trump's policy positions also had important implications for the rest of the region. For decades, the US has been a relatively consistent economic presence in Latin America – albeit slightly less so in South America. Washington has long encouraged free trade through both bilateral and multilateral agreements. With a GDP almost double that of the rest of the Americas, the US is the economic centre of gravity in the Western Hemisphere. It is the largest or second-largest trade partner of all but a few countries in the region. Multinational companies based in the US – along with corresponding investments, products and financial services – remain influential across Latin America.

Since the end of the Cold War, the US has also been a consistent advocate of human rights and democracy in the Western Hemisphere (at least in principle). Support and funding from Washington has been important for the Organization of American States (OAS) and the Inter-American System, a human-rights body. At times, the stated goals of these organisations have come into conflict with many Latin American countries' values of sovereignty and independence. Although the US has often been accused of using support for democracy and human rights as a cover for interventionism, such critiques became relatively muted under the Obama administration.

For many Latin Americans, the US has historically offered the promise of a better life, tempting many of them to escape war, other violence or economic crises by emigrating to the country. The US is home to around 55 million Latin Americans, a number markedly larger than the population of Colombia. As a result, cultural and historical ties between the US and Latin America run deep, encompassing many diaspora communities.

Before Trump's inauguration, US policy on Latin America was fairly predictable on a wide range of other issues. For decades, Washington was a strong proponent of anti-drug policies and an important source of funding for various security efforts. Pressure from the US, largely through multilateral financial institutions, has helped shape macroeconomic and fiscal policies in many countries in Latin America since the end of the 1980s, the region's 'lost decade'. Development aid from Washington has been especially important to Colombia, Central America and the Caribbean. Even the relative value of the US dollar is critical to the economies and public finances of most Latin American countries.

From a Latin American perspective, most or all of these seemingly stable factors were immediately called into question by Trump's election, after a divisive campaign built on an anti-trade, anti-immigrant 'America first' platform.

On the surface, most Latin American leaders reacted carefully to these shifts and approached the first six months of the Trump administration with caution. Countries particularly dependent on US trade or still interested in forging new ties – such as Argentina, Brazil and Peru – quickly made overtures to Trump. Even Mexico, which initially reeled from Trump's campaign and election, swiftly developed a careful strategy designed to hedge its bets and engage with his administration. Many others seemed to avoid the subject, defaulting to the status quo and attempting to avoid disruption. Yet there was a clear divergence in the geopolitical strategies and interests of the US and most of Latin America. Trump accelerated two existing processes: Latin American countries' growing independence from the US and their pursuit of new economic and political ties with the rest of the world, China above all.

On his fourth day in office, Trump pulled out of the Trans-Pacific Partnership (TPP). This effectively ended negotiations on the formation of the trade bloc, dealing a major blow to Mexico, Peru and Chile, its three Latin American signatories. Other countries that hoped to continue opening their economies to the world, including Argentina and Brazil, were similarly disappointed by the long-term implications of the decision (although, in the short term, they avoided the competitive disadvantage of exclusion from a trade bloc with considerable market access).

Elsewhere, many traditional recipients of US development and security assistance – such as Honduras, Guatemala, El Salvador, Colombia and several Caribbean countries – worried that this support might fall victim to budget cuts. Pro-democracy and human-rights activists across Latin America feared that, under Trump, the US would no longer be an effective champion of their values in the region.

Washington's rapprochement with Cuba, a historic initiative announced by the Obama administration in late 2014, also appeared to be in limbo. On the campaign trail, Trump initially seemed open to maintaining relations, but later promised to roll back the efforts of his predecessor. After the election, Trump tweeted, 'if Cuba is unwilling to make a better deal for the Cuban people, the Cuban/American people and the U.S. as a whole, I will terminate deal.' The White House stated in February 2017 that it was in the midst of a full review of US policies on Cuba, but it remained uncertain what – if anything – would be reversed.

Perhaps the most significant effect of Trump's election in Latin America occurred in public perceptions. The first controversy Trump caused while campaigning came from his statement that 'when Mexico sends its people, they're not sending their best … They're bringing drugs. They're bringing crime. They're rapists. And some, I assume, are good people.' His pledge to 'build a wall' on the southern US border and 'make Mexico pay for it' angered many in the region. Nowhere was this truer than in the Latin American country closest to, and most intertwined with, the US.

Fraying Mexican politics

Partly because of the ripple effect of Trump's election – but also due to chronic voter dissatisfaction with corruption, insecurity and the slow pace of economic reform – Mexico's political landscape grew more fractious and volatile in the year to mid-2017.

The president, Enrique Peña Nieto, saw his approval ratings fall to the lowest of any Mexican leader in the modern era. By early 2017, only 12% of Mexicans approved of his performance in office. This collapse was largely caused by his failure, since relatively early on in his term, to address perceptions of corruption and ineffectiveness on the part of his government and the Mexican state more broadly.

Peña Nieto's government – the first led by the Institutional Revolutionary Party (PRI) since it was ousted in 2000, following seven decades of one-party rule – entered office in December 2012 with an ambitious reform agenda. He aimed to simultaneously modernise and liberalise the energy, telecoms and television sectors, along with labour laws and the education system. In doing so, he hoped to tackle many of the structural challenges perceived as having held Mexico back in the past.

Although Peña Nieto's first year in office was productive and generated optimism, voters quickly became disenchanted with a relatively lacklustre economy and a series of corruption scandals at various levels of government. He was personally named in connection with several allegations, including the particularly damaging claim that a construction company had built and paid for a US$6.3m mansion for his wife just as it was being awarded a multibillion-dollar government contract. In another striking case, Javier Duarte, governor of Veracruz State and a former rising star in Peña Nieto's party, spent six months on the run after allegedly siphoning millions of dollars from state-government coffers. He was eventually arrested in Guatemala in April 2017.

The government's popularity declined further in early 2017, when – in response to a devaluing peso, the limitations of the country's energy reforms and ongoing fiscal shortfalls – it cut fuel subsidies. In response, energy prices rose by 20% in most parts of Mexico. Known locally as the *gasolinazo* (gasoline blow), the measure spurred anger and protests across the country. Even many of the president's supporters criticised his decision to cut fuel subsidies all at once rather than gradually.

Many Mexicans also considered Peña Nieto – a telegenic career politician married to a former model, singer and *telenovela* actress – to be unable to improve the country's crime and security situation. For instance, many of them viewed the government as unwilling to seriously investigate or respond to the massacre of 43 students from Ayotzinapa Rural Teachers' College in September 2014. Overall, the murder rate ticked up sharply: 20,792 homicides were reported in Mexico in 2016, a 22% increase from 2015 and 35% more than in 2014 (although still far below the most recent peak, in 2011), according to the Executive Secretary of the National System for Public Security. In the first six months of 2017, seven journalists were killed in the country. Mass murders and shoot-outs continued to be common occurrences in many parts of Mexico.

To be sure, there were several successes in Mexico's campaign against drug cartels. Most notably, the capture and extradition to the US of Joaquín 'El Chapo' Guzmán, Mexico's most wanted drug lord, partially resolved an embarrassing and frustrating episode for the government. Guzmán, who was first captured in 1993, had twice escaped from Mexican prisons. His second escape, in July 2015, through a mile-long tunnel dug underneath the prison – complete with lighting, ventilation and a makeshift motorcycle-transport system – captured the world's attention and seemed to highlight corruption and incompetency in the country's criminal-justice system. He was recaptured with the assistance of US law-enforcement agencies in January 2016. The decision to extradite him – a possibility Mexico had previously dismissed – on 19 January 2017 (the last full day of Barack Obama's term) seemed to be a partial admission of those mistakes.

The year to mid-2017 also saw the continuing break-up of some of the main cartels in Mexico, partly due to efforts to capture or kill their leaders and figureheads. Thus, competition and power struggles between the gangs increased, contributing to intensifying violence. Importantly, there were few indicators that underlying levels of drug trafficking – the fundamental cause of Mexico's insecurity – had declined.

Meanwhile, Peña Nieto's perceived political weakness grew far worse as Trump's campaign gained ground and many Mexicans looked to their leader to defend their country. Instead, anxious to reassure financial markets that Mexico would be able to work with Trump should he win, Peña Nieto's government invited both US presidential candidates to Mexico City. While the Democratic candidate, Hillary Clinton, declined the invitation, Trump accepted.

Politically, this was a severe miscalculation by the Mexican government. The optics of the meeting and the press conference outraged much of the country. Standing at 5′7″, Peña Nieto appeared diminutive and unable to stand up to the much taller Trump; many Mexicans saw their president as unable to directly challenge the US businessman on his rhetoric or policies, especially the proposed border wall. Worse, they felt that Peña Nieto had unwittingly given Trump the opportunity to appear presidential and diplomatic on the world stage without first having to temper his rhetoric against Mexicans. Luis Videgaray Caso, secretary of finance and public credit, had organised the visit, reportedly concerned that the markets saw Mexico as unable to work with Trump. He resigned amid the resulting uproar. After Trump won the US election in November 2016, Videgaray was regarded as having been vindicated (within the government, at least) and returned to his former post. Peña Nieto's reputation largely failed to recover.

Effectively, the president instead became a lame duck almost two years before the end of his six-year term. This injected an early sense of urgency into the upcoming presidential elections scheduled for July 2018. As Mexican elections lack a run-off system – the party with a plurality of the vote wins – they tend to be unpredictable. However, by mid-2017, the two frontrunners in the polls appeared to be Margarita Zavala, from the centre-right National Action Party (PAN), and Andrés Manuel López Obrador, the leader and founder of the new National Regeneration Movement party. Peña Nieto's PRI party had yet to select a candidate, but was expected to finish in third place.

Zavala, the wife of former president Felipe Calderón, who governed between 2006 and 2012, represented relative continuity for Mexican politics. While she was cautious to avoid being too closely linked with her husband's tenure – which was marked by a controversial security and anti-narcotics strategy that many Mexicans saw as bloody and ineffective – most of her policy proposals are in line with the traditional centre-right.

In contrast, López Obrador (commonly known by his initials) is a distinctive and polarising force in Mexican politics. The charismatic former mayor of Mexico City ran for president in 2006 and 2012. In his first campaign, he ran as a left-wing populist critical of trade and privatisation – leading many of his opponents and several international observers to compare him to Venezuela's Hugo Chávez. After losing to Calderón by less than one percentage point, he refused to concede defeat. Instead, he accused the government of tampering with the vote count and declared himself to be the 'legitimate president' in a rally in Mexico City's central square.

In his second election attempt, López Obrador sought to moderate his image considerably, reaching out to Mexico's traditional business class and elites. In contrast to his first campaign – in which he focused on inequality and poverty – he worked to present himself as a pragmatic operator able to reinvigorate Mexico's political system and economy. He focused many of his criticisms on Calderón's security policies. This strategy was also unsuccessful: he lost to Peña Nieto by more than six percentage points.

In this third campaign, López Obrador has carved out another new strategy, one that focuses on corruption and Mexico's relationship with the US. While Zavala and the other candidates have also been sharply critical of Trump's rhetoric, López Obrador has been the most forceful in arguing that Mexico should rebuff Washington. His image of personal austerity and independence from Mexico's three main political parties – having cut ties with the left-wing Party of the Democratic Revolution after the 2012 election – also helped him effectively criticise corruption in the political system. Polls show that he is viewed as the strongest on anti-corruption reforms and standing up to Trump, both expected to be driving electoral issues.

Therefore, the winner of the 2018 election was likely be determined by two factors. The first centred on whether López Obrador – who despite two decades on the national political stage had positioned himself as an outsider – was able to assuage the lingering concerns of wealthy and middle-class Mexicans about his populist and anti-market tendencies. Disappointed with the return of a PRI government, as well as the tenure of the two preceding PAN governments, it was possible that many industries would support López Obrador. The second factor related to whether the Trump administration would maintain its hostile rhetoric and positions on Mexico.

Against this background, there was no sign that the growing divisions, hostility and sense of cynicism among the Mexican electorate would dissipate quickly. Mexican politics arguably remained more unstable than at any time since the 1994 elections, which were disrupted by the assassination of the leading candidate. This instability was compounded by significant institutional challenges and security concerns, as well as persistent drug trafficking, corruption, impunity, fiscal shortcomings and structural obstacles to economic growth. None of these challenges was likely to become less daunting in the short term.

Venezuela's crisis and regional diplomacy

Throughout the year to mid-2017, Venezuela's economic and political implosion – Latin America's worst crisis in decades – became increasingly severe. The country's GDP shrank by at least 10% in 2016. As its left-wing *chavista* government, headed by President Nicolás Maduro, grew more repressive and authoritarian, there was little evidence that a resolution was at hand. The country remained in gridlock, with widespread violence and shortages of basic goods. Perhaps the only positive development was that Latin American governments, long hesitant to criticise the Venezuelans, slowly began to express more concern about the crisis.

Many international observers were alarmed by the growing humanitarian disaster in Venezuela. As the economy continued to spiral downwards, inflation reached more than 800% by many credible estimates. According to one study, 93% of Venezuelans said that they lacked the income to buy sufficient food, while 75% reported having lost weight due to hunger. The medical system deteriorated, often lacking basic medicines and supplies. Doctors were reportedly forced to operate on bloody tables, as they lacked water to clean them.

The price of oil, the country's primary export and the lifeblood of its economy, remained far below its peaks in 2007–13. Government mismanagement and a lack of investment also continued to hobble the state-owned oil company, PDVSA, resulting in a steady decline in production. Both the government and the oil sector were deeply indebted, largely to Chinese state-owned banks, with no clear means to repay outstanding loans. Thus, the unsustainable fiscal and economic distortions in the Venezuelan economy steadily grew more intractable.

In 2016 the newly elected opposition majority in the National Assembly was systematically stymied by the *chavista*-controlled presidency, Supreme Court and National Electoral Council. In practice, members of the opposition were left with little power to make laws or constrain the executive.

Instead, the opposition decided to turn their efforts to implementing a constitutionally sanctioned recall referendum that could remove Maduro from office. Opinion polls showed that most Venezuelans would support his ouster. However, for the referendum to be meaningful, it would have had to occur before 10 January 2017 – the halfway point of Maduro's term. Before that date, a successful recall would trigger snap elections. Afterwards, his vice-president would replace him.

In the second half of 2016, the *chavista* government carefully employed legal and administrative mechanisms to disrupt the recall effort. These mainly involved delaying a series of steps to gather signatures, each of which required the approval of the National Electoral Council. Nonetheless, the opposition scrambled to collect the millions of signatures required to trigger the recall. In turn, the government slowed the process by voiding large numbers as illegal, delaying signature counts and mandating various audits. Although many members of the opposition claimed to have the requisite number of signatures, the de facto deadline eventually passed.

On 29 March 2017, the Supreme Court announced a surprise ruling that effectively neutralised the National Assembly and allowed the courts to become the country's legislative authority. Although the Supreme Court quickly reversed the ruling in the face of protests and an international outcry, the decision set off a wave of unrest. In subsequent weeks, Caracas and other cities experienced massive clashes between demonstrators, the security forces and government-backed militias known as *colectivos*. Almost 30 people died in the first month of the protests.

Meanwhile, the government often deployed the military to quell the demonstrations, and to try some demonstrators before military tribunals rather than in civilian courts. On 8 April 2017, Henrique Capriles, governor of Miranda State and the opposition's presidential candidate in the 2012 and 2013 elections, was banned from political activity for 15 years. On 1 May, Maduro announced the establishment of a 'constituent' national assembly in an attempt to rewrite the constitution. He claimed that a new constitution would help reduce tension, but the opposition and many international observers regarded the measure as designed to concentrate power in Maduro's hands, marginalise his opponents and avoid the risk of contending elections scheduled for December 2018. According to most counts, Venezuela continued to incarcerate more than 100 political prisoners, including former mayor of Caracas Antonio Ledezma and Leopoldo López, leader of the Popular Will party.

Three factors differentiated Venezuela's crisis from similar episodes in Latin American history, and partially explained why the challenge facing the country remained so difficult to resolve. Firstly, even in the face of declining revenues, the country's oil economy provided the government with the enormous resources required to sustain itself through the crisis. Secondly, the military had become deeply integrated with the civilian leadership – both politically and ideologically. This focused the capability to deploy force within the *chavista* movement. Thirdly, according to most accounts, many members of the government were involved in drug trafficking and other illicit activity. In February 2017, the US placed sanctions on Tareck El Aissami, the first vice-president, due to his alleged 'significant role in international narcotics trafficking'. According to international observers, members of the *chavista* government had accrued millions of dollars in revenue from drugs, bribes, graft and other illegal activity. This factor, perhaps above all, explained the government's determination to retain power. Expulsion from office threatened to expose Venezuela's leaders to extradition and prosecution on charges of narcotics trafficking and corruption, as well as human-rights violations and other crimes. As a consequence, traditional international measures designed to promote democracy, such as diplomatic pressure and sanctions, were relatively unlikely to have their intended effect.

As conditions in the country grew worse, there were growing international calls to respond to the crisis. Within the OAS, whose remit includes defending democracy and human rights, Venezuela's base of support began to erode. Led by the OAS Secretary-General Luis Almagro, a Uruguayan former diplomat, a coalition of countries – most of them in Latin America – became more vocal in criticising and confronting the Venezuelan government. Although there did not appear to be consensus on the idea of potentially suspending Venezuela's membership of the OAS under the terms of the Inter-American Democratic Charter, an increasing number of countries – including for the first time some of Venezuela's traditional allies in South and Central America (most notably, Brazil) – came to believe that inaction was no longer permissible. Mexico also emerged as a particularly vocal leader in pressing for action. This was a significant development for a country that had long spoken against interventionism in most forms, an approach that many observers saw as a means to ensure it never faced similar scrutiny. The change of heart reflected both the severity of the Venezuelan crisis and Mexico's pressing need to take a more assertive role in setting the diplomatic agenda in the Trump era.

In a move likely intended to pre-empt suspension or further sanctions, the Venezuelan government announced on 26 April that it would begin the two-year process of leaving the OAS. The effort deepened Venezuela's isolation, a country that only ten years earlier had been perhaps the most diplomatically influential in Latin America.

However, this regional realignment had numerous causes beyond the humanitarian and political crisis. With declining oil production and a struggling economy, Venezuela was no longer able to use its oil wealth to reinforce alliances and maintain a network of dependent states. This was particularly true in the Caribbean, where the country's generous oil-subsidy programme, Petrocaribe, had a significant effect between 2005 and 2013. The programme was designed to taper off when the oil price fell, and did so from 2014 onwards. For the 18 countries that benefited from Petrocaribe – most of them small, energy-starved Caribbean and Central American states – Venezuela had been a critical source of support. This earned Caracas a substantial reserve of goodwill and diplomatic backing. Although some residual loyalty among these states remained, by 2017 it was abundantly clear that Venezuela would not be able to afford generous subsidies again even if the oil price rose.

Secondly, a wave of anti-incumbent political sentiment across the region largely targeted the left-wing governments that had been Venezuela's natural allies. Many of them were ousted. Between 2013 and 2017, centre-right governments took power in Argentina, Brazil, Paraguay, Peru and Jamaica. Moreover, even some of the leftist governments that remained in office felt electoral pressure to distance themselves from Venezuela as the crisis grew worse, painting the issue as a domestic conflict that needed to be resolved internally. Lenín Moreno, the left-wing candidate who narrowly won the election to succeed Rafael Correa as president of Ecuador on 2 April, called for a dialogue between the government in Caracas and the opposition, urging other countries to respect Venezuela's right to self-determination. 'They must take it to their people, let the Venezuelan people decide', he said. El Salvador, a country led by former left-wing guerrilla Salvador Sánchez Céren, adopted a similarly hands-off position.

It remained unclear how this ongoing realignment would affect Latin American diplomatic relations in the long term. And, even as the coalition of concerned countries grew, it appeared to lack the influence required to alleviate the crisis in Venezuela.

Colombia's fractured peace process

Colombia's peace process, and its transformation into a prosperous and stable country after decades of widespread violence, was a historic accomplishment for Latin America. The conflict with FARC, which killed an estimated 220,000 people and displaced more than 5m Colombians, had been a major security and development challenge for Colombia and its neighbours for half a century. Due to the instability, Colombia had, at various points in history, become a locus for the production and trafficking of drugs, particularly cocaine. FARC had been involved in the drug trade since the 1990s, if not earlier. Terrorism, murder, kidnapping, assassination and other forms of violence and intimidation had become a part of life for many Colombians. There were rampant human-rights violations in the country – committed not just by the guerrillas, but also by the armed forces and the right-wing paramilitaries that emerged to oppose FARC. The conflict disproportionately affected Colombia's rural poor, indigenous groups, Afro-Colombians and other vulnerable and minority groups. For many of these victims, peace meant a chance for a better future. Despite marked progress, events in the year to mid-2017 showed that these challenges had not been entirely resolved. By 24 August 2016, when the final details of the peace accord were announced in Havana, many of its underlying weaknesses had become clear.

Crucially, the deal was extraordinarily polarising within Colombia. Although President Santos was able to negotiate with FARC, he was unable to convince a large portion of the country that the accord was good enough. Opponents viewed the deal as offering impunity to terrorists, murderers and drug kingpins. Many believed that FARC had been on the brink of a battlefield defeat when Santos effectively provided it with a lifeline. Others were simply unable to accept many of the concessions in the deal, especially the Special Jurisdiction for Peace in Colombia, a tribunal under which FARC commanders who freely admitted their crimes could face only house arrest and community service rather than jail time. Worse, many viewed the incentives for the guerrillas to focus on electoral politics rather than violence – such as observer seats in congress – as granting them undeserved legitimacy. Some Colombians even believed that their country was on a path to being governed by FARC-led *castrochavismo* (an unlikely scenario, given the guerrillas' pervasive unpopularity).

Publicly, the movement opposing the deal was led from the right by Senator Alvaro Uribe, Santos's predecessor as president. Uribe, a hardline conservative whose father was killed by FARC in a botched kidnapping attempt in 1983, argued passionately against almost all concessions. He viewed Santos, who had previously served as Uribe's defence minister and was effectively his anointed successor, as having betrayed his political legacy by negotiating with the group. Thus, Uribe repeatedly referred to Santos as a 'traitor' whose accord would bring neither justice nor peace.

There were fears on the other side of the political spectrum that the deal would result in relative amnesty for human-rights violations committed by military leaders and right-wing paramilitary groups, including the many who were deeply involved in drug trafficking and other criminal activity. According to some estimates, as many as 2,000 military officers and soldiers accused or convicted of crimes planned to submit to the transitional-justice system to receive lenient treatment. Of particular concern was the so-called 'false positives' scandal, in which members of the military murdered poor or mentally ill civilians to present their bodies as those of combatants, thereby gaining bonuses and promotions. More broadly, there continued to be concern over the role of the military – one of the largest and most professional in Latin America – in a post-conflict environment. Reportedly, the peace process created tension between the military and civilian leaderships that threatened to persist throughout the development and transitional-justice processes.

Amid bitter divisions over the peace process, discontent with a slowing economy, concerns about corruption and fear that the security environment was deteriorating as the illegal-narcotics trade grew, Santos's approval ratings fell sharply. Throughout 2016 and 2017, polls found that fewer than 20% of voters generally approved of his government. Large majorities thought that Colombia was moving in the wrong direction. Many believed that Santos was only concerned with his rosy image abroad and was willing to cede anything to achieve an accord that would define his legacy. To these critics, the official signing ceremony in the Caribbean port of Cartagena on 26 September was proof. The grand outdoor event was attended by the UN secretary-general and dozens of other heads of state, dignitaries and celebrities all dressed in white to signify peace. While the luminaries applauded, many Colombians watching on television felt uncomfortable with the image of the FARC commander standing equal to the elected president.

All of these factors contributed to the result of the referendum on the peace deal. In practical terms, the loss was more symbolically damaging than legally debilitating. Less than two months later, Santos and his allies passed a restructured (but generally similar) deal through congress and declared it to be fully in force. Only Santos's sizeable majority in congress prevented Uribe and the other critics from blocking the agreement outright. Thus, the implementation phase of the accord, intended to be a unifying moment for Colombia, began haltingly amid controversy. The accord faced substantial challenges that its political weakness was sure to exacerbate.

As FARC fighters began to gather in 26 disarmament zones across the country, under the careful observation of UN monitors, the government scrambled to address a host of obstacles and concerns. The first of these was reliance on extraordinarily complicated logistics: 7,200 FARC guerrillas were to gather over the course of six months amid delays in the construction of so-called 'demobilisation zones' and other setbacks. From the beginning, the timeline of the process seemed unrealistic. Another 6,000–10,000 members of FARC (primarily supporters and personnel living in cities) were to be registered. More than 14,000 weapons were to be handed over to the UN mission. The transitional-justice process quickly encountered further controversy due to the passage of a new piece of legislation perceived as watering down some of its provisions.

Many in the US and elsewhere expressed deep concern about the soaring rate at which coca (the main ingredient of cocaine) was being produced in Colombia. In March 2017, the US government estimated that the territory given over to coca cultivation there had grown to 188,000 hectares in 2016, an increase of almost 20% from 2015. Analysts argued that this was partly because of a decision in 2015 to cease aerial spraying to eradicate the crop, a controversial and chemically intensive process. Moreover, the peace process created a perverse incentive for poor rural farmers to plant more coca in the expectation that they would later gain compensation by switching back to another crop, especially given the government's hesitance to launch aggressive new anti-drug offensives into FARC territory during the negotiations.

As part of the effort to prevent criminal groups from filling the power vacuum left by departing guerrillas, the government began to implement an ambitious rural-development, security and land-reform plan. Although many Colombians expected that there would eventually be a 'peace dividend' for the economy, the government's investment in schools, roads, job-creation programmes, police forces, local administrations and reconciliation-tribunal processes required significant funding in the short term. With the domestic economy growing relatively slowly, the Santos government hoped that the international community would help fill the gap. However, it was unclear whether President Trump would fulfil his predecessor's commitment to increase US annual support to US$450m as part of the Peace Colombia initiative. The budget passed for the remainder of 2017 sustained the funding, but Trump's proposed 2018 budget cut support for Colombia by 36%. Even without this cut, there was no guarantee that Colombia would receive the funds it needed to achieve its goals.

A separate peace process between Bogota and the National Liberation Army (ELN) – a relatively small, leftist guerrilla group unconnected to FARC – made little progress, as the group's fighters continued to clash with government forces after the negotiations between the sides began. Given that the ELN tended to be more decentralised and disorganised than FARC, there was persistent doubt about its leaders' capacity to comprehensively represent fighters on the ground. Equally, Santos's political weakness made it difficult for the government to make credible commitments as part of the process. Finally, with FARC engaged in the demobilisation process, the ELN had a considerable opportunity to expand into the territory and criminal markets vacated by the larger group.

It became clear that the process of implementing the peace accord with FARC would extend well beyond the end of Santos's term, in 2018. As a result, the coming presidential campaign was viewed as a de facto second referendum on the peace process. Uribe had yet to back any of his party's candidates, but the eventual recipient of his support was likely to enter the run-off against someone friendlier to the peace process. Even long before the referendum, the election seemed destined to be the final hurdle for the peace accord due to Colombia's deep political divisions.

Brazil's diminished influence

With 44% of Latin America's landmass, 34% of its economic output and 33% of its population, Brazil has often been seen as a central player in the region – a perception that dates as far back as the country's 'unwritten alliance' with the US in the first half of the twentieth century. In recent years, Brazil has had global ambitions, perpetually craving a permanent seat on the UN Security Council.

However, by 2017 the country's regional and global ambitions, as well as its diplomatic standing, had been almost entirely subsumed by internal turmoil. The country's worst recession in two decades, caused by a collapse in commodity prices, continued: the economy shrank by 3.6% in 2016, following a 3.8% drop in 2015. The crisis had exposed deep fiscal weakness and unsustainable government spending that forced the government to carry out painful cuts. Political fights over budgets and methods for breaking out of the downward spiral provoked further chaos in Brasilia as President Michel Temer (who came into office after the removal of his predecessor, Dilma Rousseff, in May 2016) continued to push through austerity measures and reforms. Although they were arguably necessary, these measures undermined services and limited the economy in the short term. Moreover, corruption investigations into Temer and other political figures looked set to suspend the reform effort.

This austerity trap severely limited Brazil's domestic and foreign policy, with the result that it could no longer afford to maintain a robust diplomatic presence on the regional or world stage. The government cut international-cooperation budgets and embassy staffs. The quality of the country's foreign service started to decline, as did its visibility in capitals around the world. Like Venezuela, Brazil has at times in recent years fallen considerably behind on its payments to the United Nations and the Organization of American States (for slightly different reasons). The absence of Brazilian leadership in UNASUR and Mercosur created dysfunction and stagnation within both organisations.

Meanwhile, Temer's approval ratings rarely topped 10% in 2017. Much of his cabinet, largely comprising members of the centrist Brazilian Democratic Movement Party, was targeted in corruption investigations. On 18 May, there emerged tapes of Temer appearing to endorse bribes to Eduardo Cunha, former speaker of the house. With Temer refusing to resign, the resulting public outcry further destabilised Brazilian politics. Unless Temer stepped down, the allegations were likely to lead to a constitutional stand-off between the president and the Supreme Court. Even if he did resign, he had no clear successor; the only plausible option was a caretaker government led by a member of congress or the judiciary. Some commentators suggested that Fernando Henrique Cardoso – president during 1995–2003, and in his mid-80s – could return to office until new elections were held.

As the crisis continued, Brazil's diplomatic power in Latin America was replaced with a different sort of transnational influence: networks of corruption partially exposed by the economic downturn and growing public concern about graft. The *Lava Jato* (Car Wash) corruption investigation – the largest in Brazilian, and perhaps world, history – uncovered immense misdeeds and a network of impunity that passed through almost all political parties and state institutions. Centred on Petrobras, the Brazilian state oil company, the scandal reportedly involved billions of dollars in bribes, amounting to tens of billions in losses for the company and the state – mostly due to the overvaluation of assets. The investigation revealed everything from secret Swiss bank accounts to illicit campaign slush funds; it implicated hundreds of business leaders and politicians representing all of Brazil's major parties, including the heads of both legislative chambers and multiple cabinet ministers. For the first time in Brazilian history, a large number of powerful figures were charged, prosecuted and jailed.

The scandal expanded far beyond Brazil. Odebrecht, a Brazil-based company and Latin America's largest construction conglomerate, became a flashpoint for an expanded set of corruption revelations. One of the dozens of companies that admitted paying bribes as part of the *Lava Jato* probe, the Odebrecht case soon took on a life of its own. Between 2015 and early 2017, 77 company executives, including Chief Executive Officer Marcelo Odebrecht, were prosecuted and jailed. Because many of its operations went through US-based financial institutions, a large number of Odebrecht's dealings fell under the jurisdiction of the US Department of Justice.

In December 2016, Odebrecht announced a deal in which it would pay at least US$2.6bn to US and Swiss authorities, the largest corruption fine in history. As part of its investigation, the US released details of Odebrecht's bribery activities in ten countries. This created a cascade of scandals in Colombia, Panama, the Dominican Republic, Ecuador and other countries. The most damaging allegations related to Peru, at least two of whose former presidents were implicated in several bribery schemes. As a consequence, in January 2017, the Peruvian government cancelled a US$7bn Odebrecht project to build a natural-gas pipeline. Due to the cancellation of the initiative, delays to other public-works projects and an expected chilling effect from the scandal, the Peruvian finance ministry cut its 2017 growth forecast by a full percentage point.

The dilemma of these corruption scandals is that they appear to bring both progress and disruption. In the long run, the exposure and prosecution of corruption cases is a profoundly positive development. Not only do anti-corruption movements have a salutary effect on the quality of government, they can also improve the efficiency of economies and improve citizens' trust in the state. However, in the short run they do the opposite: governments are paralysed, economies slow and public trust is shattered. Thus, the key question for Latin America concerned whether the public's patience would hold and reformist resolve would be maintained amid rising cynicism, ambivalence and dysfunction.

Region of contradictions

In the year to mid-2017, Latin America's trajectory was neither wholly positive nor entirely negative. The region ended its last active insurgency, but many countries remained among the most violent in the world. There was huge progress in exposing corruption, but the fight against impunity remained inconsistent and halting overall. Almost every country continued to be governed by freely elected democratic leaders, but exceptions such as Venezuela starkly defied this norm. Although Latin America took some steps towards greater regional independence and autonomy, its voice on the world stage was muted. Citizens took to the streets to demand their political and civil rights, yet in many countries there was a decline in democracy and political freedom. While the worst of the economic downturn appeared to have passed for most countries, the short-term outlook was daunting: many observers feared that the region would experience lacklustre growth for years to come. Several states had made significant gains in equality, political inclusiveness and sustainable development, but the list of pending challenges on the economic-development and governance agenda was long, and it was likely that there would be further setbacks in coming years. Perhaps most concerning of all, the failure to meaningfully improve the security situation or make gains against drug cartels loomed over many Latin American countries. Venezuela experienced the most severe deterioration in security, but violence also spiked in Brazil and Mexico, and remained stubbornly high in Honduras, El Salvador and Guatemala. Without a fundamental change in counter-narcotics efforts – including on the demand side, primarily in the US – drug trafficking would almost certainly continue to hobble Latin America's progress.

In the face of this mixed and unsteady outlook, the dynamics of the region continued to shift. Trump and the economic slowdown seemed to offer new incentives for the pursuit of an economically integrated and politically unified Latin America. Mexico was especially active in attempting to establish new ties with other countries in the region, partly as a means of reducing its reliance on the US. Previously divergent trading blocs the Pacific Alliance and Mercosur – the former encompassing Chile, Colombia, Mexico and Peru, and the latter Argentina, Brazil, Paraguay and Uruguay (following Venezuela's suspension in December 2016) – made tentative steps towards cooperation. Many of the political barriers to cooperation and collective action seemed less immutable.

However, even amid these changing dynamics, Latin America seemed unlikely to engage in a regional-integration programme strong enough to boost productivity and improve its global competitiveness, at least in the short term. Many of the structural obstacles to cooperation, growth, prosperity and good governance remained stubbornly intact. As a consequence, Latin America struggled to keep up with the rapidly changing geopolitical environment.

Chapter 11

North America

A historically divisive and ugly presidential campaign; the shock election of Donald Trump as president; subsequent months of turbulent politics, featuring scandal and erratic presidential pronouncements but little legislative action: these were the chief elements of an extraordinarily eventful and disruptive period for the United States during the year to mid-2017.

They left other governments around the world unsure whether long-standing tenets and assumptions about the US still held, and whether the US still aspired to leadership of the free world, as had all its presidents in living memory. Some leaders espied opportunities to advance their nations' interests in personal diplomacy with Trump, a businessman and television celebrity who had no experience of government. Others, especially in Europe, wondered whether they could still count on Washington as a firm ally.

Uncertainty in the United States

The US had become an increasingly divided country during the eight years of Barack Obama's presidency. While this had been a period of steady recovery from the near-collapse of the financial system in 2008, among the white working class there was a sense of being left behind, and a rising anti-establishment perception that the Democratic

YUKON TERRITORY
NORTHERN TERRITORIES
BRITISH COLUMBIA
Alaska (United States)
ALBERTA
MANITOBA
SASKATCHEWAN
QUEBEC
NEWFOUNDLAND
CANADA
ONTARIO
PRINCE EDWARD IS.
NEW BRUNSWICK
NOVA SCOTIA
MAINE
Ottawa
VERMONT
NEW HAMPSHIRE
MASSACHUSETTS
RHODE ISLAND
CONNECTICUT
NEW YORK
PENNSYLVANIA
NEW JERSEY
DELAWARE
MARYLAND
Washington DC
Pacific Ocean
Atlantic Ocean
WASHINGTON
OREGON
IDAHO
MONTANA
WYOMING
NORTH DAKOTA
SOUTH DAKOTA
MINNESOTA
WISCONSIN
MICHIGAN
NEVADA
UTAH
COLORADO
NEBRASKA
IOWA
ILLINOIS
INDIANA
OHIO
WEST VIRGINIA
VIRGINIA
UNITED STATES
CALIFORNIA
KANSAS
MISSOURI
KENTUCKY
NORTH CAROLINA
TENNESSEE
ARIZONA
NEW MEXICO
OKLAHOMA
ARKANSAS
SOUTH CAROLINA
MISSISSIPPI
ALABAMA
GEORGIA
TEXAS
LOUISIANA
FLORIDA
Capital
Borders
0
500 miles
0
500km
© IISS

Party had become devoted to identity politics that consistently privileged ethnic minorities, women, gays and transgender people, as well as favouring banks and corporations over working people. Trump tapped into this dissatisfaction in a populist campaign that deployed racist messaging, anti-Muslim fear-mongering and personal attacks on his opponent, Hillary Clinton. Both candidates, in their different ways, were polarising figures who had the highest disapproval ratings of any candidates in the previous ten presidential elections. The tone of the campaign was epitomised by Trump's repeated encouragement of his audiences to chant 'lock her up' when discussion turned to Clinton's use of a private email server during her 2009–13 tenure as secretary of state.

Trump was an unorthodox Republican Party candidate, and he ran an unorthodox campaign of which iconoclasm was the hallmark. He challenged established conventions of US policy, as well as the international order that Washington had played a major part in creating. He decried the global trading system, including the World Trade Organisation (WTO) and the North American Free Trade Agreement (NAFTA), as harming US prosperity and exporting jobs abroad. He railed against US alliances, which he portrayed as allowing rich nations in Asia and Europe to free-ride on US military protection. He dismissed as naive idealism the US practice of promoting democracy and human rights abroad. And he rejected the science of climate change as a hoax devised by foreign states, especially China, to stop the US from developing its hydrocarbon resources. To halt illegal immigration from Latin America, Trump promised to build a wall along the US border with Mexico, and to deport millions of illegal immigrants. He advocated a ban on the entry of refugees from Muslim countries to the US, as well as setting aside US reservations about dealing with the Assad regime in Syria so that the US could annihilate the Islamic State, also known as ISIS or ISIL, in Syria and Iraq. Whereas his post-Second World War predecessors had viewed the US as the leader of the free world, Trump offered a different credo. During his presidency, it would be 'America first'.

Two controversies in the campaign stood out. One was the hacking of the Democratic National Committee server to obtain sensitive and embarrassing emails exposing internal tension, including the emails of Clinton's campaign chairman John Podesta, which were released via the website WikiLeaks. It quickly became apparent that this was done by Russian hackers. The other was the decision of James Comey, FBI director, to write a letter to Congress just two weeks before the election concerning the investigation into Clinton's use of the private email server. Comey reported that the FBI had become aware of additional emails and he had authorised investigators to look into whether they contained classified information or would have a bearing on the investigation. The controversy reduced Clinton's slender opinion-poll lead and dominated press coverage for the remainder of the campaign.

Trump defied the polls to secure a clear majority of 304 of 538 votes in the Electoral College – which constitutionally determines the victor – although he received almost three million fewer popular votes than Clinton nationally. The result reflected the Democrats' dominance in major cities and on the east and west coasts, and Republicans' geographically wider support in the South, the Midwest and the western interior. The new House of Representatives was decisively Republican, by a margin of 238 seats to 193; the new Senate narrowly so, by 52 seats to 46, with two independents caucusing with the Democrats.

Turbulent start

In his first six months in office, Trump acted on some but not all of his pledges. He sought to impose a temporary travel ban on people entering the US from six Muslim-majority countries, causing chaos at airports until his order was stayed by the courts. He pulled the US out of the Trans-Pacific Partnership (TPP), a mooted trade agreement under negotiation for years by the Obama administration. In June 2017, he began a process to withdraw the US from the landmark COP-21 global agreement on climate change that had been reached in Paris in December 2015, also after many years of difficult negotiations. He sent mixed messages on the American commitment to NATO, while harrying his allies to increase their spending on defence. In a sign of his priorities and of his approach to international relations and security, his first budget proposed a US$57-billion increase in military spending while visiting cuts of one-third on the State Department and foreign aid.

Trump's arrival made for turbulent and disorderly politics. His cabinet contained right-wingers who sought to execute a highly conservative agenda, for example in the areas of justice and education. But his efforts to carry out Republican promises such as reform of the tax system and replacement of Obama's signature healthcare system were stymied by a lack of clear policy direction from the White House and by discord among Republicans.

Trump led a fractious administration, often undermining his own officials through his aggressive use of social media. The president's close family, especially his daughter Ivanka and her husband Jared Kushner, were playing important roles in the White House. So too was Stephen Bannon, the anti-establishment former head of the right-wing Breitbart News, who was White House chief strategist. Underlining the fact that this was not a normal administration, at mid-year most government positions that required nomination by the president and confirmation by the Senate remained unfilled. Administration officials often expressed conflicting positions on a range of issues, and congressional action on much legislation was handicapped by disagreements among the Republican majorities.

Russia's long shadow

The latter months of the campaign, and the first six months of the administration, were heavily overshadowed by investigations into contacts between Trump aides and Russians. In the run-up to the election, Trump had fuelled suspicion that his campaign was colluding with Russia to sway the result by, among other things, publicly inviting Moscow to reveal Clinton's unaccounted-for official emails. His victory was tainted by suspicion of Russian interference in the electoral process through cyber operations, an issue which the US intelligence community had raised well before the elections and for which the

Obama administration had imposed sanctions that included the expulsion of Russian diplomatic (and presumably intelligence) personnel from the US.

In the interim between the elections and Trump's inauguration, his national-security adviser-designate Michael Flynn met with Russian officials and subsequently appeared to have improperly reassured them that the sanctions would be lifted. On 13 February, after he dissembled about the substance of these discussions in a conversation with Vice President Mike Pence, Flynn was forced to resign after only 25 days in office. It later transpired that during the transition, Obama had advised Trump not to appoint Flynn as national-security adviser. Moreover, six days after Trump became president, then-acting attorney general Sally Yates informed the Trump administration that Flynn was under investigation and vulnerable to blackmail. During the subsequent months, new revelations about contacts between Trump aides and Russians repeatedly fuelled suspicions of collusion.

On 2 March, Attorney General Jeff Sessions recused himself from the Russia investigation, because of inaccuracies in his confirmation-hearing statements about meeting Russian Ambassador Sergey Kislyak in 2016. The depth of the president's anger at this move by Sessions, a long-serving senator from Alabama who had been an early supporter of Trump's candidacy, was to become evident later.

On 20 March, Comey disclosed to the House Intelligence Committee that the FBI was not only 'investigating the Russian government's efforts to interfere in the 2016 presidential election' but also looking into 'the nature of any links between individuals associated with the Trump campaign and the Russian government, and whether there was any coordination between the campaign and Russia's efforts'. Leaks then revealed that at least one campaign associate, Carter Page, was the subject of FBI surveillance under a Foreign Intelligence Surveillance Court warrant. This meant that the agency had presented the court with probable cause that he was acting as a foreign agent.

US intelligence agencies had already provided some details, jointly assessing in January that

> Russian President Vladimir Putin ordered an influence campaign in 2016 aimed at the US presidential election. Russia's goals were to undermine public faith in the US democratic process, denigrate Secretary Clinton, and harm her electability and potential presidency. We further assess Putin and the Russian Government developed a clear preference for President-elect Trump. We have high confidence in these judgments.

Some of Trump's supporters argued that Russia's campaign had not been effective because the White House subsequently did not lift sanctions on Russian entities or enact a major change of policy on the Ukraine conflict or NATO, and had launched airstrikes against the Moscow-backed regime of Syrian President Bashar al-Assad. They cited these sources of tension as evidence that the Trump administration had not coordinated with Russia. However, according to a declassified US intelligence-community assessment, the primary goal of Moscow's efforts was not to prompt radical policy shifts in Russia's immediate national interest but rather to delegitimise the US democratic system and weaken whoever became the next president. Moscow may have viewed a critically damaged Trump presidency perpetually enmeshed in scandal as a better result than a potentially hawkish Clinton presidency.

Trump denied all accusations and employed familiar tactics of distraction through outlandish claims. He alleged that former Obama-administration officials had leaked classified material, and accused his predecessor of 'wiretapping' Trump Tower, his home and business base in New York – a charge that Comey, National Security Agency Director Michael Rogers and former director of national intelligence James Clapper all denied.

Congressional committees pursued inquiries into the Russia links. But further controversy was engendered by the bizarrely partisan behaviour of House Intelligence Committee Chairman Devin Nunes. During the 20 March hearing, he focused on leaks rather than the substance of Russian actions or possible links with Trump associates. Nunes subsequently held a press conference outside the West Wing, announcing that he had just seen intelligence reports corroborating accusations that the Obama administration had surveilled the Trump campaign. The episode sparked outrage because intelligence products are supposed to be provided to Congress directly, not via the White House. Moreover, only Nunes – not his Democratic counterpart Adam Schiff nor the rest of the committee – had seen the alleged reports. Nunes eventually recused himself from the Russia investigation.

The Senate Intelligence Committee, led by Chairman Richard Burr of North Carolina and Vice Chairman Mark Warner of Virginia, functioned in a more collegial, professional and bipartisan manner. Burr declared that 'this investigation's scope will go wherever the intelligence leads'.

On 9 May, amid growing evidence of contact between the Trump campaign and Russian officials, the president dismissed Comey from his post. Trump justified the decision with reference to Comey's late intervention in the election campaign, which at the time he had praised. Many observers saw the dismissal as an attempt to halt the Russia investigation. Within eight days, political pressure had mounted to the extent that Deputy Attorney General Rod Rosenstein appointed Comey's predecessor as FBI director, Robert Mueller, as special prosecutor. As Mueller assembled a team and pursued the investigation in a low-key manner, the congressional hearings continued. In June, Comey and Sessions testified in public Senate hearings. Comey asserted that Trump had pressured him to stop investigating Flynn and the Russia connection.

Among Trump aides who were implicated in alleged links to Russia were Flynn, who was revealed to have discussed lifting sanctions with the Russian ambassador, and who in 2015 had accepted a US$45,000 fee to speak at a dinner at which he sat next to Putin at a table populated by Kremlin leaders, three of whom were under US sanctions; Paul Manafort, Trump's campaign manager for part of 2016, who was forced to resign after disclosure of payments from former Ukrainian president Victor Yanukovych, an ally of Moscow; Roger Stone, a friend and adviser of Trump who served briefly in the campaign and communicated with the Russian-aligned hacker Guccifer 2.0, who alerted him to forthcoming WikiLeaks email dumps; and Kushner, who took part in meetings with Russians but insisted there was no collusion. Virtually all of these men retained criminal lawyers. So did other key figures in the administration, including Trump himself.

By mid-2017, there was no conclusive, publicly available evidence that the Trump team had coordinated with the Russians to influence the 2016 election. But there remained unanswered questions about the nature and content of contacts between Trump aides and Russians who were used by the Kremlin to maintain deniability – in particular, a June 2016 meeting attended by Donald Trump, Jr, Kushner and Manafort, which Trump, Jr, had accepted on the premise that the Russians would provide damaging information about Clinton. Mueller's investigation proceeded discreetly and resolutely, while the Senate Intelligence Committee indicated that it would exhaustively pursue its investigation.

Disordered foreign policy

At the outset of Trump's presidency, there was trepidation in Washington's foreign-policy community about the possible effects of Trump's impulsiveness, his limited knowledge of international affairs and his reliance on trusted but inexperienced advisers. Trump's expressions of contempt for the intelligence agencies exacerbated this unease.

Although Trump had disparaged parts of the military during his campaign, he named a cadre of generals and former generals to key positions, including James Mattis, a former four-star Marine general, as secretary of defence and H.R. McMaster, a serving three-star Army general, as national-security adviser following Flynn's departure. Critics hoped that these appointees, together with Secretary of State Rex Tillerson, former head of ExxonMobil, would restrain the president's impulsiveness and thwart the ambitions of the unilateralist and quasi-isolationist Bannon. Indeed, Trump gave Mattis broad authority on operational decisions such as troop levels in Iraq, Syria and Afghanistan.

However, there were significant risks in relying on military figures to moderate the actions of the executive branch, not least the implicit subversion of institutionalised civilian control of the military. By mid-2017, it seemed that the generals had failed to coherently shape US foreign policy in at least three major regions. In the Asia-Pacific, the Trump team was ineffective in handling a crisis over North Korea's nuclear-bomb and ballistic-missile testing – though this would constitute an immense strategic problem for any administration. Trump initially attempted to intimidate Pyongyang with assertive rhetoric and a show of force, deploying a carrier strike group to the Sea of Japan in April 2017. After North Korea refused to change its behaviour, Trump indicated that the US was counting on Beijing to pressure Pyongyang. But he also praised North Korean leader Kim Jong-un and offered to negotiate with the regime. This inconsistency raised serious doubts about the credibility of US threats and longer-term strategy. Trump appeared to abandon the policy of relying on China on 20 June, following the death of Otto Warmbier, a 22-year-old American whom North Korea had recently returned to the US in a coma after detaining him for 17 months. But this still left Washington's strategy unclear.

In the Middle East, Washington sowed confusion about US policy on the Syrian regime; incited regional powers' political and economic isolation of Qatar, the host of an important US air base; and encouraged a destabilising strategic confrontation between Saudi Arabia and Iran that even Mattis – known for his hawkishness on Iran – and most senior Pentagon officials opposed. In spring and summer 2017, the Trump administration appeared to be inclined to confront the Syrian regime, which Iran closely supported. On 7 April, the US fired 59 *Tomahawk* cruise missiles at Shayrat Air Base, from which regime aircraft had recently launched a chemical-weapons attack on civilians in the town of Khan Sheikhoun. Subsequently, manned and unmanned regime aircraft flew closer and closer to areas in which US-supported rebel forces operated, and US aircraft shot down several of them, including a Russian-made Su-22 warplane on 18 June. Moscow, which directly supported the regime, subsequently claimed that it had suspended a long-established US–Russia military-to-military deconfliction channel for air operations.

In Europe, Trump failed during his first NATO summit to allay fears raised during the election campaign about the US commitment to NATO. On a subsequent trip to Poland he did affirm the US commitment to Article 5 of the Washington Treaty – the linchpin of Europe's collective security vis-à-vis Russia – but he also continued to hector European members of the Alliance to spend more on defence. Transatlantic relations remained shaky, with German Chancellor Angela Merkel stating bluntly that Europe could no longer rely on the US.

The Trump administration's erratic approach to Russia seemed to stem from a desire to control perceptions of its cosiness with Moscow. The transactional mindset that had served Trump so well in his business career appeared ill-suited to international relations. This was particularly the case at a time when the US faced a revanchist Russia and a rising China increasingly jealous of American influence in the Asia-Pacific – generational strategic challenges. In common with past activist administrations, Trump's plans rested on an assumption that opponents would simply accede to US demands; hence, he failed to plan for scenarios in which they did not. Even if some considered Obama to have been too cautious internationally, many foreign-policy professionals worried that Trump's failure to ask 'what next?' would create trouble for the US – or even lead it into war.

Alternatively, and more commonly, presidential bluster would be followed by quick retreat. This too could have costs. The administration's cruise-missile strikes on Syrian-regime military targets in April 2017, in response to the use of a nerve agent against civilians, may have strengthened US deterrence of the regime's use of chemical weapons, and made Trump's administration look tougher than Obama's. Yet the lack of accompanying initiatives meant that it did little to suppress Assad's indiscriminate use of force against civilians.

Personnel and institutional challenges

Trump appeared to present a uniquely difficult challenge to senior national-security officials. He proved unwilling to acknowledge the unhelpfulness of his policy interventions or to accept responsibility for them. He publicly scapegoated the military for politically damaging episodes, such as an unsuccessful 29 January counter-terrorism raid in which up to 30 Yemeni civilians and one navy special-warfare operator died. Openly at odds with Mattis, Trump demonised Islam; refused to affirm NATO's primacy; failed to fully fund the State Department or support diplomatic efforts in military crises; called for the seizure of Iraq's oil; and advocated flouting international laws and norms (including the prohibition of torture).

Nonetheless, after McMaster replaced Flynn, the National Security Council (NSC) was supposed to be able to fulfil its main directive: corralling the heads of multiple agencies – in particular, Mattis, Chairman of the Joint Chiefs of Staff General Joseph Dunford and then-secretary of homeland security John Kelly – to formulate and implement policies that all branches of government would follow. But by mid-year the NSC had not established a coherent policymaking process. Trump indulged his penchant for policy improvisation and seemed neither to have elicited nor comprehended most of the policy options and recommendations that his staff provided. For instance, Trump appeared not to have consulted the NSC before inviting Philippine President Rodrigo Duterte to the White House (the council would almost certainly have advised against this due to Duterte's poor human-rights record). Tillerson and UN Ambassador Nikki Haley made inconsistent statements on several issues, including regime change in Syria. Only later did the State Department in Washington and the US Mission to the United Nations in New York – which is part of the department – begin to coordinate their positions. In past administrations, harmonising policy statements across all relevant agencies had been standard operating procedure.

Dunford was in theory the president's primary military liaison and adviser, but he rarely had one-on-one meetings with Trump, and at one point became merely a discretionary attendee at meetings of the Principals Committee – the critical NSC mechanism for orchestrating significant policy shifts. Kelly, a former Marine general, shared some of Trump's policy preferences, including that of reducing immigration. But he too failed to moderate Trump. In a tweet impugning the Department of Justice for softening his travel ban, Trump implicitly tarred even Kelly, who had questioned the order's legality in relation to permanent US residency and work authorisation.

Moreover, it was impossible to maintain a robust NSC process without adequate staffing across the spectrum of government agencies involved in national-security affairs, including the State Department and the Pentagon, as well as the NSC itself. By June 2017, Trump had failed to formally nominate anyone for 442 of 559 key positions requiring Senate confirmation, and only 5% of senior administration jobs had been filled. Crucially, the empty slots included the deputy secretaries of state and defence – two of the essential players in Deputies Committee meetings, the NSC's key mechanism for day-to-day policy implementation – because Trump ruled out several of the secretaries' choices. At the outset, many observers in the US capital wondered whether Tillerson was intent on hollowing out the upper and middle management of the State Department so as to weaken and conquer the institution. By mid-2017, having failed to secure Trump's approval for his nominees, Tillerson appeared a beleaguered figure who lacked authority. The State Department was drained of morale and institutionally disengaged. To fix foreign policy, Trump would have to both empower the bureaucratic structure and pay attention to what it produced. He showed little inclination to do either.

Stymied agenda

Trump had been expressing critical opinions of governments of all hues for decades before deciding to stand for president. But after opting to run for the Republican candidacy, he had firmly aligned himself with the far right on domestic issues to appeal to his anti-establishment political base. In turn, many of his domestic cabinet appointments reflected his objective of undoing programmes favoured by Obama, and in some cases seemed to be based on contempt for the departments they headed.

Attorney General Sessions appeared determined to roll back voting rights, reignite an ineffective 'war on drugs', continue mass incarceration and exclude immigrants from the US. Education Secretary Betsy DeVos had no experience with public schools and was hostile to them. Secretary of Health and Human Services Tom Price opposed federal funding for abortions, including those performed when the life of the mother was at risk. Administrator of the Environmental Protection Agency Scott Pruitt was a climate-change denier who aimed to dismantle environmental regulation. Secretary of Housing and Urban Development Ben Carson had no experience with public housing, and appointed a Trump family wedding planner to head his agency's New York operations.

Trump's domestic agenda encountered obstacles in Congress and the courts. The executive orders he used to clamp down on immigration and curb environmental regulation faced legal challenges, including Supreme Court review. His administration's efforts to repeal and replace Obama's Affordable Care Act, which had increased the number of Americans with health insurance by around 15m, stalled first in the House and then in the Senate. A crudely prepared budget proposing deep tax cuts that would purportedly be offset by increased economic growth faced significant scepticism and resistance. The Republican Party's plans for comprehensive legislative tax reform gained little traction.

By July 2017, Trump's approval rating was hovering at around 35–40% – low for a new president – and some Republican members of congress were expressing doubt about his fitness for office. However, the US economy remained buoyant and polls suggested that Republican voters were still prepared to give him time, as a majority of Republicans approved of his performance. A special election in a traditionally Republican congressional district in Georgia in June proved a fillip for the president and his party. In November 2016 the district had voted for Trump over Clinton by just one percentage point, 48% to 47%. Although the moderate Democratic candidate, Jon Ossoff, had raised a record amount of money, his Republican rival, Karen Handel, won by a margin of nearly four percentage points. This lent credence to the view that most Republicans would give Trump the benefit of the doubt for some time, despite his indiscretions. He also benefited from the Democrats' difficulties in unifying their party after the presidential elections and finding a strategy to reverse their fortunes. Many in the Democratic Party appeared to be pinning their hopes on the Russia investigation bringing down Trump, but they were making little headway in addressing the popular concerns that Trump had exploited so effectively. Much, therefore, depended on the outcome of the Russian investigations. Yet the ability of Trump's administration to develop coherent policy in the face of the president's volatile behaviour also appeared to be a crucial factor. Republican politicians, many of them uneasy about Trump from the start, seemed increasingly concerned about their future electoral prospects if they continued to fail to put their campaign promises into practice.

Canada's unsettling year

Canada faced a series of unexpected challenges in the year to 1 July 2017, its 150th anniversary. Most of these difficulties related to the election of Trump, whose policies were often directly opposed to those of the Liberal government led by the prime minister, Justin Trudeau. Canada's support for free trade, a rules-based international order and the COP-21 agreement on climate change all became points of contention. As a consequence, Trudeau and his ministers scrambled to understand the priorities of the new US administration and to mitigate potential damage to the economy.

Many other governments engaged in similarly rapid readjustment. But Canada is more reliant on the US for trade than any other country, aside from Mexico. The US purchased three-quarters of Canada's goods exports in 2016 and supplied half of its goods imports. Washington's changing domestic and foreign policies forced Ottawa to reconsider and, in some cases, alter its approach in a range of areas, including defence, security, immigration, climate change and energy. However, Canada felt the impact of Trump's presidency most on trade.

The new US president blamed NAFTA, a 1994 deal with Canada and Mexico, for the loss of American jobs and investment to Mexico, threatening to scrap it if it could not be renegotiated in favour of the US. In May 2017, the White House notified Congress that it intended to renegotiate NAFTA, initiating a 90-day consultation period prior to trilateral talks. Among the aspects of NAFTA Washington aimed to renegotiate were the deal's dispute-settlement mechanism (which allows firms to sue states before special tribunals), rules of origin and provisions on public procurement.

The Canadian government tried to present the process as an opportunity. The foreign-affairs minister, Chrystia Freeland, said that Canadian negotiators were ready to 'modernise' the agreement. Unlike Mexico, Canada said little in advance about what it wanted from the deal, except that it would have to include a fair mechanism for settling disputes. Stephen Poloz, governor of the Bank of Canada, said he welcomed a 'dust-off' of the deal to include sectors omitted from the original version and those that had become more important in the preceding two decades, such as the softwood-lumber trade and e-commerce respectively. Trudeau continued to exude optimism, saying in late June that he had no 'Plan B' for NAFTA and was certain the agreement would be in place in mid-2018, due to its importance to the US and Canada. Ottawa launched an intensive lobbying effort to persuade Americans that the deal was crucial to the US economy.

Canadian firms did not share the government's positive outlook. Commercial investment remained subdued because of concerns that increased US protectionism and regulation would undermine their competitiveness. As a result, Canadian companies pressed the government to speed the process of trade diversification. Ottawa reached an important milestone in this effort on 8 July 2017, when it agreed – after eight years of negotiations – to provisionally implement the Comprehensive Economic and Trade Agreement (CETA) with the European Union the following September. There also appeared to be building momentum among Canada and ten other prospective members of the TPP to proceed with the deal, as Japan assumed the position of leadership abandoned by the US in January. Canada began in September 2016 to explore a free-trade deal with China, and continued its seven-year negotiations on a free-trade agreement with New Delhi. Ottawa was likely to focus more on all these talks if the NAFTA negotiations fell short of the Canadian government's expectations.

Concern about the Trump presidency was also evident in Canada's new foreign, defence and international-aid policies. In a speech on 6 June, Freeland laid out the country's commitment to a rules-based international order, free trade, gender equality and measures to combat climate change. She acknowledged the important role the US played in the world but bemoaned the fact that it was questioning 'the very worth of its mantle of global leadership'. In an unusual move for a Liberal minister, she noted that Canada could not depend solely on diplomatic and cultural influence, and would resort to force where required. Canada risked becoming a 'client state' of the US if it continued to rely solely on the American security umbrella, she said.

Freeland, who opposes Russia's seizure of Ukrainian territory, also described Russian military expansionism as a strategic threat to the liberal-democratic world of which Canada is a part. She stated her support for a bill mirroring US and UK Magnitsky laws – named for Sergei Magnitsky, a lawyer who died in custody in Russia after exposing an alleged money-laundering scheme linked to the country's security services – that would sanction states engaging in human-rights violations or large-scale corruption.

On 7 June, Minister of National Defence Harjit Sajjan elaborated on Canada's new defence policy. Despite saying little about defence procurement during the 2015 election campaign, the Liberals committed to a series of major procurements, including the replacement of aging CF-18 fighter jets with 88 new aircraft (up from the 65 called for by the previous government), and the procurement of 15 new surface combatants to replace existing frigates and destroyers. The government also pledged to refurbish four problem-plagued nuclear-powered submarines, increase the size of the regular force from 68,000 to 71,500 troops and invest in satellite-surveillance and cyber capabilities.

The announcements followed Trump's repeated scolding of NATO members whose military spending fell below the agreed goal of 2% of GDP. Trudeau defended Canada's record, stating that the country had done more than its share for the Alliance, even leading a battle group in Latvia as part of a mission to discourage Russian aggression. Nonetheless, the decision to increase defence spending reflected a significant change in policy. The budget of the Department of National Defence (excluding the Department of Veterans Affairs) was positioned to grow on an accrual basis from C$17.1bn (US$12.9bn), or 0.8% of GDP, in 2016–17 to C$24.6bn (US$18.7bn), or an estimated 1.0% of GDP, in 2026–27. Although this still fell short of the NATO goal, it seemed to be enough to satisfy Trump, who praised the move.

Ottawa was less mindful of US interests in its new international-aid policy, which allowed organisations that provide abortions to receive Canadian aid funding. This contrasted with both US policy under Trump and that of the previous Conservative administration in Canada. Critics of Trudeau's government were quick to point out that it had not increased the aid budget.

Ottawa undertook a major overhaul of counter-terrorism policy in June, placing Canadian security agencies under the oversight of the newly created National Security and Intelligence Review Agency. The organisation was designed to ensure that the agencies complied with the constitution. It also provided one of them, the Communications Security Establishment, with new powers to launch offensive and defensive cyber operations against foreign states and suspected terrorists.

Domestic Canadian politics was relatively subdued. The two main opposition parties, the Conservative Party and the New Democratic Party (NDP), began 2017 without permanent leaders. The Conservatives elected Andrew Scheer, a career politician and former speaker of the House of Commons, as their leader on 27 May. The NDP contest was to be decided in October.

Nonetheless, the stance of the new US administration sometimes compelled the Liberal government to re-examine domestic policy.

Ottawa built on the COP-21 agreement by publishing a plan to reduce the impact of climate change. Including a national carbon price, the plan aimed to reduce greenhouse-gas emissions by at least 30% below 2005 levels by 2030. Trump's decision to withdraw the US from the climate pact and to review his predecessor's plan to restrict greenhouse-gas emissions from coal-fired power plants raised concerns among Canadian exporters, which feared they would become uncompetitive in the US due to the need to abide by stringent environmental legislation. Despite this, Trudeau stuck with his original plan to price carbon.

The two leaders supported the Keystone XL pipeline, a project to bring crude oil from Alberta to refineries in the southern US that Obama had opposed. Trudeau also backed the proposed Edmonton–Vancouver Trans Mountain Pipeline extension. Although these positions caused consternation among his supporters who regarded the pipelines as antithetical to climate-change initiatives, the prime minister said that energy production was key to the Canadian economy even as the country sought to reduce its dependence on fossil fuels.

Trump's anti-immigrant rhetoric had the potential to help Canada attract more of the skilled workers it needed. The country's technology companies welcomed a programme the government launched in June to ease the process of applying for a work permit for highly skilled foreigners.

The economy grew at an annualised rate of 3.7% in the first quarter of 2017, up from 1.5% in 2016. Some of that increase came from the government's postponement of deficit-reduction measures to stimulate the economy through infrastructure spending. But the major driver was the housing market, which grew particularly quickly in Toronto and Vancouver, generating fears of a property bubble that could damage the broader economy. Canadian household-debt levels were at a near-record high of C$1.70 of debt for every C$1 in disposable income, primarily due to mortgage debt. The Bank of Canada raised its benchmark rate from 0.5% to 0.75% on 12 July. But it continued to fret that a shock to the economy or a sudden increase in interest rates would cause an economic slump, as did the IMF. A major change to NAFTA could create such a shock. The situation recalled the view of North American relations held by Trudeau's father Pierre, a former prime minister who in 1969 described living next to the US as 'in some ways like sleeping with an elephant. No matter how friendly or temperate the beast, one is affected by every twitch and grunt.'

Index

C

D

Q

R

S

T

U

V

W

X

Y

Z